Learning Japanese for Real

Learning Japanese for Real

A Guide to Grammar, Use, and Genres of the *Nihongo* World

Senko K. Maynard

University of Hawai'i Press
Honolulu

Library of Congress Cataloging-in-Publication Data
Maynard, Senko K.
Learning Japanese for real : a guide to grammar, use, and
genres of the Nihongo world / Senko K. Maynard.
p.   cm.
Includes bibliographical references and indexes.
ISBN 978-0-8248-3482-1 (hard cover : alk. paper)—
ISBN 978-0-8248-3540-8 (pbk. : alk. paper)
1. Japanese language—Study and teaching—English speakers—
Handbooks, manuals, etc.   I. Title.
PL519.M33 2011
495.6'82421—dc22
2010033493

Designed by Wanda China
Printed by Sheridan Books, Inc.

Contents

Preface

Welcome to the world of *Nihongo,* the Japanese language. So you have decided to learn *Nihongo* as a foreign language. The project you are about to launch is challenging. But it will also be, I trust, an exciting, eye-opening, and rewarding experience.

I wrote this book with one aim in mind: to help you learn the essentials of the Japanese language.

You may be a high school or college student planning to take *Nihongo* courses. You may be a professional having contact with Japan or someone out there genuinely interested in Japanese language and culture. Or maybe you are currently taking *Nihongo* courses. Perhaps you are studying on your own. Regardless of your situation, you will find *Learning Japanese for Real* useful. It will help you chart this new territory of your mental and emotional adventure.

Learning Japanese for Real provides a concise and simplified overview of the information helpful for your learning. Sure, a single book such as this may not capture the complete universe of knowledge related to *Nihongo.* But short of completeness, I am confident *Learning Japanese for Real* will become your go-to source for learning Japanese.

I have kept each entry section and chapter as short and as simple as possible. The accumulation of each entry will gradually construct the overall structure of your task. Gaining a bird's-eye view of what it takes to acquire *Nihongo* gives you a clearer goal. Instead of randomly learning a few words and blindly understanding some grammatical features, knowing the complete picture will help you organize necessary information, giving you perspective. Once you understand the core knowledge structure, you can always build upon that foundation as you advance.

The materials covered in *Learning Japanese for Real* range from elementary to intermediate to advanced *Nihongo* courses. To read authentic text samples introduced in Chapter 18, a knowledge of advanced-level Japanese is required. Above all, this is a guidebook that you will refer to many times throughout your three-to-four year project.

If you have already studied Japanese for a few years, this book will be useful as a comprehensive review. It will help you deepen your understanding of *Nihongo* in a renewed sense and perhaps from a different perspective.

I must confess that if you are interested in picking up a few expressions to use when greeting Japanese people or visiting Japanese restaurants, this book is out of your league. However, if you are a serious student of Japanese, this book will prove useful. To really speak your mind in Japanese, you need to generate sentences from scratch. In meaningfully interacting with Japanese-language speakers, you must know the grammar and how to (and how not to) use the sentences you create. And to understand those sentences in social and cultural context, you must learn about the genres of the *Nihongo* world. This book offers precisely such information.

Learning Japanese for Real is written with English speakers in mind. English may not be your native language, but it is a world language through which I can reach many readers. As a result, the explanations and characterizations of the Japanese language are presented in contrast with the English language.

I am personally involved in the project you are about to launch in two ways. First, I was born and educated in Japan through college and learned English as a foreign language. The fact that I am a native speaker of Japanese will never change, and my personal experience of learning English continues to make me think about language education in general.

Second, I was trained as a linguist and have spent many years conducting research on the Japanese language. I have taught Japanese as a foreign language to college students at several institutions. My years of experience in research and teaching have resulted in the publication of seventeen books and eighty or so articles. I believe what I have learned can offer constructive guidance.

As you probably know already, information about the Japanese language is available in printed form and elsewhere, especially on the Internet. Directions, suggestions, advice, and various tools abound. But they are often unorganized, randomly selected, and may become unavailable unexpectedly. This information overload can be confusing, and you can waste your time reading scattered tidbits of information. Worse yet, some of this information may be wrong or useless.

Searching for information crucial to learning Japanese is frustrating when you realize you are simply going around in circles. This book, on the other hand, gives it to you straight. It leads you to the essentials quickly and systematically. Once you gain the basic knowledge, you can make use of information available in various media. Part VII of this book guides you in how to make the most use of available resources.

Because this book is virtually an anthology of grammar, use, and genres of the *Nihongo* world, Japanese teachers may also find it a useful reference. However, given the necessary conciseness of the content, I want to remind teachers that broader and more detailed information is available in many of my other works, listed at the end of this volume.

For many years, I have enjoyed teaching Japanese language and linguistics at various institutions. While I was a graduate student, I taught at the University of Iowa, the University of Illinois at Chicago, and Northwestern University. Then I went on to teach at other universities (in chronological order, the University of Hawai'i, Connecticut College, Harvard University, and Princeton University), and currently I teach at Rutgers University. I thank the students and colleagues I have met at various locales for their friendship, inspiration, and encouragement. This book is dedicated to past, present, and future students of the Japanese language at Rutgers University. It is also dedicated to students learning Japanese on their own or at many institutions worldwide.

I would like to express my gratitude to the following for granting permission to duplicate the visual images: Ten'ya Yabuno and Shogakukan for *Inazuma Irebun,* which appeared in *Korokoro Komikku* (September 2008 issue, pp. 446–448), and Q. P. Corporation and Orenji Peeji for Chuuka Suupu no Moto advertising, which appeared in *Orange Page* (December 2, 2007, p. 202).

I would like to thank Patricia Crosby, executive editor at the University of Hawai'i Press, for her continuing faith in me and her warm support throughout this project. And Michael, thank you, as always, for your support and cheerleading.

SKM
"On the Banks of the Old Raritan"

PART I

Preliminaries

CHAPTER 1

Introduction

1.1. Learning *Nihongo* for Real

I titled this book with specific reasons in mind. By "for real" in the title, I mean the real *Nihongo,* the Japanese language, used by native speakers. Examples used in this book are similar to authentic Japanese, and they can be used for real communication. Although the necessity of presenting only simple expressions early on made it difficult to be totally natural, I have made every effort to create sentences as close as possible to real Japanese.

I also emphasize the importance of learning for real, that is, learning not just a few happenstance words, but acquiring knowledge necessary to achieve real and meaningful communication. The chapters and entry sections selected for this book cover a wide range of topics necessary to realize that goal.

Unlike grammar books explaining grammatical rules only, unlike conversation books giving conversation samples and strategies only, and unlike advanced reading books primarily introducing written texts only, this book provides critical information for you to be comfortable in the *Nihongo* world. We need to learn real Japanese, the kind actually used in real human communication.

Now, what do we mean by *Nihongo?* Does it refer to idealized expressions that often appear in textbooks? Overly emotional speech you find in comic magazines? Headlines you access on newspaper Web sites? Unfamiliar words listed in an elaborate sushi menu? Whatever examples you encounter, it is important to understand that they represent only a part of the whole. In this book, I strive to represent the kind of widely and ordinarily used *Nihongo* in everyday communication. We must make such real Japanese the target of our study.

This leads to the issue of language variation. The Japanese

language comes in various styles and varieties. Depending on your social and personal needs and depending on a particular situation, you are expected to speak in a certain way. As in any language, but more clearly in Japanese, it is critical to choose and shift among appropriate styles and varieties. As if that wasn't enough of a challenge, these styles and varieties are constantly changing, and so is the significance of the factors motivating such changes. Because of this fluidity in language, we must remain flexible and resourceful when learning *Nihongo.*

This book is based on the most current use of *Nihongo,* but soon new expressions will evolve while some old ones will fade. I will address this issue later, but at this point, we must bear in mind that language is never static, and we must keep up with what constitutes the real Japanese language.

Although language is in perpetual flux, the fundamental features remain fairly constant. What you learn in this book will serve as a core on which you can build your accrued knowledge. You can add more subtle aspects of current and future *Nihongo* to these fundamentals.

1.2. *Nihongo* as a Foreign Language

LANGUAGE AND THOUGHT

Learning *Nihongo* is rewarding in itself, but how is it related to the way we think and feel? To answer this question, we must first consider the relationship between language and thought.

The relationship between language and thought has been extensively discussed in academia. The most reasonable conclusion is that language does not necessarily control one's thought but that language as a whole (not just a vocabulary item or a certain grammatical structure) encourages certain ways of viewing the world. After all, we gain knowledge through our native language. We interpret our life experiences through human interaction enabled by that very language. We cannot ignore the characteristics of a medium through which we actualize our daily lives.

It is reasonable to assume that certain ways of thinking are encouraged in the *Nihongo* world while certain others are not. This does not mean that a Japanese speaker is imprisoned by certain ways of thinking. Rather, certain thoughts are easier to access in Japanese, which may or may not be different from the way of thinking in other languages.

Another way to understand the relationship between language and thought is to pay attention to how we develop our mental capacities. Our native language is internalized, and it functions as a means to facilitate our psychological and social development. We acquire language through early interaction with those close to us. The very way we socially interact with them is internalized. Think of the constant question-answer interactions that take place between a child and a parent. Such social experience is internalized to organize, form, and promote higher mental functions such as the problem-solving process and cause-effect reasoning. In this sense, one cannot deny that our native language deeply influences how our minds work.

In addition, the ways we interact with people in our language are linked to the kinds of emotions we feel. Think of a situation where you witness two people parting. You may be moved by the scene, but if a friend describes it in words, you are likely to be moved even more. You may personally recall a situation where your emotions became clear when you labeled them with words.

When a Japanese expression of emotion is used, the kind of emotion specifically associated with it comes alive. Although emotion is personal, because you feel it through language, it is social as well. In this way, language is undeniably tied to our deep emotions and feelings.

THE MEANINGS OF LEARNING *NIHONGO*

Given the close association between our native language and our way of living, learning a foreign language becomes an all-inclusive experience. It reaches your mind and heart. Learning Japanese will open new ways of looking at things, thinking about issues, solving problems, socializing with others, and experiencing emotions. Learning a foreign language makes you a new person. Unchained from a mono-language universe, you will live in multiple worlds.

As is by now clear, language functions in various ways. It conveys information, expresses emotion, and connects to others. But more fundamentally, language helps define our identity. In the process, the foreign language learner creates a kind of self unattainable otherwise. This is why learning *Nihongo* challenges you deep in your sense of self. It is a "real" experience that echoes through your soul.

You may have concrete reasons for learning *Nihongo*—finding a job in or related to Japan, communicating with Japanese friends or relatives, being interested in the traditional and current culture of Japan, and so on. You may be a speaker of multiple languages and simply wish to add Japanese to your repertoire. All these practical reasons are important. But in addition, you will find special and privileged meanings unavailable in a world absent of the *Nihongo* experience.

In many ways, the world of *Nihongo* is similar to the world you know. But it is also filled with different ways of expressing yourself, understanding people, appreciating nature, and identifying yourself. Just as with learning any foreign language, learning Japanese will increase your level of self-awareness and sensitivity to different kinds of human life.

YOU'RE NOT ALONE

According to a 2006 worldwide survey conducted by the Japan Foundation, around thirteen thousand institutions employing over forty-four thousand teachers are offering Japanese language instruction. Worldwide, nearly three million students are studying Japanese as a foreign language. You are not alone, indeed.

Throughout Japan's bubble economy of the 1980s and despite the prolonged economic recession since the 1990s, the number of students learning Japanese as a foreign language has steadily increased. Over the past thirty years, it has increased tenfold. The majority of students are native speakers of Korean and Chinese. Australians studying Japanese constitute approximately 12 percent of the total, followed by students in Indonesia, Taiwan, and the United States. In the United States in 2006, over 117,000 students were studying Japanese at various institutions.

1.3. Organization of This Book

This book is divided into seven parts. Part I, "Preliminaries," gives introductory information about the Japanese language and its background. Part II, "Sounds and Scripts," explains the sound system and scripts, including *hiragana, katakana,* and *kanji.* It is particularly important that you pay close attention to Chapter 5, where you will be expected to learn *hiragana* and *katakana.* From that point on, I will assume you can read *hiragana* and *katakana* without difficulty.

Part III, "Words," is divided into two chapters. Chapter 6 discusses the characteristics of various word types, including loan words and onomatopoeic words. Chapter 7 looks at words from a grammatical perspective and presents grammatical categories such as Japanese nouns, adverbs, and adjectives (which function differently from their English counterparts). The words in this chapter are mostly content words (except particles). Other word categories (i.e., function words), such as conjunctions and modal verbs, appear later, when they are introduced in separate entry sections. This chapter also provides verb and adjective conjugations, to which you will be referring throughout your study.

Part IV, "Grammar," gives a bird's-eye view of Japanese grammar. I have divided this part into four chapters. Chapters 8 and 9 introduce simple sentences, while Chapter 10 discusses complex sentences. These chapters cover essential grammar such as verb sentences, questions, grammatical particles, preferred word order, negation, conditionals, clausal modification, and quotation. In addition, Chapter 11 takes a look at grammar in terms of how it expresses emotion. Here you will find entries such as attitudinal adverbs, exclamatory phrases, interjections, and rhetorical questions, all of which carry emotive meanings.

Part V, "Use," goes beyond grammar and discusses how *Nihongo* is used in interaction. When engaging in Japanese communication, how should you behave? What expressions should you choose or avoid? What level of formality and politeness should you maintain? Communication strategies such as requesting, apologizing, and inviting are discussed in Chapter 12. Chapter 13 illustrates how to interact when you participate in Japanese conversation. This chapter introduces you to such strategies as prefacing your utterances, sending listener responses, and repairing your utterances.

In Parts III, IV, and V, each chapter contains many entries. Each entry comes with Key Expressions, Explanations, and an optional Graffiti section. I have purposely arranged entries from simple to complex, using easy to understand examples. However, especially with the initial entry sections, some things have not yet been explained. But as you proceed, it will all make more sense to you.

We all know that gestures carry important messages in communication. Chapter 14 offers a quick overview of Japanese gestures such as hand signals, bowing, and head nods. Chapter 15 returns to language itself and introduces representative rhetorical figures of speech in Japanese. Metaphor and tautology are universal rhetorical figures, while the frequent use of puns and the lingering effect of *yojoo* are specific to Japanese.

In Chapter 16, the final chapter under Part V, I discuss how Japanese discourse is organized. Here we study how multiple sentences are tied together to create coherent and cohesive discourse units. Particularly significant is the four-part organizational principle known as *ki-shoo-ten-ketsu*. Also important are the concept of topic structure and the staging effect associated with the use of *wa* and other topic markers.

Part VI, "Genres," first introduces the world of *Nihongo* in terms of genre categories. In Chapter 18 I present popular culture discourse samples taken from a comic strip, variety show, television drama, print advertising, magazine essay, and cell-phone novel. You are exposed to the authentic language and discourse created and consumed in today's Japan. Each sample discourse comes with an English translation and specific features to be noted.

Finally, in Part VII, "Learning *Nihongo*," I discuss concrete methods and tools for learning Japanese. The information in this part is useful when you need practical ideas. Chapters 19 and 20 contain information on learning tools, but it is limited. You are encouraged to search for additional up-to-date information on the Internet and elsewhere.

At the end of the volume, you will find a list of my works, some in English and others in Japanese. If you are interested in the field of Japanese linguistics, specifically the areas of conversation analysis, discourse analysis, linguistic emotivity, and linguistic creativity, you may find some of my work helpful.

1.4. How to Use This Book

Learning Japanese for Real is a guidebook for your Japanese learning project. It is best used as a supplement to your textbooks in elementary to advanced courses. You may read from the beginning to the end, but it is more likely you will seek specific entries as you prepare for or review certain points.

Because this book contains words you may not be familiar with, you should have access to a Japanese-English dictionary (see Chapter 20, section 20.2). This is particularly true if you are studying on your own or if you are a beginning student. I must also warn you that early on in the book, grammatical features may appear that have not yet been introduced. In those cases, please return to them after you have covered the basics introduced in Chapters 8, 9, and 10. At various critical points I have so noted or have suggested that you refer to the relevant entry sections (for example, see section 10.1).

It is best to study Parts I through IV in order. When you are interested in Japanese conversation, Chapters 12 and 13 will be particularly useful. When you write or read Japanese, refer especially to Chapters 15 and 16. And, as mentioned earlier, Chapters 19 and 20 offer basic learning strategies that you can always update with information obtainable on the Internet.

Having a supplementary reference book such as this one by your side offers comfort and excitement. As you take Japanese language courses, when you feel you need help for certain aspects, you can consult specific entries. When you feel you are ahead of the class and need to be challenged, you can jump ahead. In the process, you will grasp the total picture of what it takes to be proficient in the Japanese language. Because *Learning Japanese for Real* contains a critical mass of information, it is ideal for reviewing your overall knowledge about Japanese. Those of you who have studied Japanese for a couple of years will find the latter half of the volume particularly useful.

Instructors can use this book as a required or recommended reference that guides students in their studies outside the classroom. Students may be asked to read certain sections in preparation for planned classroom activities. Because the book is written in English, students can, on their own, become familiar with the grammar and proper use of the Japanese language. This will save precious classroom time, and instructors can insist on speaking in Japanese with the knowledge that students already have the necessary background information. Certain chapters may be assigned to students for review purposes. Chapter 18 contains authentic popular culture samples and can be studied in the classroom. Particularly in advanced Japanese courses, the authentic sources introduced here offer inroads to encourage students to explore additional "real" Japanese, an essential step toward being truly proficient in *Nihongo*.

Because this book contains many entry sections and each section is purposely brief, I want to remind the reader that more detailed information is readily available elsewhere, as suggested in Chapter 20. Three of my own books—*An Introduction to Japanese Grammar and Communication Strategies, Principles of Japa-*

nese Discourse: A Handbook, and *Expressive Japanese: A Reference Guide to Sharing Emotion and Empathy*—offer fuller accounts of Japanese grammar, discourse organization, and interpersonal communication.

I hope *Learning Japanese for Real* will serve students and instructors alike as a useful guide in learning *Nihongo* as a foreign language. And it is my hope that this book will inspire the reader to continue learning *Nihongo* well beyond its covers.

1.5. Notes on Transcription

Japanese expressions are presented in the normal script, combining *hiragana, katakana,* and *kanji.* Sometimes the same phrase may appear in different scripts. This variation is conventionalized in the Japanese print media, and accordingly I have used varied scripts.

Almost all Japanese examples are transcribed by using Romanization *(roomaji),* that is, the English alphabet. Romanization follows the Hepburn style but features the following slight variations: (1) long vowels are represented by double vowels; (2) the glottal stop is represented by *t* instead of a double consonant *(itchi* instead of *icchi);* and (3) the syllabic *n,* when followed by a vowel, is presented as *n' (ren'ai).* Also, note that the glottal stop *tsu* at the word-final position is spelled *tt.* Based on these principles, Tokyo is spelled "Tookyoo" in *roomaji,* although the conventional spelling of Tokyo is used in the English translation. I will use this *roomaji* presentation throughout unless conventionalized otherwise.

Once Japanese scripts are introduced in Chapter 5, *kanji* characters are accompanied by *hiragana* readings either in parentheses or in a separate column. When Japanese sentences are presented separately, each sentence is given in Japanese orthography, followed by the *roomaji* transcription and an English translation. All English translations are mine. When translating into English, I followed the original Japanese as closely as possible, but my translation is not the only acceptable rendition. The English translations are given for reference purposes only to help clarify the meaning. Throughout the book, some Japanese terms appear in *roomaji,* mainly to avoid confusion.

When offering explanations, for purposes of contrast I use some examples that are ungrammatical or inappropriate. These expressions appear with an asterisk (*), and you should pay special attention to them so that you will know to carefully avoid them.

CHAPTER 2

Background

2.1. *Nihongo:* The Japanese Language

WHO SPEAKS *NIHONGO*?

Nihongo is the national language of Japan, and it is spoken by approximately 127 million people. As a rule, Japanese nationals speak Japanese, and conversely, speakers of Japanese are Japanese nationals. In Japan, a substantial number of foreigners speak Japanese with varying proficiency levels. Japanese is also spoken in Japanese emigrant communities around the world, most prominently in Hawai'i and Brazil. It is also spoken by Japanese nationals who temporarily reside in major cities throughout the world. In addition, it is estimated that a few million people speak Japanese as a second or a foreign language. Still, unlike the English language spoken by multiple nationals, Japanese is very much the language of a single national entity.

BASIC CHARACTERISTICS OF *NIHONGO*

Although a genetic relationship remains obscure, Japanese is suggested to be distantly related to Korean and therefore to the Altaic languages.

Japanese is classified as an agglutinating language, one that combines many separable elements, such as particles and modal suffixes. Bits of meaningful units are strung together to form a larger structural unit. For example, *tabesaserareta* is a combination of *taberu* 'to eat', *saseru* (causative), *rareru* (passive), and *ta* (past tense). The combined meaning is something like 'was forced to eat'.

Japanese takes the basic SOV (Subject-Object-Verb) word

11

order, whereas in English the word order is SVO (Subject-Verb-Object). For example, compare the following two sentences.

(a) Joo ga manga o yonda.
(b) Joe read a comic book.

In (a), the object *manga* 'a comic book' appears before *yonda* 'read'. In (b), English puts *read* before *a comic book*.

Overall, Japanese is a topic-comment prominent language, where a topic (i.e., something being talked about, not necessarily a grammatical subject) plays a significant role. It includes particles that express not only grammatical cases but also personal emotion and attitude. Non-specification of topics, subjects, objects, and particles is common.

Japanese has a rich system of formality and politeness levels. Depending on the formality of a situation, formal (i.e., *desu/masu*) or informal (i.e., *da*) styles are chosen. Politeness is achieved not only by choosing the appropriate formal styles but also by choosing appropriate expressions such as respectful and humble forms.

This said, as you can easily imagine, Japanese speakers do not always use polite forms. Conflicts are a part of life, and under certain circumstances, blunt forms, emotive interjections, and curses are abundantly used. Although Japanese is known for its indirectness in communication, when necessary, speakers express themselves directly through various emotion-revealing means. It should be noted in passing that familiarity plays a more important role than formality among younger speakers. As a result, young people often use familiar informal styles mixed in with formal styles to express their desire for emotional closeness.

List of Basic Features

The list that follows summarizes the basic characteristics of the Japanese language.

1. Verb in final position
    The basic rule for ordering elements in a sentence is to place the verb (optionally followed by suffixes and particles) at the final position.
2. Adjectives as predicates
    The *i*-adjective (a type of adjective ending with *i*) behaves like a verb. It can constitute a predicate by itself.

3. Topic-comment prominence

    The notion of topic plays a vital role in organizing infor-
    mation. Topic is marked by a number of topic-marking parti-
    cles, and if it appears, it usually does so at the sentence- and
    discourse-initial positions.

4. Not saying the obvious

    Not verbally specifying the elements obvious to the com-
    munication partners is frequent.

5. Varied styles

    Japanese uses different devices to mark formality and
    politeness levels.

6. Rich variations

    Different varieties of language are used, often associated
    with demographics (age, gender, region, etc.). In addition, dif-
    ferent varieties and their mixtures may be borrowed for mark-
    ing social identity. Speakers may choose styles for personal,
    emotional, and creative reasons.

7. Modifier preceding the modified

    The basic word order for modification is that the modi-
    fiers (e.g., adjectives and clausal modifiers) come before the
    modified (e.g., nouns).

8. Postpositional particles

    Particles mark grammatical relations (grammatical parti-
    cles) as well as interpersonal feelings and attitudes in inter-
    action (interactional particles), and they are placed after the
    element whose relation is defined.

9. Verb and adjective conjugation

    Verbs and adjectives are conjugated and change forms
    based on tense. They also change forms depending on the
    speaker's views and attitudes but not on those of the gram-
    matical person (i.e., first, second, or third person).

10. Nouns and counters

    Japanese does not mark a distinction between the singu-
    lar and plural forms of a noun. There is no device comparable
    to the English plural marker -s. When specifying quantity,
    Japanese employs a set of counters.

11. Not specifying the agent

    Japanese tends to describe the world as a natural state
    or a change brought about by some force. Specification of a
    subject or agent (i.e., the person performing an act) is not as
    prominent a factor as it is in English.

2.2. The Country Called Japan

GEOGRAPHY

Japan *(Nippon, Nihon)* is an island country lying at the eastern periphery of Asia.

The four main islands extend in northeast and southwest directions, forming an arc. These four main islands are, from the northeast, Hokkaido *(Hokkaidoo)*, Honshu *(Honshuu)*, Shikoku, and Kyushu *(Kyuushuu)*. In terms of size, Japan is slightly larger than Germany and somewhat smaller than California. It is approximately one-twenty-fifth of the United States.

The Japanese climate is temperate, with a rainy season in June (except in Hokkaido) followed by a hot and humid summer. The variation in temperature between northern and southern Japan is considerable. The four seasons are distinct, and the Japanese have traditionally been highly sensitive to and appreciative of the distinctions among the seasons. The country is not exempt from frequent natural disasters, including earthquakes and volcanic activity. Annual typhoons strike the country in the fall.

Modern Japan is a highly industrialized and urbanized society, and its major cities are concentrated along the seaboard of Honshu, facing the Pacific. These are cities such as Sendai, Tokyo *(Tookyoo)*, Yokohama, and Nagoya. Osaka *(Oosaka)* and Kobe *(Koobe)* are located along the Inland Sea (between Honshu and the Shikoku Islands). Other major cities include Fukuoka in Kyushu, Sapporo in Hokkaido, and the ancient city of Kyoto *(Kyooto)* near Osaka. Although modernized, communities in the countryside generally maintain traditional customs.

SOCIETY

Many observers characterize Japan as a society that emphasizes social hierarchy and group membership. Although the "group" orientation exists, it is also true that Japanese society praises individualism.

The desire to belong to a group and the wish to remain independent as an individual occur in all societies. These two forces pull us toward opposing directions, it seems. More broadly, we can understand this phenomenon through the concept of self and society, which shape all other sociocultural concepts. What is critical is the way we relate to society and the way we define our selves in relation to others. Characterizing the Japanese view toward self and society in contrast with that of the traditional American culture, in my earlier work I introduced the concept of "relationality."

Relationality refers to the reciprocal influence exerted by two different elements that are reflexively characterized by each other. In other words, it refers to the mutual relationship of self and society.

The starting point for the Japanese lies in society, while the starting point for traditional Americans lies in the concept of self. Here the "starting point" means the primary and deep-rooted self-concept with which one is encouraged to identify early in life. In Japan, social accommodation, responsiveness, and cooperation are the dominant, although not the only, training one receives in the socialization process. The relationship one identifies as one's psychological foundation is based on, anchored to, and defined in relation to society. The Japanese, however, express individuality more as they mature and achieve comfort within society. The direction of opposing forces between society and self in Japan is from-society-to-self, that is, society-relational.

For many Americans, the concept of self is fundamental. Socialization is important, and each person is expected to be on friendly terms with others, but more important is exercising individuality. Being on one's own and speaking up for one's interest are more important than learning to accommodate others. However, after a certain degree of individuality is learned, many Americans find solace in family and group. This tendency can be labeled from-self-to-society, that is, self-relational.

Of course, we are creatures of contradiction, and we find ourselves simultaneously pulled toward self and society. A Japanese person often finds balance between self and society by moving from "social dependence" toward "psychological independence." An American tends to find such balance by moving from "social independence" toward "psychological dependence." Cultural forces in Japan and the United States tend to encourage opposing directions in the relationality of self and society.

Depending on your native language and society, you will find your own view of self and society more or less similar to that of the Japanese. The comparison will reveal your sense of self and the characteristic of your native country in an interesting way.

2.3. Social Concepts

Among the concepts known to characterize the Japanese society, four approaches are worth mentioning: (1) *amae,* (2) *meue* and *meshita,* (3) *uchi* and *soto,* and (4) *tatemae* and *honne.*

AMAE

Amae refers to the psychological and emotional sense of dependence, and it is considered a concept that explains certain aspects of the Japanese people's psychological and social behavior. *Amae* is etymologically related to *amai* 'sweet' and refers to sweet, tender, and all-forgiving love, similar to parental love, particularly a mother's love. *Amae* is the warm, all-accepting, and dependent relationship Japanese people enjoy among intimates. It is enjoyed by people not only during their childhood but, more important, throughout their lives. *Amae,* above all, involves the desire to be passively cared for by another. When the *amae* relationship is established, one can be selfishly dependent and still be accepted and forgiven.

For the *amae* relationship to work, at least two persons must be involved, one to seek the other's dependence and the other to accept it. Once such a relationship is recognized by both parties, the manner of interaction changes. For example, interactional particles are frequently used, familiar and friendly vocatives appear, and a self-centered mode of communication is, in general, likely to be accepted.

MEUE AND *MESHITA*

The word *meue* literally means 'above eye level'. A *meue* person is someone who is socially higher in status. In contrast, *meshita* literally means 'below eye level' and refers to someone who is socially lower in status. A number of factors determine whether your status is higher or lower in relation to a person with whom you interact or a person you mention. Some comparisons are listed below.

Meue	*Meshita*
Boss at work	Younger worker, with lower rank
Older person	Younger person
Male	Female
Doctor	Patient
Lawyer	Client
Teacher	Student
Upper class at school	Lower class at school
Person with prestigious job	Person with less prestigious job
Person offering a favor	Recipient of the favor
Buyer, customer	Seller, salesperson

Identifying social status is critical in Japanese communication because you must choose the appropriate speech style based on such awareness.

UCHI AND SOTO

Uchi 'in, insider, internal, private, hidden' and *soto* 'out, outside, external, public, exposed' refer to social and psychological spaces identified among Japanese. People belonging to a specific group (such as a workplace, association, or other social circle) usually consider themselves *uchi* members. Japanese speakers refer to an affiliation by using the very phrase, as in *uchi no kaisha* 'our company'. Also, as a self-referencing term, *uchira* 'we, the members of a group' is used, implying the significance of a group unity. *Uchi* members share a sense of *amae,* and they are likely to use expressions that would enhance and strengthen the feeling of *amae.*

It should be added that depending on the occasion, *uchi* and *soto* worlds shift. For example, at a party held for university alumni, every graduate considers himself or herself an *uchi* member. But just as there are groups within groups, an inner *uchi* group (e.g., members of the ski club) would consider other alumni to be part of the *soto* world. Depending on these in-group/out-group relationships, the style and manner in which you communicate will shift.

The sense of being *uchi* or *soto* plays a significant part in social scenes. Even when a person is *meue,* if he or she is considered an *uchi* member, less polite and more frank expressions are used. In Japanese society, *uchi* and *soto* are the most powerful elements controlling one's social behavior.

Although social contexts such as *uchi* and *soto* offer frameworks within which we select our communication styles, the styles themselves also function to define the context of which they are a part. In other words, by choosing styles permitted to *uchi* members (to the extent it is allowed), the *amae* relationship is nurtured. In addition, by strategically choosing a less polite and therefore a less distant style, you may encourage familiarity and intimacy. In this sense, communication styles are used to create the social context as well.

TATEMAE AND HONNE

A Japanese person is known to distinguish between *tatemae* 'principle, public face' and *honne* 'private true thoughts and feelings'.

Tatemae should be followed based on one's principles and social expectations. *Honne,* on the other hand, is what a person truly thinks and feels. For Japanese, it is important to maintain *tatemae* in many public situations, but at the same time, it is important to share *honne* with people who share the *amae* relationship.

In general, Japanese expressions used to show *honne* are direct and self-revealing, although people select formal and distancing styles when maintaining *tatemae.*

2.4. Popular Culture

For years, Japanese popular culture has attracted worldwide attention. Most popular are *manga* (comic books) and anime (animation games, TV programs, and movies). The art of *manga* and anime can be traced to the works of Osamu Tezuka (1928–1989). Tezuka was a *manga* artist and animator whose works include *Astro Boy (Tetsuwan Atomu)* and *Phoenix (Hi no Tori).* More recently, a series of anime movies by Hayao Miyazaki, including *Nausicca of the Valley of the Wind (Kaze no Tani no Naushika), Spirited Away (Sen to Chihiro no Kamikakushi),* and *Ponyo on the Cliff by the Sea (Gake no ue no Ponyo),* have gained popularity abroad.

Japanese comic magazines and comic books continue to occupy a significant part of printed media. Many of the comic stories are produced as anime, television dramas, and special movies released in theaters. Some representative series include *Meitantei Konan, Kindaichi Shoonen no Jikenbo, Nodame Kantaabire,* and *Nana.* There are literally thousands of *manga,* and information is available not only through thousands of books but also on the Internet.

In addition, Japanese television dramas, movies, music (J-pop), and electronic games are popular in Asia and elsewhere. Japanese cooking and pop art have produced some world-recognized chefs (e.g., Masaharu Morimoto) and pop artists (e.g., Takashi Murakami). Japanese architects (e.g., Tadao Ando) and fashion designers (e.g., Kenzo Takada, Rei Kawakubo, and Junya Watanabe) are also recognized worldwide.

Various images of Japan have been created through consumer culture as well. The phenomenon of Cos-play *(kosu pure),* or costume play, at Akihabara in Tokyo is well known. Some coffee shops and eating places feature service staff wearing "maid" costumes.

Some characters (such as Sanrio's Hello Kitty) personify "cuteness," a recognized value in Japanese culture. Cuteness *(kawaisa)* and cute *(kawaii)* are ubiquitous, and they are easily spotted in the trends of popular culture, the entertainment business, fashion, snacks, and toys. Although a preference for *kawaii* may be considered childish and immature, it is widely used in marketing a variety of commodities and remains a familiar value in Japanese culture.

The familiarity of Japanese popular culture has brought the Japanese language to the world stage. The Japanese language used in some of these media bears distinct characteristics and features. *Manga* contain extensive onomatopoeic and action-enhancing expressions. J-pop uses many English and other foreign loan words and foreign-sounding expressions.

Nihongo in these consumer venues differs from ordinary natural speech. However, it is in this context that you are often exposed to Japanese, and Japanese popular culture provides useful resource for students. Still, it is important to know that the varieties depicted in the mass media resemble the naturally occurring *Nihongo* only in varying degrees. In Chapter 18, we will study the Japanese language representing some of the popular culture genres.

CHAPTER 3

Variation and Change in *Nihongo*

3.1. Variations in Language

When we refer to "the Japanese language," we tend to assume there is one language. In reality, however, the Japanese we speak represents one variety among many, all of which belong to the Japanese language.

A *Nihongo* student should be aware of the functions of different varieties. Choosing the wrong form at the wrong time can be awkward. Youth language addressed to an audience of seniors, for example, would be not only rude but also silly, and such usage would be considered characteristic of a *jooshiki shirazu,* a person who lacks social grace.

There are at least three major factors associated with linguistic variation: (1) the traditional concept of gender, (2) the speaker's age and generation, and (3) the speaker's regional background. This chapter offers a general overview on the nature of variation. Details on different varieties will be given in Chapter 12.

3.2. More Assertive "Masculine" and Less Assertive "Feminine" Styles

Traditionally some Japanese speakers have made a clear distinction between masculine speech (or men's language) and feminine speech (or women's language). Although a clear distinction between these varieties has largely faded and speakers use both styles for expressive purposes, it is necessary to understand their characteristics. Moreover, older speakers tend to retain the distinctions, so it is unwise to use gender-associated varieties carelessly without understanding the possible social consequences.

Differences between masculine and feminine speech styles are not so prominent in formal Japanese as in casual speech. In casual speech, the gender differences appear more significantly, partly because the speaker feels less constrained to express feelings and partly because differences may be used to emphasize one's gender identity in intimate relationships.

In general, feminine speech is more gentle, and masculine speech, more blunt. The overall impression of gentleness or bluntness can be achieved through a number of linguistic and other means.

It is important to realize that female speakers sometimes choose a rather blunt style, and male speakers, a gentle style. In reality, feminine and masculine speech should be viewed as tendencies, as a matter of degree. Masculine and feminine speech styles are not mutually exclusive, and Japanese speakers may use both styles across genders.

3.3. Gender-Associated Styles in Transition

Traditionally feminine speech was considered the kind of language women should use. Numerous books are available to tell women how to talk. However, such discourse itself reflects an ideology that discriminates against women. It makes more sense to understand feminine speech as an option available for all speakers.

In fact, Japanese women's speech is becoming more like men's speech, and gender differences in language use, particularly among youth, are becoming something of a myth. Women are viewed as being more aggressive than once thought, particularly in private and casual situations. The language used by young women and for young women in the media also has taken on features traditionally considered restrictively masculine.

3.4. Generation and Variation

Variations in *Nihongo* are observed among different age groups. Naturally we speak differently and use different vocabulary as we age. In Japanese, a young male speaker may always use *boku* 'I' in childhood, but later in his life he is expected to identify himself as *boku, ore, watashi,* or *jibun* depending on the context.

The formal style followed by the particle *naa,* as in *Samui desu naa* 'It is cold, isn't it?', is considered *ojisan-kotoba* 'middle-aged men's language'. It is not normally used when the speaker is young. In other words, certain expressions are used at different stages of one's life. Age-sensitive variations convey different messages about the speaker's identity. In this way, generational differences in speech style communicate both personal and social meanings.

3.5. Youth Language

Among generational variations, youth language is often noted in the media for its newness, cleverness, and peculiarity. Youth language is the language spoken by teens and those in their twenties under certain circumstances (see section 12.4). Some features of the so-called youth language, however, cross over generations. Some youth expressions have taken root in the speech style of people in their thirties and even in their forties.

The following are some of the known characteristics of youth language.

1. Shortening of existing phrases
   Kimoi instead of *kimochi ga warui* 'feeling (physically) sick' is used. *Kimoi* is used in a more restricted sense; it is used only when feeling emotionally bad.
2. Change of meanings
   Yabai (or *yabee*), which originally meant 'in danger, risky', is also used to mean 'extremely and/or surprisingly good, overwhelmingly excellent'. For example, when eating something very delicious, a young speaker may say, *"Kore yabai"* 'This is too delicious'.
3. Emphatic expressions
   Choo, mecha, metcha, and *mutcha* are used. For example, *choo yasui* 'unbelievably inexpensive' and *mecha kawaii* 'super cute'.
4. Objectifying and self-alienating expressions
   The speaker describes one's own behavior as if objectively observed by someone else. For example, *Kesa, okitara atama mo itai shi, metcha, buruu haitteru mitaina* 'This morning when I got up, I had a headache, and I was under the impression that I was really depressed'. This and other objectifying and self-alienating expressions give the impression that the speaker is being solicitous of and considerate to his or her partner.

3.6. Regional Variations

Although there are many regional variations in Japan, the major dialect divisions are between the Ryukyuan dialects (of Okinawa) and the mainland dialects. The mainland dialects are customarily divided into three large groups: eastern Japan, western Japan, and Kyushu. There are, however, major differences between the eastern group, on the one hand, and the western *(Kansai)* and Kyushu group on the other.

The language of the Kansai area is called the "Kansai dialect" *(Kansai-ben)* and, more restrictively, the "Osaka dialect" *(Oosaka-ben)*. It shows some contrast with the dialect of the Kanto area, or Tokyo speech.

The principal differences are in some vocabulary, in certain word formations, and in the tone system. For example, the verb form *Moo haratta* 'I already paid' in the Tokyo speech is *Moo ha-roota* in the Kansai dialect. Adverbs also differ. *Takaku natta* 'It became expensive' in the Tokyo speech is *Takoo natta* in the Kansai dialect. For the negative *nai* in the Tokyo speech, the Kansai dialect uses *n* or *hen,* as in *Kyoo wa ika-nai* 'I won't go today' versus *Kyoo wa ika-n* or *Kyoo wa ika-hen.*

The tone system difference between the two varieties is also quite noticeable. For example, *ko-ko-ro* 'heart' is pronounced in Tokyo with low-high-low tone but with high-low-low tone in Osaka. Regional variations show differences in conversational style as well. Tokyo speakers express personal opinions and views while soliciting those of others'. In contrast, Osaka speakers are known to involve everyone in the conversation, creating an intensely collaborative discourse.

The majority of Japanese people are exposed to a number of varieties on a daily basis, with the dominant variety being Tokyo speech. In fact, depending on the situation, most Japanese speakers shift between their local speech and the common or standard variety *(kyootsuugo)*, that is, the media-supported Tokyo speech. Most of the media follow Tokyo speech, except in certain entertainment industries where the Kansai dialect appears frequently. In an *uchi* situation, it is more likely that the local speech will be chosen, although in a formal *soto* situation, *kyootsuugo* is likely to be used.

In the past, regional dialects were considered inferior to *kyootsuugo*. However, in recent years, particularly among youth, regional dialects have been taken as something curious and even fun. Select phrases from different dialects are introduced in the mass media for entertainment purposes as well. The value of dialects has increased in general, although in formal occasions people choose *kyootsuugo*.

Among Japanese, the ideal speech is the kind that broadcasters in the NHK (*Nihon Hoosoo Kyookai,* the public broadcasting system in Japan) use in reading the daily news. It is a good idea to listen to their Japanese as a model for the most acceptable accent, speed, and tone.

3.7. New Dialects

Particularly interesting among dialects is the new dialect, called *shin-hoogen.* A new dialect emerges in three ways. First, changes occur within a dialect, and new forms gradually take over. For example, in the northeastern regional dialect *(Toohoku-ben),* among seniors *yokan be* is dominant, although young speakers prefer *ii be* 'it's good'.

Second, new expressions particular to certain speech variations emerge. For example, in Tokyo, instead of *mitai, mitaku* 'like' is used. Instead of *nanigenaku, nanigeni* 'without intention' is preferred. These new forms are not necessarily restricted to youth, and they appear somewhat consistently in ordinary speech. Third, an expression may migrate from its original place to another region. For example, *jan* 'isn't it?', originally spoken in Yamanashi, was introduced into Shizuoka, then to Tokyo. Once it has become popular in Tokyo, particularly due to its use in media, the expression spreads throughout Japan. This is considered a new dialect, although it seems to be on its way to becoming a part of *kyootsuugo*.

Whatever happens to the specific newly created expression, the new dialect is expected to thrive as long as speakers are interested in using it. These expressions are often used for fun and for enhancing a sense of camaraderie among speakers.

3.8. Stylistic Variations

Two of the most prominent speech styles in Japanese are formal and informal. They are marked by the verb form, either formal *desu/masu* or informal *da. Desu* is a formal style of the *be*-verb *da,* and *masu* is a formality marker for other verbs and adjectives. For example, *iku* 'to go' is informal, while *ikimasu* 'to go' is formal.

You use formal style unless there are reasons to do otherwise. It is the style of choice in public and official situations. In general, the formal style is chosen on all occasions where you interact with partners to whom you want to be polite and from whom you want to maintain a distance. Using the formal style is an important part of expressing politeness.

Informal style is used in private situations, though also in public situations if interpersonal familiarity and intimacy are already established. You choose the informal style when the situation does not require formality and when you sense that a familiar and casual attitude is either tolerated or appreciated.

Blunt style is another speech variation. You use it when it is not necessary to pay attention to how you should speak or when you are overtaken by raw emotions such as anger and frustration. Because the blunt style is straightforward and closes the psychological distance between you and your partner, in certain circumstances it can also convey intimacy and closeness. Some blunt expressions are slangy and vulgar and are limited to very casual situations.

In this book, the formal and informal styles appear without markings. When the speech style requires special attention, it is noted in square brackets, that is, [blunt style]. When styles are discussed in the text and they are self-evident, such markings do not appear.

In association with politeness, Japanese can be either polite or supra-polite. Polite expressions use formal forms as well as other moderately polite vocabulary and strategies. Supra-polite expressions use formal style, respectful and humble verb forms, the prefixes *go-* and *o-*, and other very polite strategies. When necessary, the supra-polite style is marked as such, again in square brackets.

3.9. Written, Spoken, and Speech-like Written *Nihongo*

Depending on the methods of communication, three different styles are recognized in *Nihongo:* (1) spoken, (2) written, and (3) speech-like written. Spoken style includes official speech, speech exchanged in formal meetings and business conversations, and casual personal and intimate conversations, among others. Written style is used in letters, documents, novels, print media such as newspapers and magazines, and so on.

The speech-like written style is a recent development and

requires some explanation. In the early 1980s, a style bearing straightforward and unconventional speech characteristics was introduced by a limited number of writers. In the 1990s the speech-like written style (called *shin-genbun-itchitai*) began to rise as a stylistic trend. This style was originally used by youth in communications on the Internet, in magazines targeted at youth, and in many romance novels for girls. Although the Japanese is written, it is written as if one were talking to a friend. It frequently uses interjections, particles (such as *ne, sa,* and *yo*), sound changes (e.g., *suggoku* 'extremely' instead of *sugoku; naantonaku* 'somehow' instead of *nantonaku*). Because of its spontaneity, speech-like written style tends to be simple, sporadic, and emotion-filled.

Currently the speech-like written style is widely used in publications addressed to adult readers, including some magazine articles, essays, and novels. Japanese is becoming increasingly more casual in style, and the speech-like style is spreading across genres.

3.10. Digital Communication

Digital communication on the Internet or on the cell phone *(keetai)* has encouraged a new kind of language use. Some Japanese expressions are used almost exclusively in text messaging on the cell phone (e.g., the final particle *pyoon*). Text messaging encourages short sentences and a spoken style.

Often in digital communication, visual signs are used. They basically come in two types: *kaomoji* and *emoji. Kaomoji,* also called emoticons or smilies, use different keys to form facial expressions. These appear in e-mails and other communications through computer terminals. Many of them are common across languages.

Emoji 'picture characters' are a visual presentation of messages and feelings and are mostly used in cell-phone text messaging. Depending on the cell-phone service with which you contract, different *emoji* icons are available. The use of *emoji* in cell-phone text messaging is prevalent in Japan, particularly among young female users. These picture icons accompany verbal messages to convey overall friendliness and to share feelings. Messages without *emoji* are thought to be too direct. In a way, *emoji* are used like the wrapping paper for a gift, making the communication more pleasing.

The *keetai* culture has produced a popular literary field called *keetai shoosetsu* (cell-phone novels). Certain *keetai* novelists are very popular, and some of the novels are later published as printed books and produced as television dramas and movies. The language used in *keetai shoosetsu* is short, conversational, and youth-oriented. We will examine one such example in Chapter 18.

3.11. Meanings of Variation

On one hand, technological advancements in communication and the saturation of the media have contributed to the decline of traditional differences among varieties of language usage. On the other hand, social and psychological motivations have led to linguistic variability. Think of the language variety shared by closely connected group members. A certain dialect may be used away from the region where it is normally spoken. For example, people from Osaka may carry on a conversation in Osaka dialect in Tokyo to strengthen their sense of unity. A certain speech style may be shared among high school clique members to mark group identity. A specific variety, because it differs from other varieties, functions as a source for emotional bonding that enhances group identity and the sense of group belongingness.

It is important to note that the choice of a certain variety is not based on one's biological or social factors alone. A person in Tokyo may use the speech variety of his or her friend (outside of Tokyo) for expressing intimacy. A female student may use a blunt masculine variety to play with gender identity unexpected in society. Although we choose language varieties on the basis of social conventions, they also function as tools for creating and realizing our identity. Curiously these varieties, because they are associated with biological and social factors, may be used against those very assumptions and expectations.

3.12. Language Change and Learning *Nihongo*

Language constantly undergoes changes, and so do its varieties. As in the case of a new dialect, changes may occur in a single variety. Certain expressions may be transformed by another dialect's influence, or new phrases may be created within a dialect, influenced by the media-supported Tokyo speech.

Changes may be brought about by the media, where certain dialects are used for entertainment purposes. The *Kansai-ben* used by teen idols in television variety shows becomes more acceptable in ordinary communication, for example.

It is customary that the mature adult population tends to be frustrated by rapid changes in language. But language is in constant flux, and there is no way of stopping it. It is interesting that sometimes similar language changes are observed across time. In 2007, a group of Japanese phrases using strings of letters was introduced as a part of the youth language. A prominent example is KY, made up of the first letters of the two words *kuuki yomenai* 'cannot understand the social and situational atmosphere'. But fifty years earlier, a similar mechanism was at work, and MMK was used to refer to *motete motete komaru* 'being extremely popular among the opposite sex'.

The relative importance among the three factors associated with variations (i.e., gender, age, and location) may also shift. Today the age factor seems strongest, and the differences based on location and gender are somewhat declining. These changes influence how Japanese varieties morph through time.

We must recognize that language is always undergoing changes, and a book such as this one can capture only a certain moment in time. Consequently it is important for the student to remain vigilant of constant changes. Publications that comment on new popular expressions, including youth language, are available (e.g., Shuueisha's *Imidas* and Asahi Shinbunsha's *Chiezoo,* published on a yearly basis, some available free on the Internet).

Japanese Internet sites also provide information related to youth language (若者言葉、わかものことば *wakamono kotoba*). Use key words such as 流行語 *ryuukoogo* 'popular phrases' and 新語 *shingo* 'new words' to search for additional information about changes and shifts in *Nihongo*. Most current language changes won't be found in old textbooks, so it is important to remain sensitive to the changes that occur in "real" Japanese.

PART II

Sounds and Scripts

CHAPTER 4

The *Nihongo* Sound System

4.1. Overview

A precise description of the sounds of a language is difficult, and you can fully master Japanese sounds only by imitating what you hear. However, your efforts will be better directed if you are familiar with the system and are aware of predictable problems.

Keep in mind that students of any foreign language must be exposed to the natural flow of the spoken words of the target language. It is important to pay close attention to native speakers' speech in person or through the media. For those of you who are not taking courses and have little access to classroom Japanese, CDs, DVDs, and other audio and visual materials are available. Some sites on the Internet provide Japanese sounds for the words you type in. (These resources are discussed in Part VII.)

Two basic points should be noted about the Japanese pronunciation system, especially relevant to English speakers. The first is making a distinction between short and long vowels, and the second is avoiding the English-style stress. For example, you are familiar with the capital of Japan, Tokyo. How would you pronounce it? The way English speakers normally pronounce "Tokyo," it consists of two short syllables with the accent placed on the first, that is, Tó-kyo.

The accurate pronunciation consists of four units, *to-o-kyo-o*, where *to* and *kyo* are short, but they are both elongated with the duplicated vowel *o*. No stress is placed on *to*.

4.2. Morae

Before we begin, we must familiarize ourselves with the word "mora" (and its plural form, "morae"). A "mora" refers to a unit of

31

time, particularly the duration of a sound. In *Nihongo,* each mora is of approximately the same length, and it carries about the same weight. Instead of syllables, Japanese is supported by mora. (Tokyo is To-o-kyo-o, a four-mora word.) The word *Nihongo* consists of four morae, *ni-ho-n-go,* pronounced with four rhythmical units of sound.

Japanese morae are presented below. Morae are accompanied with *hiragana* (to be introduced shortly) for convenience. Basic morae take the form of (1) the sound "n," (2) vowel, (3) consonant + vowel, and (4) consonant + y + vowel.

4.3. The Sound "N" as One Mora

Special attention must be paid to the sound "n." *N* (ん) is one mora, and accordingly it occupies the same length of time as other morae. The *n* in *nihon* carries the same weight as *ni* and *ho.*

Ni-ho-n	にほん	Japan
sa-n-po	さんぽ	walk
ko-n-ba-n-wa	こんばんは	good evening

4.4. Vowels

There are five vowels in Japanese:

a	i	u	e	o
あ	い	う	え	お

Special attention should be paid to the sound "u." Unlike in English, it is pronounced without rounding or protruding the lips.

4.5. Consonant + Vowel

The consonant + vowel combination forms the primary sound system in Japanese, as listed below.

k/g	ka	ki	ku	ke	ko	ga	gi	gu	ge	go
	か	き	く	け	こ	が	ぎ	ぐ	げ	ご

s/z	sa	shi	su	se	so	za	ji	zu	ze	zo
	さ	し	す	せ	そ	ざ	じ	ず	ぜ	ぞ

t/d	ta	chi	tsu	te	to	da	ji	zu	de	do
	た	ち	つ	て	と	だ	ぢ	づ	で	ど

n	na	ni	nu	ne	no
	な	に	ぬ	ね	の

h/b/p	*ha*	*hi*	*fu*	*he*	*ho*	*ba*	*bi*	*bu*	*be*	*bo*	*pa*	*pi*	*pu*	*pe*	*po*
	は	ひ	ふ	へ	ほ	ば	び	ぶ	べ	ぼ	ぱ	ぴ	ぷ	ぺ	ぽ

m	ma	mi	mu	me	mo
	ま	み	む	め	も

y	ya	yu	yo
	や	ゆ	よ

r	ra	ri	ru	re	ro
	ら	り	る	れ	ろ

w	wa
	わ

A couple of points regarding Japanese consonants follow. First, the Japanese "r" differs from the English "r" and "l," both of which are absent in Japanese. It is produced by the tongue tip flicking the hard gum ridge slightly behind the upper teeth, in a forward and downward movement. Note, in contrast, that the English "r" (as in *run*) is pronounced without touching the palate. Actually, the Japanese "r" is closer to the English "d." Japanese native speakers find the English phonemic distinction between "l" and "r" difficult. Japanese students of English are often warned that *rice* and *lice* are two different things, but in many cases they come out the same.

Second, note that the "th" and "f" sounds are absent in *Nihongo*. Use the "s" and "z" sounds for "th." "Smith," for example, is pronounced *su-mi-su,* and "mother," *ma-za-a*. When pronouncing "fu," instead of the "f" sound, use "h" as in *who. Furuta,* for example, is pronounced *hu-ru-ta.*

4.6. Consonant + Y + Vowel (Contracted Sounds)

A group of sounds is contracted by inserting a "y," creating the following combinations. Note that for the combinations of sy, zy, and ty, we are using "sh," "j," and "ch."

ky/gy	*kya* きゃ	*kyu* きゅ	*kyo* きょ	*gya* ぎゃ	*gyu* ぎゅ	*gyo* ぎょ			
sy/zy	sha しゃ	shu しゅ	sho しょ	ja じゃ	ju じゅ	jo じょ			
ty	cha ちゃ	chu ちゅ	cho ちょ						
ny	nya にゃ	nyu にゅ	nyo にょ						
hy/by/py	hya ひゃ	hyu ひゅ	hyo ひょ	bya びゃ	byu びゅ	byo びょ	pya ぴゃ	pyu ぴゅ	pyo ぴょ
my	mya みゃ	myu みゅ	myo みょ						
ry	rya りゃ	ryu りゅ	ryo りょ						

4.7. Long Vowels (Duplication of Vowels)

Japanese long vowels are duplicated short vowels, as shown below.

aa	ii	uu	ee	oo
ああ	いい	うう	ええ	おお

They are used in expressions such as the following:

aa	ああ	yes	[casual speech]
iie	いいえ	no	
uun	ううん	no	[casual speech]
ee	ええ	yes	

4.8. Double Consonants

The consonants *k, s, t,* and *p* commonly occur in a duplicated form (i.e., *kk, ss, tt,* and *pp*). For example, *k* is duplicated in *sakki* 'a while ago'. This consonant also constitutes a mora, and it is spelled with small *tsu* in *hiragana*. So *sa-k-ki* has three morae.

zasshi	ざっし	magazine
yottsu	よっつ	four
rippa	りっぱ	fine

4.9. Word Accentuation

Beyond vowels and consonants, Japanese sound is characterized by accentuation. As a general tendency, Japanese accentuation is mainly a matter of pitch (high versus low), while English accentuation involves more of a stress (or loudness). Under normal circumstances, accentuation in Japanese is lighter than in English, devoid of a clear distinction between strong and weak sounds. However, some words are strongly and clearly pronounced for emphatic effect.

Although accentuation differs among different regional dialects, here we will focus on Tokyo speech, which makes use of two levels of relative pitch with two basic principles. First, the first two morae in a word are always at different pitch levels. Second, there can be no more than a single drop of pitch within a word. It should be noted parenthetically that the first principle is not always followed in Tokyo speech today; instead, flat pitch is spreading.

In the examples to follow, ¬ marks a change from higher to lower pitch, and □ marks a change from lower to higher pitch.

ha¬shi	はし	chopsticks
ha□shi	はし	bridge
ta□bako	タバコ	cigarette
ta□ma¬go	たまご	egg

Additionally, a notable contour change occurs when combining words. For example, note the words *tori* 'bird' and *shima* 'island'. Although these words share identical pitch, when they occur in a sentence, they trigger a different sound contour in the consequent

sound. In the case of *tori o miru* 'to look at a bird', a high pitch is
sustained at the sound of *o*, while in the case of *shima o miru* 'to
look at an island', *o* takes a lower pitch.

to□ri	とり	bird
shi□ma	しま	island
to□ri o mi¬ru	とりをみる	to look at a bird
shi□ma¬o mi¬ru	しまをみる	to look at an island

As you can see, the pitch assignment in Japanese is rather
complex. The best way to learn is to imitate the natural speech. It
is a good idea to be sensitive to the pitch and to train yourself so
that you can imitate a sound as closely as possible.

4.10. Sound Changes for Emphasis

Japanese sounds are expressively used for emphatic and stylistic
effect. Usually an increase in volume and length indicates an emphasis in meaning. The elongation of vowels brings an emphatic
effect, for example, *yooku* 'really well', instead of *yoku* 'well'. The
elongation is usually transcribed with a bar (—).

(a) Hai hai, yooku wakarimashita.
はいはい、よーくわかりました。
Yes, sure, I understand it well.

Another sound change is the insertion of a glottal stop (a sound
represented as a small っ and ッ), which creates a more emphatic
or more emotive effect. For example, the emphatic *zenttzen* ぜんっ
ぜん 'absolutely not' occurs instead of *zenzen* ぜんぜん 'not at all'.
The glottal stop can be added at the end of an utterance when the
speaker wants to make an extraordinarily strong assertion.

(b) Ikunatt.
行くなっ。
Don't go, ever!

CHAPTER 5

Scripts

5.1. Overview

The Japanese writing system is known to be complex. The most notable feature is its combination of a few distinct scripts. The three basic scripts are *hiragana, katakana,* and *kanji.* While *hiragana* and *katakana* are based on sound units, *kanji* is used on the basis of meaning. In addition, the Latin alphabet *(roomaji)* and Arabic numerals are used.

To see some Japanese writing samples, visit the Web sites of the major Japanese newspapers such as *Asahi Shinbun, Mainichi Shinbun,* and *Yomiuri Shinbun,* and click on the Japanese language icon. Or take a look at Japanese magazines and books if you have access to them. And obviously your Japanese language textbooks will contain some writing samples.

A typical online newspaper site is likely to contain writing samples such as the following.

YOMIURI ONLINE 読売新聞
スポーツ
サッカーW杯予選に代表２５人

Note the different scripts:

roomaji	YOMIURI ONLINE, W
hiragana	に (grammatical particle)
katakana	スポーツ 'sports', サッカー 'soccer'
kanji	読売新聞 *'Yomiuri Newspaper'*, 杯 'cup', 予選 'preliminary matches', 代表 'representatives', 人 (counter for people)
Arabic numerals	２ ５

Notice W杯 'World Cup', a combination of the Latin alphabet "W" and *kanji* for the word "cup." The three lines presented above showing the name of the newspaper and the headline roughly mean the following:

> *Yomiuri* Online   *Yomiuri Newspaper*
> Sports
> Twenty-five representatives chosen for the World Cup soccer preliminary matches

5.2. History

The *kanji* used in Japan today is the Japanese adoption of the Chinese character script. Chinese characters were the first form of writing introduced to Japan around the fifth century. Because the grammatical structures of the two languages differ, writing strictly in *kanji* proved to be problematic. Japanese has conjugations and particles, for which Chinese characters were not suitable.

The solution was to develop *hiragana* and *katakana. Hiragana* was created through the cursive style of writing certain *kanji,* and *katakana* by taking parts of some *kanji.* For example, the cursive style for the character 宇 was used for the *hiragana* う, and the top part of the 宇, to create the *katakana* ウ. *Hiragana* was originally used by female writers, but it became widespread by the tenth century.

5.3. *Kanji*

You use *kanji* when writing independent phrases (especially nouns and parts of verbs), except for *wago* (indigenous Japanese words) and loan words. Using *kanji* is particularly important for words that are distinguished by *kanji* characters. For example, you can write *miru* in two ways: (1) by using *kanji:* 見る 'to see, to look at', and (2) by avoiding *kanji:* みる 'to try and see'. The word *kiku* can be written using different *kanji* characters, among them 聞く 'to hear' and 効く 'to be effective, to take effect'.

Along with Chinese characters, the Japanese borrowed vast numbers of Chinese words. These words were written by using their original Chinese characters. The Chinese word for "water," 水, was borrowed as *sui* from Chinese. This reading is called *on*-reading. At the same time, the Japanese extended the use of *kanji* to represent native Japanese words as well. 水 was used to represent the word *mizu* '(cold) water'. This reading is called *kun*-reading. In this way, Japanese *kanji* typically acquired two readings, *on* and *kun,* normally with closely related meanings.

| *on*-reading | 流水 | ryuu-sui | running water |
| *kun*-reading | 氷水 | koori-mizu | ice water |

Currently 1,945 *kanji* characters are used as *jooyookanji* (*kanji* for general use), of which 1,006 must be learned in the first six years of compulsory education. In addition, nearly one thousand *kanji* characters are authorized for use in personal names. Both native and non-native learners must master more than two thousand basic *kanji* characters to read the Japanese print media. The magnitude of this task accounts for the length of time required to attain a reasonable reading proficiency in Japanese.

5.4. *Hiragana*

Hiragana is the first script most students (and Japanese children) learn. Mastering *hiragana* is absolutely necessary when learning Japanese. The readings of *kanji* are often given by small *hiragana* characters (called *rubi*) placed to the right side or the top of each *kanji.*

You use *hiragana* for native Japanese words, words without *kanji* representation, and particles and to show the conjugated parts of verbs. The *hiragana* system contains forty-six basic symbols and an additional twenty-five variations.

Basic symbols

あ a	い i	う u	え e	お o
か ka	き ki	く ku	け ke	こ ko
さ sa	し shi	す su	せ se	そ so
た ta	ち chi	つ tsu	て te	と to
な na	に ni	ぬ nu	ね ne	の no
は ha	ひ hi	ふ fu	へ he	ほ ho
ま ma	み mi	む mu	め me	も mo
や ya		ゆ yu		よ yo
ら ra	り ri	る ru	れ re	ろ ro
わ wa		を (w)o	ん n	

Additional symbols

が ga	ぎ gi	ぐ gu	げ ge	ご go
ざ za	じ ji	ず zu	ぜ ze	ぞ zo
だ da	ぢ ji	づ zu	で de	ど do
ば ba	び bi	ぶ bu	べ be	ぼ bo
ぱ pa	ぴ pi	ぷ pu	ぺ pe	ぽ po

Note the following exceptions:

1. The particle *wa* is spelled は, the particle *e* as へ, and the particle *o* as を.
2. The verb *yuu* 'to say' is spelled いう.
3. *Oo* is normally represented as おう with a few exceptions:

おおきい	ookii	big
とおい	tooi	far
とおる	tooru	to go through
こおる	kooru	to freeze

4. The sound *zu* is transcribed in two ways. The general rule is to spell it as ず. The alternative is づ, and it is used where the sound *zu* corresponds to つ in a related word. For example, *kizuku* 'to notice' is transcribed きづく because it is related to *tsuku* of きがつく 'to notice'. Also, when the preceding *hiragana* is つ, づ is used, as in つづく 'to continue'.
5. A similar phenomenon exists for the sound *ji*. Although generally じ is used, in rare cases, ぢ is used where the sound corresponds to ち in a related word. For example, はなぢ 'nosebleed' is transcribed with ぢ because it is associated with the word ち 'blood'. The continuation of ちぢ occurs in ちぢむ 'to shrink'.
6. In some casual writing styles, long vowels may be marked by the elongation marker, ー. おはよー may be used instead of おはよう, and ねー instead of ねえ.

5.5. *Katakana*

You use *katakana* primarily when writing Western loan words and some plant and animal names and for emphatic and expressive effect. In addition, some Japanese words are frequently written in *katakana,* as in マジ 'serious(ly)'.

More recently, with increased frequency *katakana* words have been appearing for stylistic reasons. Words written in *katakana* connote an aura of being "in," pointing out what is new, or just communicating specialness. For example, the Japanese Major League Baseball player Ichiroo Suzuki spells his name as イチロー. This *katakana* representation is considered fashionable, and it adds to his status as a celebrity.

The *katakana* system contains the following symbols.

Basic symbols   Additional symbols

ア a	イ i	ウ u	エ e	オ o

カ ka	キ ki	ク ku	ケ ke	コ ko	ガ ga	ギ gi	グ gu	ゲ ge	ゴ go
サ sa	シ shi	ス su	セ se	ソ so	ザ za	ジ ji	ズ zu	ゼ ze	ゾ zo
タ ta	チ chi	ツ tsu	テ te	ト to	ダ da	ヂ ji	ヅ zu	デ de	ド do
ナ na	ニ ni	ヌ nu	ネ ne	ノ no	バ ba	ビ be	ブ bu	ベ be	ボ bo
					パ pa	ピ pi	プ pu	ペ pe	ポ po

ハ ha	ヒ hi	フ fu	ヘ he	ホ ho
マ ma	ミ mi	ム mu	メ me	モ mo
ヤ ya		ユ yu		ヨ yo
ラ ra	リ ri	ル ru	レ re	ロ ro
ワ wa		ヲ (w)o	ン n	

For long vowels, ー is used in *katakana* script.

You may notice a similarity between ソ and ン, as well as ツ and シ. When writing ソ and ン, watch out for the direction of the second stroke. *Katakana* ン requires an upward stroke similar to *hiragana* ん. A good way to remember the difference between ツ and シ is that they follow the basic stroke direction of their *hiragana* counterparts つ and し.

Given that loan words carry sounds absent in Japanese, the transcription process has resulted in the use of special sound combinations. The following are established cases.

ティ ti	ディ di		
シェ she	ジェ je	チェ che	
ファ fa	フィ fi	フェ fe	フォ fo

5.6. Learning the Japanese Scripts

The best way to learn the Japanese scripts is to witness how your teacher writes them. Alternatively, get access to some of the *hiragana* and *katakana* learning Web sites. Usually the sites sponsored by Japanese language textbook publishers or academic institutions are the most trustworthy. Some sites offer moving images that follow correct stroke orders. In writing Japanese scripts, it is particularly important to follow the correct stroke order.

One warning: the *hiragana* も is written with the central line (resembling し) first, followed by the two cross lines. I have seen many cases where both students and teachers make mistakes in this stroke order.

The most effective way to memorize the scripts is to write the symbols time and time again. You can also make flash cards and test yourself. You should master both the reading and writing of *hiragana* and *katakana*. Most important, you must be able to instantly recognize the sounds assigned to the characters.

From this point on, when *kanji* characters appear in independent phrases in the text or when they appear in lists, I will provide the *hiragana* reading, sometimes in parentheses. Note that only the first occurrence of the *kanji* within each entry section will come with the *hiragana* reading. It is particularly important to carefully study the Key Expressions that are provided because those words, when they appear again within an entry, will not be provided with *hiragana*. For sentences containing *kanji*, I provide a *roomaji* transcription immediately underneath.

5.7. Fonts

As soon as you observe Japanese writing, you will notice that a variety of fonts are used. Fonts in the ゴシック, 明朝 (みんちょう), and 楷書 (かいしょ) styles are reproduced below.

ゴシック体	漢字	ひらがな	カタカナ
明朝体	漢字	ひらがな	カタカナ
楷書体	**漢字**	ひらがな	カタカナ

The ゴシック (Gothic) style is widely used in advertisements, announcements, and multiple print media. 明朝 is the standard font used in books and magazines.

I personally like the 楷書 font for students of Japanese. This style mimics the calligraphy brush strokes more accurately than the other two. In 楷書, you can appreciate how each stroke is balanced in the character space, and you can also observe the differences between the fixed and released strokes. However, following the conventions of the print media, this book will use the 明朝 style.

5.8. Punctuation

Perhaps the most surprising thing about Japanese writing to English speakers is the lack of word separation. An entire sentence may appear without an empty space. Also, there is no distinction corresponding to English capitals and lower cases.

Basic punctuation marks include 句点 (くてん 。) and 読点 (とうてん 、). These are called 句読点 (くとうてん), and they roughly correspond to the period and comma. A raised dot functions to separate closely linked elements of the same type as well as the first and last parts of a foreign name, as in アダム・スミス. Quotation marks are called かぎカッコ, and they appear as single quotations 「 」 as well as double quotations 『 』.

Paragraph division is indicated by one empty character space at the beginning of the first sentence of the paragraph.

5.9. Vertical and Horizontal Writing

Although the text in this book is presented horizontally, Japanese can be written vertically. In fact, traditional writing comes almost exclusively in the vertical style. Japanese readers face both vertical and horizontal writing on a daily basis. Horizontal writing is used in scientific publications, as well as in other cases that may include horizontal foreign languages and numbers. Printed newspapers maintain the vertical style, although online newspapers follow the horizontal style.

More recently, a preference has developed toward horizontal writing. In 2008 for the first time, some classic novels were published in the horizontal style. Cell-phone novels are also published in the horizontal style, following how they were first produced as cell-phone text messages. Young people generally prefer horizontal writing, but older people prefer vertical writing. One drawback of horizontal writing is the impossibility of connecting characters, especially in *hiragana*. In traditional writing, connecting a few *hiragana* characters (called *renmentai*) is conventionalized, but this is possible only when writing vertically.

It is particularly important to know that punctuation takes different forms and positions in vertical and horizontal writing.

Paragraphs A and B are identical in content, but they are written in the horizontal and vertical styles respectively. Note the differences in the direction of the elongation bar, the way quotation marks are used, and the positions of 句読点 (くとうてん).

Paragraph A
　今、日本のポップカルチャーは世界の若者の注目を集めている。先日、アメリカの若者に「日本について何か知っていますか」とたずねてみたが、「アニメやマンガ」という答えが返ってきた。

　　日本語を勉強する動機には、このようなポップカルチャーへの興味
がある。それはそれですばらしいことだが、日本の伝統的な文化も大い
に楽しんでもらいたいものである。

Paragraph B

　今、日本のポップカルチャーは世界の若者の注目を集めている。先
日、アメリカの若者に「日本について何か知っていますか」とたずね
てみたが、「アニメやマンガ」という答えが返ってきた。
　日本語を勉強する動機には、このようなポップカルチャーへの興味
がある。それはそれですばらしいことだが、日本の伝統的な文化も大
いに楽しんでもらいたいものである。

　　The *hiragana* readings for the *kanji* used in Paragraphs A and
B are as follows:

今	いま
日本	にほん
世界	せかい

若者	わかもの
注目	ちゅうもく
集めて	あつめて
先日	せんじつ
何か	なにか
知って	しって
答え	こたえ
返って	かえって
日本語	にほんご
勉強	べんきょう
動機	どうき
興味	きょうみ
伝統的	でんとうてき
文化	ぶんか
大いに	おおいに
楽しんで	たのしんで

Here is the English translation:

Currently, Japanese popular culture is attracting young people's attention from all over the world. The other day, I asked an American youth, "Do you know anything about Japan?" and the answer "Anime and *manga*" came back.

The reason for studying Japanese is supported by this kind of interest in popular culture. That in itself is a wonderful thing, but it would be nice if they fully enjoyed traditional Japanese culture as well.

5.10. Calligraphy as Language Art

Although handwriting has become rare, it is still used for special functions such as traditional announcements, a very personal letter, or special seasonal greetings.

Handwriting is also the essential part of the Japanese art of calligraphy. Both lay and professional calligraphers learn to write various styles of Japanese (and some Chinese) scripts with bamboo brushes. *Sumi* ink and various types and sizes of rice paper are used for this purpose. Calligraphy lovers practice intensively and participate in contests. Various local, regional, and national exhibitions of calligraphy are held throughout the year.

Many private calligraphy studios, called 書道教室 (しょどうきょ
うしつ) or 書道塾 (しょどうじゅく), offer courses for everyone from
schoolchildren to seniors.

Novice students start at the lowest rank and work through
over a dozen levels before they are conferred the highest rank of
master. Calligraphy training offers an excellent opportunity for
learning Japanese writing. But more than that, Japanese calligraphy is called 書道 (しょどう) 'the way of writing', and it offers a kind
of spiritual training as well.

In calligraphy, three styles for 漢字 (かんじ) are best known: 楷
書 (かいしょ), 行書 (ぎょうしょ), and 草書 (そうしょ). These were all
developed in China, and each has classic representative works produced by master calligraphers. 楷書 is created with sharp strokes;
行書, with cursive strokes; and 草書 is the most cursive of all. See
my calligraphy (Figure 1) for the character 風 (かぜ) 'wind' in three
styles. From top to bottom, the character 風 appears in 楷書, 行書,
and 草書.

For writing *hiragana,* there are two styles: 仮名 (かな) and ひ
らがな. When 仮名 were developed during the Heian period, each
sound was represented by several different 仮名. These classic 仮
名 are known as *hentaigana* (変体仮名 へんたいがな), and they are
used only in calligraphy. In ordinary writing, you use ひらがな consistently. See my calligraphy (Figure 2) for an example of 変体仮名.

Figure 1. The character *kaze* 'wind' in
kaisho, gyoosho, and *soosho.*

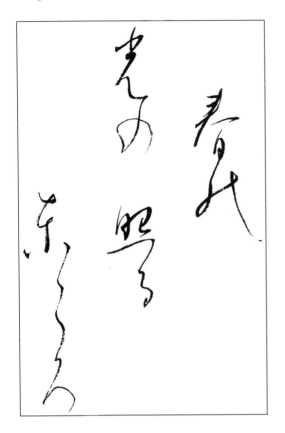

Figure 2. Writing sample of *hentaigana.*

The vertical writing in Figure 2, written horizontally in contemporary script, follows.

春の光の照るところ
haru no hikari no teru tokoro
the place where spring light shines on

PART III

Words

CHAPTER 6

Kinds of Words

6.1. *Wago* and *Kango*

Key Expressions

貧 (まず) しさ	poverty
貧困 (ひんこん)	poverty
旅 (たび)	travel
旅行 (りょこう)	travel
入学試験 (にゅうがくしけん)	entrance examination
入試 (にゅうし)	entrance examination

Explanation

WAGO (NATIVE WORDS)

Indigenous Japanese words are called *wago* (和語 わご). 和語 include native Japanese vocabulary, particles, and conjugation suffixes. These are normally written (1) in ひらがな (and occasionally in カタカナ), (2) in combination with 漢字 (かんじ), as in 貧しさ, and (3) in 漢字 with *kun*-reading, as in 旅.

KANGO (CHINESE-DERIVED WORDS)

Throughout history, the Japanese language has borrowed many words from foreign countries, the most important from China, as early as the Nara period (710–794 AD). During the Heian and Edo periods (ninth through nineteenth centuries), Chinese words continued to enter into the language, and many were integrated to the extent that they are no longer considered foreign "loan" words.

Words borrowed from Chinese or coined in Japan on the basis of classical Chinese are called *kango* (漢語 かんご) or Chinese-derived words (or Sino-Japanese words). More than half of the total

Japanese vocabulary is thought to be influenced by 漢語. See the examples in the Key Expressions: 貧困 and 旅行, which correspond to 貧しさ and 旅 respectively.

漢語 typically contain two meaningful units, using two 漢字 characters. For example, by combining 学 'learning', 生 'living things', and 校 'place for learning', compounds such as 学生 (がくせい) 'student' and 学校 (がっこう) 'school' are formed.

When there are four consecutive 漢字, they are often shortened by taking the first and the third characters, as in 入試 instead of 入学試験 'entrance examination'.

USEFULNESS OF *KANJI*

It is important to use 漢字 when using 漢語. This is because many homophones (different words that sound alike) exist in *Nihongo,* and it is through the assignment of correct 漢字 that we can tell the semantic differences.

| せんたく | 選択 selection | 洗濯 washing |
| さいきん | 最近 recently, lately | 細菌 bacteria, germ |

FORMING ADJECTIVES AND VERBS WITH *KANGO*

漢語 are categorized as nouns. They form な adjectives and する verbs.

便利な	べんりな	convenient
新鮮な	しんせんな	fresh
勉強する	べんきょうする	to study
出発する	しゅっぱつする	to depart

Graffiti

Handwritten 漢字 is becoming rare among Japanese. However, it is crucial to recognize correct 漢字. When a word processor is used, ひらがな input is changed into different 漢字 combinations, and you must be able to choose the correct one. I encourage you to learn as many 漢字 as possible. Minimally you should learn how to read them.

6.2. Loan Words

Key Expressions

コーヒー	coffee
チョコレート	chocolate
メルアド	mailing address (e-mail and cell phone)
セクハラ	sexual harassment
プロ野球 (やきゅう)	professional baseball
デパ地下 (ちか)	department store's basement floor (where food items are usually sold)
ネット検索 (けんさく)	Internet search
ゲットする	to get (obtain) something
トラブる	to get into trouble
ショッキングな	shocking

Explanation

HISTORY

Around 1600 AD, the Japanese language began to borrow many Western words, particularly from Portuguese and Dutch (during the Edo period, 1603–1868 AD). Additionally, German, French, and most of all English loan words have been introduced since the beginning of the Meiji era (1868 AD).

PRONUNCIATION

Western loan words are written in カタカナ and are pronounced according to Japanese phonological rules, mostly in the form of available Japanese morae. The sounds you hear for English words in Japanese may be very different from the original English and may in fact be incomprehensible. How do コーヒー and チョコレート sound to you?

SHORTENED FORMS

Long loan words are often reduced to four morae, as in メルアド for メールアドレス 'mailing address', and セクハラ for セクシャルハラスメント 'sexual harassment'.

マスコミ	mass communication
スタメン	starting member (of a baseball team, for example)
パソコン	personal computer
インカレ	intercollegiate

FORMING WORDS WITH LOAN WORDS

A loan word can be combined with Japanese or other foreign words to produce a compound noun.

The word パン 'bread' (from Portuguese *pão*), for example, is combined with several meaningful units to form the following:

食 (しょく) パン	loaf of bread
フランスパン	French bread
ライ 麦 (むぎ) パン	rye bread
むしパン	steamed bread

Among the Key Expressions presented above, プロ野球 'professional baseball' and デパ地下 'department store's basement floor' are worthy of our attention. Here the shortened loan words (from *professional* and *department store*) and Japanese words (野球 'baseball' and 地下 'basement') are combined. ネット検索 is another example, a combination of (Inter)net and 検索 'search'.

OTHER GRAMMATICAL MANIPULATIONS

Combining loan words and する 'to do' produces a group of verbs, including ゲットする 'to get (obtain) something'. Adding る also produces a group of verbs, including トラブる 'to get into trouble'.

Loan words are used as い adjectives as well as な adjectives, as in the case of the Key Expression ショッキングな. Additional examples follow.

| エロい | erotic |
| ユニークな | unique |

Graffiti

Can you understand the following loan-word-filled expressions? The *Nihongo* used for marketing purposes, as in (a), often employs many loan words, to the extent that they are sometimes incomprehensible to the older generation.

(a)

キッチンを私色にデザインしよう！
柿色、白、シルバーのコントラストがモダン。

Kitchin o watashiiro ni dezainshiyoo!
Kakiiro, shiro, shirubaa no kontorasuto ga modan.

Why not design your kitchen in your own favorite color!
The contrast among persimmon, white, and silver adds a
modern touch.

Note the following loan words contained in these sentences.

キッチン	kitchen
デザイン	design
シルバー	silver
コントラスト	contrast
モダン	modern

6.3. Made-in-Japan "Foreign" Words

Key Expressions

ナイター	baseball night games
サービス	free of charge
ペットボトル	plastic bottle
リアルタイム	live, concurrently happening events

Explanation

There are pseudo-loan words made in Japan. These are foreign-sounding words, but they are created by Japanese with meanings different from (or nonexistent in) the original language. For example, ナイター, made up of the English word *night* and followed by the suffix *-er,* means baseball night games. サービス is related to *service,* but in Japanese サービス means something free of charge. ペットボトル is a combination of an acronym, PET (polyethylene terephthalate), plus the English word *bottle,* and リアルタイム comes from *real time.*

Another made-in-Japan word is クールビズ, related to the words *cool* and *business.* クールビズ is not really a loan word but was created to refer to a cool business outfit worn at the office in the summer to conserve energy. An example of "cool business" attire is the Japanese businessman working without a tie.

An interesting development in word creation is found in イケメ
ン, a combination of イケてる 'cool' and メン 'men'. イケメン refers
to nice-looking men. You may be interested in knowing that メン is
a pun on the Japanese phrase 面 (めん) 'face'. A similar combination is used for ドタキャン 'last minute cancellation'. This is formed
by using the first two morae of the words どたんばで 'at the last
minute' and キャンセル 'cancellation'.

NAMES AND BRAND NAMES

Phrases written in カタカナ and *roomaji*, ローマ字 (じ), give the
impression that they are loan words. With that "with-it" effect in
mind, foreign-sounding names and brand names are created. They
are so ubiquitous in Japan that they no longer sound foreign.

セブンスター	cigarette brand
Shiseido Elixir	cosmetic line
Dime	magazine title
SMAP	idol group name
KAT-TUN	idol group name

Graffiti

Some made-in-Japan pseudo-loan-word product names may raise
eyebrows. As incongruous as they are, all are very popular brands
in Japan.

ポカリスエット (Pokari Sweat) (sweat?)	sports drink
カルピス (Calpis) (sounds like cow piss?)	soft drink
クリープ (Creap) (creep? creepy?)	coffee creamer

6.4. Numerals and the Number System

Key Expressions

一 (いち)	one
十 (じゅう)	ten
百 (ひゃく)	one hundred

Explanation

TWO NUMBER SYSTEMS

There are two number systems up to number 10: (1) numbers of Japanese origin (和語 わご), and (2) numbers of Chinese origin (漢語 かんご).

The 和語 number system is limited in use. You use it for counting objects without counters and for describing ages up to ten years old. You also use it for dates up to the tenth of the month and for a few other combinations.

The 漢語 number system is more extensively used. You use it for mathematical calculations, for combinations that make higher numbers, and in combination with various counters.

	和語	漢語
1	ひとつ	いち
2	ふたつ	に
3	みっつ	さん
4	よっつ	し（よん）
5	いつつ	ご
6	むっつ	ろく
7	ななつ	しち（なな）
8	やっつ	はち
9	ここのつ	きゅう（く）
10	とお	じゅう

UNITS OF NUMBERS

100,000,000,000	一千億	いっせんおく	one hundred billion
10,000,000,000	百億	ひゃくおく	ten billion
1,000,000,000	十億	じゅうおく	one billion
100,000,000	一億	いちおく	one hundred million
10,000,000	一千万	いっせんまん	ten million
1,000,000	百万	ひゃくまん	one million
100,000	十万	じゅうまん	one hundred thousand
10,000	一万	いちまん	ten thousand
1,000	千	せん	one thousand
100	百	ひゃく	one hundred
10	十	じゅう	ten
1	一	いち	one
0	零, ○	れい, ぜろ, ゼロ	zero

SOME SAMPLE NUMBERS

48	四十八	よんじゅうはち
105	百五	ひゃくご
136	百三十六	ひゃくさんじゅうろく
3,792	三千七百九十二	さんぜんななひゃくきゅうじゅうに

PHONE NUMBERS

For phone numbers, just as in English, each number is read as a single digit. For example, 03–3832–5601 will be read ぜろさん、さんはちさんに、ごろくぜろいち. The particle の may be added at the hyphen.

6.5. Counters

Key Expressions

五本 (ごほん)	five long cylindrical items
三匹 (さんびき)	three small animals
七千円 (ななせんえん)	seven thousand yen

Explanation

USING COUNTERS

Counters are used for a set group of items, and they are attached immediately following the number. The use of counters is obligatory, and using numbers only should be avoided.

People

一人	ひとり
二人	ふたり
三人	さんにん
四人	よにん
五人	ごにん
六人	ろくにん
七人	しちにん、ななにん
八人	はちにん
九人	きゅうにん、くにん
十人	じゅうにん
十一人	じゅういちにん

Objects

個 (こ)	for a broad category of small and compact objects, including round fruit, balls, and boxes
冊 (さつ)	for bound objects such as books, notebooks, and magazines
本 (ほん)	for long cylindrical objects, including trees, sticks, pens, bananas, and fingers
枚 (まい)	for flat, thin objects, including paper, dishes, stamps, blankets, and boards

Animals

匹 (ひき)	for insects, fish, and small animals such as cats and dogs
頭 (とう)	for large animals such as horses, bears, and deer
羽 (わ)	for birds

Currency

円 (えん)	yen
セント	cent
ドル	dollar
ユーロ	Euro

Measuring Units

キロ	used for both kilometers and kilograms
グラム	gram
センチ	centimeter
メートル	meter
リットル	liter

SOME SOUND CHANGES

Some counters cause sound changes. For example, 本 undergoes the following changes.

一本	いっぽん
二本	にほん
三本	さんぼん
四本	よんほん
五本	ごほん
六本	ろっぽん
七本	ななほん

八本	はっぽん
九本	きゅうほん
十本	じゅっぽん、じっぽん

Graffiti

If you were to count people by 匹, that would be a joke. This would mean that you were treating people as animals! You can make mistakes by using the wrong counters, but sometimes errors or intended "wrong" use can be humorous (or offensive).

When you are uncertain about counters, use 和語 (わご) numbers up to ten, and after that, use 個, which is the most widely applicable counter.

6.6. Time-Related Expressions

Key Expressions

春 (はる)	spring
月曜日 (げつようび)	Monday
九時半 (くじはん)	nine thirty

Explanation

FOUR SEASONS

春	はる	spring
夏	なつ	summer
秋	あき	fall
冬	ふゆ	winter

DAYS OF THE WEEK

月曜日	げつようび	Monday
火曜日	かようび	Tuesday
水曜日	すいようび	Wednesday
木曜日	もくようび	Thursday
金曜日	きんようび	Friday
土曜日	どようび	Saturday
日曜日	にちようび	Sunday

DATE OF THE MONTH

Use the following for the first to the tenth of the month. For dates beyond the tenth, add the number and 日(にち), for example, 十

五日(じゅうごにち) 'fifteenth', 二十三日 (にじゅうさんにち) 'twenty-third'. Exceptions are 十四日 (じゅうよっか) 'fourteenth', 二十日 (はつか) 'twentieth', and 二十四日 (にじゅうよっか) 'twenty-fourth'. For 'which date', use 何日 (なんにち).

一日	ついたち
二日	ふつか
三日	みっか
四日	よっか
五日	いつか
六日	むいか
七日	なのか
八日	ようか
九日	ここのか
十日	とおか

MONTHS

For months of the year, add 月(がつ) to the 漢語 (かんご) numbers up to twelve. For 'which month', use 何月 (なんがつ).

一月	いちがつ
二月	にがつ
三月	さんがつ
四月	しがつ
五月	ごがつ
六月	ろくがつ
七月	しちがつ
八月	はちがつ
九月	くがつ
十月	じゅうがつ
十一月	じゅういちがつ
十二月	じゅうにがつ

TIME

秒	びょう	seconds
分	ふん	minutes
時	じ	hours
時間	じかん	duration of hours
半	はん	thirty minutes

For 分, sound changes occur as shown below:

一分	いっぷん	one minute
三分	さんぷん	three minutes
六分	ろっぷん	six minutes
八分	はっぷん	eight minutes
十分	じゅっぷん、じっぷん	ten minutes

6.7. Family Terminology

Key Expressions

母 (はは)	my mother
弟 (おとうと)	my younger brother
お母 (かあ) さん	(someone else's) mother
弟 (おとうと) さん	(someone else's) younger brother

Explanation

UCHI-SOTO DISTINCTIONS

One important feature in Japanese family terminology shows a striking contrast with English. *Nihongo* provides two distinct sets of terms depending on whether you are referring to *uchi* or *soto* persons. They also differ depending on whether you are using them for referential purposes or as terms of address. (In the list that follows, FN stands for first name.)

SOME BASIC FAMILY TERMS

| | Referential terms | | Terms of address | |
	Your own	Another's	Your own	Another's
Grand-father	祖父 (そふ)	おじいさん	おじいさん	おじいさま
Grand-mother	祖母 (そぼ)	おばあさん	おばあさん	おばあさま
Father	父 (ちち)	お父 (とう) さん	(お)父さん/パパ	お父さま
Mother	母 (はは)	お母 (かあ) さん	(お) 母さん/ママ	お母さま
Elder brother	兄 (あに)	お兄 (にい) さん	(お) 兄さん	FN + さん

Elder sister	姉 (あね)	お姉 (ねえ) さん	(お) 姉さん	FN + さん
Younger brother	弟 (おとうと)	弟さん	FN	FN + さん
Younger sister	妹 (いもうと)	妹さん	FN	FN + さん
Uncle	おじ	おじさん	おじさん	おじさま
Aunt	おば	おばさん	おばさん	おばさま
Son	息子 (むすこ)	息子さん	FN	FN＋さん
Daughter	娘 (むすめ)	娘さん	FN	FN＋さん
Husband	主人 (しゅじん) or 夫 (おっと)	ご主人	あなた	ご主人さま
Wife	家内 (かない) or 妻 (つま)	奥 (おく) さん	おまえ	奥さま

Male speakers often refer to their own family members by using おやじ 'my father', おふくろ 'my mother', 姉貴 (あねき) 'my elder sister', and 兄貴 (あにき) 'my elder brother'.

Graffiti

When talking to a child, an adult female may refer to herself as お姉さん. The speaker identifies herself in terms of how the child may place her relationally. So to refer to oneself as お姉さん, おばさん, or おばあさん becomes a sensitive issue.

The term おばさん and its intimate version, おばちゃん, are sometimes used to represent middle-aged women, mostly in derogatory terms. For example, おばちゃんの団体 (だんたい) 'a group of middle-aged women' refers to a group of middle-aged women stereotyped as pushy, insensitive, and inconsiderate. A woman labeled おばちゃん is thought to be someone who speaks in a loud voice and is prone to ignore some of the social rules.

6.8. Personal Names and Vocatives

Key Expressions

河井保奈美 (かわいほなみ)
松本弘人 (まつもとひろと)

Explanation

LAST NAMES AND FIRST NAMES

The Japanese last name comes first, and the first name, second. In the key expressions, 河井 and 松本 are last names. In formal situations, when calling out a person's name, [last name + さん] is used. As the degree of familiarity and casualness increases, [first name + さん] and first name only are used.

Calling a person by his or her first name only is widespread among younger speakers, especially among intimate *uchi* members.

INTIMATE VOCATIVES

When the intimacy increases, first names may be followed by ちゃん. In addition, a variety of vocatives and reference forms are used, as shown below.

保奈美さん
保奈美ちゃん [intimate style]
ホナミ (more stylish in カタカナ)
ほなみっち [intimate style]
弘人さん
弘人クン
弘人
ヒロト
ヒロ (shortened forms adding to familiarity and friendliness)
Hiroto

6.9. Onomatopoeia and Mimesis

Key Expressions

ワンワン	bowwow, dog barking
しとしと	rain steadily falling
ザーザー降 (ふ) り	raining cats and dogs
ポカポカ陽気 (ようき)	sunshiny, balmy, warm weather

Explanation

Japanese has a rich system of words that directly and vividly describe sounds or actions. There are two categories. The first is onomatopoeia (擬声語 ぎせいご), that is, sound-imitating words, as in

ワンワン 'bowwow'. The second is mimesis (擬態語 ぎたいご), that is, action-imitating words, as in しとしと 'rain steadily falling'.

FOUR-MORA WORDS

擬声語 and 擬態語 mostly come as four-mora words, consisting of two two-mora segments. A remarkable number of these words occur in the Japanese vocabulary. Dictionaries are available specializing in 擬声語 and 擬態語, some of which are available on the Internet.

USES OF ONOMATOPOEIA AND MIMESIS

Although in English the use of onomatopoeic words may connote childishness, in Japanese 擬声語 and 擬態語 are frequently used by great writers, and their use is not considered childish in the least. You can also find many uses of these words in マンガ.

擬声語 and 擬態語 are most commonly used as adverbs, as shown in the following examples.

(a) 雨がしとしと降る。
Ame ga shistoshito furu.
The rain falls quietly and steadily.

(b) 水を**がぶがぶ**飲む。
Mizu o gabugabu nomu.
[He/She] drinks water thirstily in big gulps.

(c) 星が**きらきら**輝いている。
Hoshi ga kirakira kagayaiteiru.
The stars are shining and glittering.

(d) 川の水が**さらさら**流れる。
Kawa no mizu ga sarasara nagareru.
The river [water] flows smoothly.

擬声語 and 擬態語 are also used as modifying phrases, creating words such as ザーザー降り and ポカポカ陽気, as given in the Key Expressions.

EXPRESSIONS RELATED TO WALKING

Walking may be described in English by different verbs. In *Nihongo*, both 擬声語 and 擬態語 are attached as adverbs in order to describe the various manners of 歩 (ある)く 'to walk'.

ぶらぶら歩く	to loiter, to roam, to stroll
ちょこちょこ歩く	to trot, to waddle
どたどた歩く	to stomp, to tramp
のろのろ歩く	to loiter slowly
すたすた歩く	to hurry
とぼとぼ歩く	to trudge
よちよち歩く	to toddle
よろよろ歩く	to stagger

CHAPTER 7

Words in Grammar

7.1. Nouns

Key Expressions

人々 (ひとびと)	people
買物 (かいもの)	shopping
バス代 (だい)	bus fare
紙袋 (かみぶくろ)	paper bag

Explanation

NO PLURAL FORMS

As alluded to already, in *Nihongo* there is no grammatical plural form marker. ペン refers to both pen and pens. Counters mark quantity, but the nouns themselves remain constant. So we have ペン一本 (いっぽん) or 一本のペン for one pen and ペン五本 (ごほん) or 五本のペン for five pens.

NOUN COMPOUNDS

Nouns are formed by combinations of various sorts, some of which are listed here.

1.   Repetition of nouns for indicating plurality
       The character 々 is used to repeat the preceding 漢字 (かんじ).

人々	ひとびと	people
日々	ひび	days

2.   [N + 代 (だい)] 'fare', 'expense'

バス代	バスだい	bus fare
本代	ほんだい	book expense

3. 漢字 compounds

These words are created by combining two independent 漢字 words, and they take the *kun*-reading.

Combination of 紙 (かみ) 'paper' and 袋 (ふくろ) 'sack':

紙袋　　　かみぶくろ　　　paper sack

Combination of 本 (ほん) 'book' and 棚 (たな) 'shelf':

本棚　　　ほんだな　　　book shelf

NOUN FORMATION

Nouns are formed by combining verbs as well. (The stem of the verb is introduced later in this chapter.)

1. [Stem of the verb + 物 (もの)] 'thing'

買物　　　かいもの　　　shopping (from 買う 'to buy')
食べ物　　たべもの　　　food (from 食べる 'to eat')
読み物　　よみもの　　　things to read (from 読む 'to read')

2. [stem of the verb + 方 (かた)] 'the way of doing'

歩き方　　あるきかた　　way of walking (from 歩く 'to walk')
泳ぎ方　　およぎかた　　way of swimming (from 泳ぐ 'to swim')

7.2. Pronouns

Key Expressions

俺 (おれ)　　　　　I [masculine speech]
私 (わたし)　　　　I
君 (きみ) たち　　　you people

Explanation

LIMITED USE

There are Japanese phrases similar to English pronouns, and depending on the speech style, different forms are chosen. Overall, the use of personal pronouns is more restricted than in English. However, pronouns appear as vocatives and for special self-identification purposes.

PERSONAL PRONOUNS

	First-person 'I'	Second-person 'you'
Very formal	わたくし	おたく, そちら
Formal	私 (わたし)	あなた
	あたくし [feminine speech]	
Casual	僕 (ぼく) [masculine speech]	君 (きみ)
	あたし [feminine speech]	
	俺 (おれ) [masculine speech]	おまえ [masculine speech]
	あんた [blunt style]	

USE OF THIRD-PERSON SINGULAR

For the third person, 彼 (かれ) 'he' and 彼女 (かのじょ) 'she' are used in a limited way. More frequently used for the third person is あのひと 'that person', meaning either 'he' or 'she'. 彼 also refers to a boyfriend or male lover, and 彼女, a girlfriend or female lover. Ex-boyfriend and ex-girlfriend are 元 (もと) カレ and 元カノ respectively.

AVOIDING PERSONAL PRONOUNS

Learning how to use Japanese personal pronouns is important, but knowing how not to use them is more important. First, there is no need to use pronouns when the persons involved are identifiable. Second, あなた should be avoided when addressing your *meue* person. Normally it is safer to address the partner by name.

Wives address their husbands by their first names followed by さん, first name only, or あなた. Husbands often address their wives by their first names or by おまえ. The pronominal address terms chosen by husbands and wives are not necessarily reciprocal.

PLURAL FORMS OF PERSONAL PRONOUNS

For plural forms, use the suffixes たち, がた (formal) and ら (casual) for the following pronouns.

たち	私たち	we
	俺たち	we, male people [masculine speech]
	あなたたち	you people
	君たち	you people [toward *meshita*]
	おまえたち	you people [toward *meshita*]
がた	あなたがた	you people [formal]

ら	私ら	we [casual speech]
	俺ら	we, male people [masculine speech]
	おまえら	you guys [blunt, masculine, toward *meshita*]

Additional plural forms include こどもたち 'children' and 山田 (やまだ) さんたち. 山田さんたち refers not to a group of people with the same last name, Yamada, but to 'Yamada and others'. For the English *they*, use あのひとたち.

Graffiti

The word おたく as a second-person pronoun has extended meanings. おたく or オタク was introduced by the essayist 中森明夫 (なかもりあきお) in the 1980s and has become the word to capture an aspect of (youth) culture. オタク refers to a devoted fan or a person absorbed (to a maniac degree) in a particular theme, topic, or activity. Although the word can be applied to anything, アニメオタク (a fan of anime) and マンガオタク (a fan of comics) are commonly used. オタク often carries a negative connotation that the person in question is overly involved and that he or she lacks common sense and good judgment. Some use the term オタク to describe themselves and their friends in positive and humorous ways as well.

7.3. Noun Prefixes and Suffixes

Key Expressions

お金 (かね)	money
ご飯 (はん)	meal
長 (なが) さ	length
かなしみ	sadness

Explanation

POLITENESS PREFIXES

In polite speech, the respectful prefixes お and ご are used for certain words. As a rule, お is added to 和語 (わご), and ご is added to 漢語 (かんご). Note, however, that お and ご are not productive. Their use is limited to select nouns only, so you must not freely add them to other nouns.

The basic function of these respectful prefixes is to show politeness and respect to the addressee or to the person referred to. These forms tend to be used more frequently in feminine speech. Note that respectful prefixes are attached to nouns associated with your *meue* person. You must not use them in reference to actions related to yourself or to your *uchi* members.

Examples

お名前	おなまえ	name
お話	おはなし	talk
お仕事	おしごと	work
ご卒業	ごそつぎょう	graduation
ご結婚	ごけっこん	marriage
ご旅行	ごりょこう	travel

い ADJECTIVE SUFFIXES

Adding さ and み to い adjectives creates nouns.

1. さ creates a noun referring to the quality or the degree.

美しさ	うつくし**さ**	beauty	from 美しい
高さ	たか**さ**	height	from 高い

2. み tends to express more emotive feelings than the さ suffix.

楽しみ	たのし**み**	fun, pleasure	from 楽しい
深み	ふか**み**	depth	from 深い

7.4. *I*-Adjectives

Key Expressions

暑 (あつ) い。	It's hot.
暑 (あつ) い日(ひ)	hot day

Explanation

い ADJECTIVE PLUS NOUN

Japanese adjectives are either い-type or な-type, and they precede the nouns they modify. All い adjectives end with い, but all words ending with い are not necessarily adjectives. 暑い 'hot' ends with い, and it is an example of an い adjective. It is used as in 暑い日 'hot day'.

い ADJECTIVE AS PREDICATE

い adjectives may also be used as predicates. 暑い can mean 'it's hot'. It may be followed by です, which makes the statement formal, that is, 暑いです. For further changes of form, refer to section 7.13, where adjective conjugation is discussed at the end of this chapter.

COMMONLY USED い ADJECTIVES

新しい	あたらしい	new
忙しい	いそがしい	busy
寂しい	さびしい	lonely
大きい	おおきい	large
小さい	ちいさい	small
近い	ちかい	near
遠い	とおい	distant
良い	よい	good
悪い	わるい	bad

Graffiti

Adjectives undergo changes, particularly among young speakers. For example, おいしい originally meant 'delicious', but it has extended its meaning, and it also refers to 'good, great, excellent'. Not only おいしいチョコレート 'delicious chocolate' but also おいしい話 'a delicious (i.e., great) deal' is used. A similar meaning change occurs in 寒 (さむ) い. Originally used strictly to mean 'cold', it is now used to mean 'bad, disastrous'.

Another interesting change is occurring. Adjectives are being treated like nouns. For example, おいしいがいっぱい 'filled with deliciousness' or かわいいを強調 (きょうちょう) する 'to emphasize cuteness'. This use, prevalent in women's magazines, gives a fashionable and friendly impression.

7.5. *Na*-Adjectives

Key Expressions

好 (す) きな人 (ひと)	person I like
静 (しず) かですね。	It's quiet, isn't it?

Explanation

な ADJECTIVE PLUS NOUN

な adjectives are marked by な when directly modifying nouns. All な adjectives end with な, but not all words ending with な are な adjectives. な adjectives are sometimes called nominal adjectives because although they function as adjectives, grammatically they behave similarly to nouns.

な ADJECTIVE AND PREDICATE

Unlike い adjectives, な adjectives cannot be used as they are as predicates. When used as predicates, they are obligatorily followed by either だ or です. な adjectives follow the conjugation of the verb だ. See section 7.13 for the conjugation.

COMMONLY USED な ADJECTIVES

暖 (あたた) かな	warm
危険 (きけん) な	dangerous
簡単 (かんたん) な	simple, easy
便利 (べんり) な	convenient
いじわるな	mean
いやな	disagreeable, offensive
きらいな	disliked, hated
きれいな	pretty, clean
好 (す) きな	preferred, favorite

7.6. Nominal Modification

Key Expressions

東京 (とうきょう) の夜 (よる)	Tokyo's night, the night of Tokyo
日本 (にほん) の 友達 (ともだち) の家 (いえ)	Japanese friend's home
妹 (いもうと) のアキ	my younger sister, Aki

Explanation

By placing の between nouns, you can create complex nouns. Here, の is a particle that links two nouns, with the first modifying the second. You can repeat this process multiple times. It is important to remember that in *Nihongo* the order of nouns is the reverse of the English [noun + of + noun] structure. Contrast between "the night of Tokyo" and 東京の夜 [lit. 'Tokyo's night'].

APPOSITIONAL USE

You may use the two nouns connected with の to express apposition. In an expression such as 妹のアキ, "my younger sister" and "Aki" are appositional, meaning 'my younger sister, Aki'.

RESTRICTIONS

1. There are some complex nouns where the linking の cannot be used.

入学試験	にゅうがくしけん	entrance examination
	(but not *入学の試験)	
社会主義	しゃかいしゅぎ	socialism
	(but not *社会の主義)	

2. In some cases, nouns linked by の and nouns without の differ in meaning.

東京大学	とうきょうだいがく	the University of Tokyo
東京の大学	とうきょうのだいがく	universities in Tokyo

7.7. Modification Phrases

Key Expressions

日本的 (にほんてき)	Japan-like, Japanese
ビジュアル系 (けい)	visually attractive
若者 (わかもの) っぽい	youth-like

Explanation

CREATING MODIFICATION PHRASES

By adding a suffix to a noun, an entire phrase becomes a modification phrase. For example, 日本 + 的 'Japan-like', ビジュアル + 系 'visually attractive', and 若者 + っぽい 'youth-like'.

Examples

(a) **日本的**な美しさ
     nihontekina utsukushisa
     Japan-like beauty

(b) 健康的な生活
kenkootekina seikatsu
healthy life style

(c) ビジュアル系のタレント
bijuarukei no tarento
a visually attractive talent

(d) ジャニーズ系の男の子
Janiizukei no otoko no ko
a pretty boy, like those boys and young men represented
by the talent agency Johnny & Associates, Inc., in
Tokyo

(e) 男っぽい人
otokoppoi hito
manly person

7.8. Adverbs

Key Expressions

すぐ	right away
いつも	always
詳 (くわ) しく	in detail
簡単 (かんたん) に	simply

Explanation

COMMON ADVERBS

Adverbs usually appear before verbs that they modify, for example,
すぐ帰 (かえ) る 'I'll return right away', いつも忘 (わす) れる 'He always forgets'. Some common adverbs are ときどき 'sometimes', よ
く 'frequently, well', なんとなく 'somehow', and きっと 'certainly, for
sure'.

と ADVERBS

Some adverbs expressing manners of action optionally take と, as
in ゆっくりと 'slowly, leisurely'. Other examples include はっきりと
'clearly' and きっちりと 'exactly'.

FORMING ADVERBS

Just as some adverbs in English may be formed by adding the suffix -*ly* to some adjectives *(happy–happily)*, Japanese is equipped with two such processes. One is to generate adverbs from い adjectives by changing the final い to く. The other method is to form adverbs from な adjectives by changing the final な to に.

(a) From 新 (あたら) しい 'new'

新しく建てられたビル
atarashiku taterareta biru
newly built building

(b) From 楽 (らく) な 'easy'

楽に読める本
rakuni yomeru hon
a book you can read easily

7.9. Demonstratives

Key Expressions

この本 (ほん)   this book
あの人 (ひと)   that person
どの店 (みせ)   which store

Explanation

Japanese demonstratives and pronouns are marked by the prefixes こ, そ, あ, and ど. Depending on how you are viewing an item, that is, from a physical, psychological, or emotional distance, different terms are selected.

USING こそあど IN THE PHYSICAL WORLD

こ   to refer to an item close to you
そ   to refer to an item close to your partner
あ   to identify items that are at a distance from both
          participants
ど   when making question words

USING こそあど IN A STORY

The こそあど system is useful when distinguishing items in an imagined world, for example, when telling a story and explaining where things are. When a new item is introduced within a frame of reference and when it is again referred to, use そ. Thus, if you introduce ルカ first in a story (or in conversation) and then refer back to her, you would use そのひと.

On the other hand, if the referent is assumed to be known by both participants and can be recalled into the current frame of discourse, choose あ. If you know that your partner already knows about ルカ, use あのひと. By using あのひと, you communicate that you are assuming a knowledge or experience in common with your partner. This strategy can create empathy.

EXTENDED USE OF こそあど

こそあど are added to form various nouns and pronouns as shown below.

1. Demonstratives

この	this (close to the speaker)
その	that (close to the listener)
あの	that (away from but identified by both speakers)
どの	which

2. Pronouns used independently

これ	this one
それ	that one
あれ	that one over there
どれ	which one

3. Locative nouns

ここ	this place
そこ	that place
あそこ	that place over there
どこ	which place, where

4. Directional nouns

こちら   this way
そちら   that way
あちら   direction toward that way over there
どちら   which way, which one

USING そこ AND あそこ

The use of あそこ differs from the English *there*. For example, in a scenario where you tell your partner that you went to Shibuya and met your friend "there," そこ is appropriate, but not あそこ. However, if you and your friend are familiar with the café that you went to, あそこ is appropriate. (Reminder: study these examples again after you finish Chapter 9.)

(a) 渋谷に行った。
Shibuya ni itta.
I went to Shibuya.

そこで友達に会った。
Soko de tomodachi ni atta.
There, I met my friend.

(b) <conversation>
A: 渋谷の例のカフェに行った。
Shibuya no rei no kafe ni itta.
I went to that café in Shibuya (I know that you know about it).
B: ふーん、あそこいつも混んでるよね。
Fuun, asoko itsumo konderu yo ne.
I see. It's always crowded there, isn't it?

7.10. Particles

Explanation

Japanese particles come in three different types: (1) grammatical particles, (2) interactional particles, and (3) topic markers. Grammatical particles mark case relations. For example, for a sentence meaning 'John drank coffee', が marks the subject and を marks the object.

(a) ジョン (John) がコーヒー (coffee) を飲んだ (drank)。

Interactional particles express personal feelings and interpersonal attitudes, the most representative ones being ね and よ. For example, used interactionally, よ conveys new information, while ね seeks confirmation. ジョンがコーヒーを飲んだよ means something like 'You may not know that, but John drank coffee.'

Additionally, a number of topic markers operate as particles, は being the most frequently used one. So (b) is a sentence marking John as the topic, that is, something that you are talking about.

(b) ジョン (John) は忙しいです (is busy)。

We will return to particles later (particularly in sections 8.6, 8.11, 11.1, 11.5, and 16.4), but for now, it is sufficient to recognize the very basics of the particles が, を, ね, よ, and は.

7.11. Verbs

Explanation

KINDS OF JAPANESE VERBS

Japanese verbs can be divided into three types: (1) common verbs, (2) *be*-verb, and (3) existential verbs. The verb comparable to English *be* is だ, and its formal counterpart is です. The verbs comparable to English existential expressions *(there is, there are)* are ある and いる. These verbs conjugate in special ways. Refer to the conjugation list presented in the next section.

Common Verbs

Common verbs are verbs excluding the *be*-verb and existential verbs. All verbs (except だ) in Japanese end with the vowel *-u,* that is, either with う or a combination of consonant plus *-u;* for example, く, む, and る. (Needless to say, not all words that end with *-u* are verbs.)

買う	kau	to buy
行く	iku	to go
飲む	nomu	to drink
食べる	taberu	to eat

Stative or Dynamic Action Verbs

Japanese verbs are further categorized based on their tendency to describe either a state of being or a dynamic action. The typical stative verbs are the existential verbs ある and いる. Typical active verbs are 買う, 行く, 飲む, and 食べる.

Transitive and Intransitive Verbs

The transitive versus intransitive contrast in Japanese verbs does not match perfectly with English. However, we can basically understand that transitive verbs require objects (on which the verbs operate) in the sentence, while intransitive verbs do not. For example, 買う 'to buy' is transitive, while 行く 'to go' is intransitive.

There are a number of transitive-intransitive verb pairs. This is similar to English, where the verb *open* can be transitive (as *I open the door*) as well as intransitive *(The door opens)*.

	Transitive	Intransitive
(a)	ドアを**開ける**。	ドアが**開く**。
	Doa o akeru.	Doa ga aku.
	I open the door.	The door opens.
(b)	お金を**集める**。	お金が**集まる**。
	Okane o atsumeru.	Okane ga atsumaru.
	I collect money.	The money is collected.
(c)	名前を**変えた**。	名前が**変わった**。
	Namae o kaeta.	Namae ga kawatta.
	They changed the name.	The name changed.

7.12. Verb Conjugation

Explanation

VERB FORMS

Japanese verbs change form according to features associated with them. Verb endings change to indicate formality levels, tense, and negation, which are covered in this entry.

In addition, verbs change form depending on the meanings added to them. These include potential, passive, causative, volitional, conditional, and command forms. Although these may not be "conjugations" in the narrow sense of the word, I refer to them as such. I will introduce these conjugations when specific forms are discussed.

Verbs are categorized into three types based on the endings of the basic or dictionary form. The basic form is the one listed in the dictionary, and it is the informal, non-past affirmative form of the verb. The three types are U-verbs, RU-verbs, and irregular verbs. These verbs conjugate differently, as shown below and throughout the book. The *be*-verb だ and existential verbs (ある and いる) will be introduced in sections 8.2 and 8.7 respectively.

In addition, important verb forms include the gerundive て form and the stem of the verb, to be mentioned later in this entry.

Verb conjugation is one area in which ローマ字 (じ) is useful. This way, we can see how a consonant and a vowel form a new mora, as in *asob-imasu* from *asob-u*.

U-VERBS

U-verbs are all verbs that are neither RU- nor irregular verbs.

遊ぶ	asobu	to play
驚く	odoroku	to be surprised
買う	kau	to buy
聞く	kiku	to hear
笑う	warau	to laugh

RU-VERBS

RU-verbs end with *-iru* and *-eru* in their basic forms.

1. *-iru* ending verbs

落ちる	ochiru	to drop (intransitive)
起きる	okiru	to get up
着る	kiru	to wear
できる	dekiru	to be able to do
見る	miru	to see

2. *-eru* ending verbs

入れる	ireru	to pour in
教える	oshieru	to teach
答える	kotaeru	to answer
捨てる	suteru	to throw away
寝る	neru	to sleep, to go to bed

Exceptions

There are a few exceptions to this basic verb categorization. The following verbs, although ending with *-iru* and *-eru*, are U-verbs and are conjugated as such.

入る	hairu	to enter
切る	kiru	to cut
減る	heru	to decrease
帰る	kaeru	to return
しゃべる	shaberu	to chat
すべる	suberu	to slide, to slip

IRREGULAR VERBS

Among commonly used verbs, there are only two irregular verbs: する 'to do' and 来る 'to come'.

The irregular verb する is very productive. It is combined with nouns of Chinese origin to make nouns into verbs (see section 6.1). Additionally, foreign loan words become verbs by adding する to them (see section 6.2).

研究する	kenkyuusuru	to conduct research
旅行する	ryokoosuru	to travel
フォーカスする	fookasusuru	to focus
シャンプーする	shanpuusuru	to shampoo

NON-PAST TENSE (AFFIRMATIVE) FORMS

Verbs in Japanese are divided into past and non-past tenses. The word "non-past" is used since it expresses English equivalents of both present and future tenses. The basic function of the non-past tense is to convey that the action or the state referred to has not yet occurred. There is no correspondence among the person (the first, second, or third person), the number (singular or plural), and the verb form.

For deriving the formal form from the basic form, the following rules apply.

U-verbs	Replace the final -u with -imasu.
RU-verbs	Replace the final -ru with -masu.
Irregular verbs	する changes to します
	来る (く) る changes to 来 (き) ます

PAST TENSE (AFFIRMATIVE) FORMS

The past tense conveys that an action or state referred to has already occurred.

To derive the formal version from the basic form, change ます

to ました. To derive informal past tense forms, the following rules apply.

U-verbs

Verbs ending with *-ku*	Replace *-ku* with *-ita*
Verbs ending with *-gu*	Replace *-gu* with *-ida*
Verbs ending with *-u, -tsu,* and *-ru*	Replace endings with *-tta*
Verbs ending with *-nu, -bu,* and *-mu*	Replace endings with *-nda*
Verbs ending with *-su*	Replace *-su* with *-shita*

RU-verbs
Replace the final *–ru* with *-ta*

Irregular verbs
する changes to した
来 (く) る changes to 来 (き) た

LIST OF VERB CONJUGATIONS (AFFIRMATIVE FORMS)

Basic		Formal non-past	Informal past	Formal past
U-verbs				
書く	to write	書きます	書いた	書きました
kaku		kakimasu	kaita	kakimashita
RU-verbs				
食べる	to eat	食べます	食べた	食べました
taberu		tabemasu	tabeta	tabemashita
Irregular verbs				
する	to do	します	した	しました
suru		shimasu	shita	shimashita
来る	to come	来ます	来た	来ました
kuru		kimasu	kita	kimashita
Be-*verb*				
だ	to be	です	だった	でした
da		desu	datta	deshita
Existential verbs				
ある	there is/are	あります	あった	ありました
aru		arimasu	atta	arimashita
いる	there is/are	います	いた	いました
iru		imasu	ita	imashita

VERB STEMS

To obtain the stem of a verb, delete ます from the ます form. For example, the stem of the verb 書く is 書き.

NEGATIVE FORMS

Negation in *Nihongo* is somewhat similar to the English process of adding negative prefixes, as in *dis*courage and *un*cover, except that in Japanese, the endings of the verbs are changed to form the negative. Negative verb forms are formed as shown below.

U-verbs

Informal non-past	Replace the final vowel *-u* with *-anai*
(For U-verbs ending in a [vowel + *-u*], replace *-u* with *-wanai*)	
Formal non-past	Replace *-masu* (of *-masu* form) with *-masen*
Informal past	Replace *-nai* (of *-anai* form) with *-nakatta*
Formal past	Add *-deshita* to *-masen* form

RU-verbs

Informal non-past	Replace the final *-ru* with *-nai*
Formal non-past	Replace *-masu* (of *-masu* form) with *-masen*
Informal past	Replace *-nai* (of *-nai* form) with *-nakatta*
Formal past	Add *-deshita* immediately after *-masen*

List of Verb Conjugations (Negative Forms)

Basic	Formal non-past	Informal past	Formal past
U-verbs			
書く　　to write	書きません	書かなかった	書きませんでした
kaku	kakimasen	kakanakatta	kakimasen-deshita
RU-verbs			
食べ　　to eat	食べません	食べなかった	食べませんでした
taberu	tabemasen	tabenakatta	tabemasen-deshita

Irregular verbs

する	to do	しません	しなかった	しませんでした
suru		shimasen	shinakatta	shimasen- deshita
来る	to come	来ません	来なかった	来ませんでした
kuru		kimasen	konakatta	kimasen- deshita

Be-verb

だ	to be	ではありません	ではなかった	ではありません でした
da		dewa arimasen	dewa nakatta	dewa arima- sendeshita
		じゃありません	じゃなかった	じゃありません でした
		ja arimasen	ja nakatta	ja arimasen- deshita

Existential verbs

ある	there is/are	ありません	なかった	ありませんで した
aru		arimasen	nakatta	arimasen- deshita
いる	there is/are	いません	いなかった	いませんでした
iru		imasen	inakatta	imasendeshita

The negative formal form may also be expressed as ないです. This form takes です immediately after the negative informal form and is less formal than the ません form.

One reminder: the verb 'to say' is written as 言う (いう, *iu*), but it is pronounced as *yuu.* This verb conjugates based on *iu,* producing *itta, iwanai, iwanakatta,* and so on.

Note that alternative negative forms (for the informal past) are also available, that is, add です to the informal past. We have 書かなかったです, 食べなかったです, ではなかったです, and so on. なかったです is considered less formal than ませんでした.

GERUNDIVE て FORMS

The gerundive form of a verb takes て (or で) endings, and therefore it is called the て form.

To obtain the て form, replace the final た of the informal past

tense of a verb with て, and だ with で. For the negative gerundive
て form, for all verbs except the *be*-verb and existential verbs, add
で to the informal non-past negative forms. See the list below for
all forms.

List of Gerundive て Forms

			て form	Negative て form
行く	iku	to go	行って	行かないで
泳ぐ	oyogu	to swim	泳いで	泳がないで
食べる	taberu	to eat	食べて	食べないで
する	suru	to do	して	しないで
来る	kuru	to come	来 (き)て	来 (こ) ないで
だ	da	to be	で	でなくて, じゃなくて
ある	aru	to exist	あって	なくて
いる	iru	to be/exist	いて	いなくて

7.13. Adjective Conjugation

Explanation

Adjectives conjugate according to formality levels and tense. (Refer
to the appendix for the conjugation lists.) な adjectives follow the
conjugation of the *be*-verb だ. So for 危険 (きけん) な 'dangerous' we
have 危険だ, 危険でした, 危険じゃない, きけんではありません, and so
forth.

い adjectives follow specific conjugation rules. Negative forms
are particularly complex and should be learned with care.

CONJUGATION RULES FOR い ADJECTIVES

From the basic/dictionary form (i.e., the affirmative informal non-
past) to obtain:

Affirmative formal non-past	Add です
Affirmative informal past	Replace い with かった
Affirmative formal past	Replace い with かったです
Negative informal non-past	Replace い with くない
Negative formal non-past	Replace い with くないです
	Replace い with くありません
Negative informal past	Replace い with くなかった
Negative formal past	Replace い with くなかったです
	Replace い with くありませんでした

LIST OF ADJECTIVE CONJUGATIONS

Basic/dictionary form	おいしい
Affirmative informal non-past	おいしい
Affirmative formal non-past	おいしいです
Affirmative informal past	おいしかった
Affirmative formal past	おいしかったです
Negative informal non-past	おいしくない
Negative formal non-past	おいしくないです
	おいしくありません
Negative informal past	おいしくなかった
Negative formal past	おいしくなかったです
	おいしくありませんでした

ADJECTIVE STEMS

An adjective stem is obtained by deleting the final い from い adjectives and the final な from な adjectives; thus we have おいし (of おいしい) and べんり (of べんりな).

Irregular Conjugation

Note the irregular conjugation for the adjective いい 'good'.

Basic/dictionary form	いい or more formal よい
Affirmative informal non-past	いい or more formal よい
Affirmative formal non-past	いいです
Affirmative informal past	よかった
Affirmative formal past	よかったです
Negative informal non-past	よくない
Negative formal non-past	よくないです
	よくありません
Negative informal past	よくなかった
Negative formal past	よくなかったです
	よくありませんでした

PART IV

Grammar

CHAPTER 8

Simple Sentences—Essential

8.1. Not Saying the Obvious

Explanation

Generally speaking, in *Nihongo,* any and all elements are left unsaid as long as they are (assumed to be) already understood. Nouns, verbs, and some particles are frequently deleted, especially in spoken language. Instead of strictly following the rule of subject-verb-object, as is the case in English, in *Nihongo* you mention only what needs to be mentioned in a specific context, all placed before the sentence-final verbal element. Mentioning unnecessary bits of information is in fact a sign of clumsiness.

WHEN NOT TO MENTION

When leaving things unsaid, follow the guidelines provided below.

1. Topic of the sentence and discourse
       Once a topic (marked with the particle は, among other topic markers) is introduced in discourse, you need not mention it again unless a specific need arises.
2. Answer to a question
       In an answer to a question, do not mention what is already stated in the question.
3. Information situationally interpretable
       Information given in the context is understood, and therefore pronouns are often deleted.
4. Culturally and socially shared information
       You need not explain what is culturally and socially shared.
5. Grammatical particles
       You may delete grammatical particles, but deletion is normally restricted to informal speech.

DELETING PHRASES AND CLAUSES IN CONVERSATION

In spoken Japanese, you may leave out even the main clause, as shown in (a). This is possible because participants readily understand the context. You may do so in English, but Japanese speakers are more free to do so.

(a) 帰ったら？
     Kaettara?
     (How about) returning?

(b) 帰ったらどうですか 。
     Kaettara doo desu ka?
     How about returning?

8.2. *Be*-Verb Sentences

Key Expressions

KE1   学生です。
           Gakusei desu.
           (I'm a) student.

KE2   明日は試験だ。
           Ashita wa shiken da.
           Tomorrow we have an exam.

KE3   それ、私のです。
           Sore, watashi no desu.
           That one, that's mine.

Explanation

だ AS A BE-VERB

In expressing 'I'm a student,' since "I" is obvious, there is no need to specify it. Simply use だ or です after 学生, as in KE1.

EXTENDED USE OF だ

だ can connect elements other than the grammatical subject and complement. In KE2 明日は試験だ, 明日 is the topic of the sentence (see section 8.11), and 試験だ offers the comment related to the topic. The straight translation into English does not make sense

(*Tomorrow is the exam). だ functions in a broader sense than the English *be*-verb.

DELETION OF だ

The informal form だ is often deleted completely and particularly so in casual situations. For example, when you are asked in casual speech whether you are a corporate employee or a student, 学生 suffices as an answer.

BE-VERB VERSUS SUFFIX

It is important to recognize here that the suffix です attached to い adjectives is different from the verb です. です attached to い adjectives only assigns a stylistic feature. Remember that while the *be*-verb takes either だ or です, い adjective predicates take only です (*高いだ).

である

Another expression associated with だ is である. である may be used in place of だ in formal written Japanese. である adds a tone of dramatic emphasis, and it is often used when a person has given some thought about an issue. It is inappropriate in a sentence pointing out a spontaneous event, as in 火事だ！ 'Fire!' (*火事である).

である is appropriate when following a statement with だ. The combined use of だ and である often occurs in this order.

(a) お金の問題か。
  Okane no mondai ka.
  Is it a matter of money, I wonder.

  そうだ。
  Soo da.
  That's right.

  そう**である**。
  Soo dearu.
  Yes, that is so.

Graffiti

だ is used when making a strong assertion. It is an utterance marker conveying that you are intentionally and strongly making an assertion. This use does not correspond with the English *be*-verb. Note that 知らないよー in (b) is a complete utterance without だ.

(b) 知らないよーだ。
Shiranai yoo da.
I don't know, I'm telling you.

Given that だ is an utterance marker, it can also be used as a stylistic marker. Adding です makes it formal. Compare (c) with its informal version サンキュ.

(c) サンキュです。
Sankyu desu.
Thank you.

8.3. Verb Sentences—Non-Past

Key Expressions

KE1   すぐ行きます。
Sugu ikimasu.
I'm going right away.

KE2   もうすぐ夏になる。
Moo sugu natsu ni naru.
Soon it will be summer.

KE3   毎日散歩します。
Mainichi sanposhimasu.
I take a walk every day.

Explanation

FUNCTIONS OF THE NON-PAST TENSE

What follows provides an explanation of how the non-past tense functions.

1.   Description of the present state (for stative verbs)

(a) 子供がいます。
Kodomo ga imasu.
There is a child.

2. Description of definite future (for active verbs)

   (b) 会議は十時に**始まる**。
   Kaigi wa juuji ni hajimaru.
   The meeting starts at ten.

3. Declaration of personal will

   (c) きっと君を幸せに**する**。
   Kitto kimi o shiawaseni suru.
   I will make you happy without fail.

4. Pointing out principles or the nature of things (for both stative and active verbs)

   (d) 水は摂氏零度で**凍る**。
   Mizu wa sesshi reedo de kooru.
   Water freezes at zero degree centigrade.

5. Description of rules, regulations, and habits

   (e) 毎朝七時半のバスに**乗ります**。
   Maiasa shichiji han no basu ni norimasu.
   I take the seven-thirty bus every morning.

6. Description of procedures

   (f) 玉ねぎは薄く**切ります**。(as in a recipe)
   Tamanegi wa usuku kirimasu.
   Onions are sliced thin.

8.4. Verb Sentences—Past

Key Expressions

KE1   きのう美術館へ行きました。
      Kinoo bijutsukan e ikimashita.
      I went to the art museum yesterday.

KE2   今日、彼と会った。
      Kyoo, kare to atta.
      Today, I met with him.

KE3   もう読んだ。
      Moo yonda.
      I already read (it).

Explanation

FUNCTIONS OF PAST TENSE FORMS

The past tense of the verb is used for multiple purposes.

1.　Descriptions of past events, as in KE1 and KE2

    (a)　きのうは雨が**降りました**。
        Kinoo wa ame ga furimashita.
        It rained yesterday.

2.　Commentary on the fulfillment of a wish or desire

    (b)　(when the bus you were waiting for finally arrives)
        バスが**来た**！
        Basu ga kita!
        The bus is here!

3.　Reaffirmation of an assumption

    (c)　田中さん**でしたね**。
        Tanaka-san deshita ne.
        You are [lit. 'were'] Mrs. Tanaka, right?

4.　Urging someone to act or to perform
      This expression appears in the past informal form. You
    should use this expression only when the person addressed
    is capable of performing the activity in question and is your
    meshita person.

    (d)　さあ、**買った**、**買った**！
        Saa, katta, katta!
        Come on, buy these

    (e)　子供たちは**帰った**、**帰った**！
        Kodomotachi wa kaetta, kaetta!
        Children, come on, go home!

PAST TENSE AS PERFECTIVE TENSE

Mainly because of the functions associated with the past tense, some grammarians call the Japanese past tense "perfective." The past tense of the verb in simple sentences can carry a strong perfective meaning (especially when accompanied by an adverb もう 'already'), as in KE3.

8.5. Adjective Sentences

Key Expressions

KE1   これ、おいしい。
       Kore, oishii.
       This is delicious.

KE2   今朝は寒いですよ。
       Kesa wa samui desu yo.
       It is cold this morning.

KE3   コンビニって、便利ですね。
       Konbini tte, benri desu ne.
       Convenience stores are quite convenient, indeed.

KE4   今日の夕日、きれいだったね。
       Kyoo no yuuhi, kirei datta ne.
       Today's evening sun, it was beautiful, wasn't it?

KE5   ああ、忙しかった！
       Aa, isogashikatta!
       Oh, how busy I was!

Explanation

ADJECTIVES AS PREDICATES

As mentioned earlier, Japanese い adjectives differ from English adjectives in that they function as predicates themselves. See sentences KE1, KE2, and KE5. な adjectives also become predicates as they conjugate as does the verb だ, as in KE3 and KE4.

Graffiti

Certain adjectives become popular and are repeated frequently in conversation. The following adjectives are currently a part of a language fad and are prominent in youth speech.

ウザい   bothersome
ダサい   not stylish, not cool, country-bumpkin-like
ヤバい   threateningly delicious, overwhelmingly good

8.6. Basic Case Markers

Key Expressions

KE1   高橋さんがビールを飲んだ。
Takahashi-san ga biiru o nonda.
Mr. Takahashi drank beer.

KE2   ここにお金を置きます。
Koko ni okane o okimasu.
I place my money here.

KE3   来週から冬休み。
Raishuu kara fuyuyasumi.
From next week, the winter break.

KE4   東京で日本語を勉強した。
Tookyoo de nihongo o benkyooshita.
I studied Japanese in Tokyo.

Explanation

CASE-MARKING PARTICLES INSTEAD OF WORD ORDER

In *Nihongo,* word order is relatively free, although there is a preferred word order (see section 8.14). In English, the position in
relation to the verb defines the grammatical case of the noun. In
Nihongo, instead of word order, you use particles to mark cases.

As we studied in section 7.10, the two most basic case markers
are が and を. The particle が marks grammatical subjects, and を,
grammatical objects.

が MARKS SUBJECTS

For action verbs, as in KE1, the subject is the agent or the per-
former of the action. For stative verbs, the noun marked by subject
marker が is the element whose state is described. For existential
sentences the subject is what exists; for a possessive sentence a
subject is what is possessed.

Active   (a)   友だちが来る。
Tomocachi ga kuru.
My friend comes.

Stative	(b)	先生**が**住んでいます。
		Sensei ga sundeimasu.
		The teacher lives there.
Existential	(c)	大きいビル**が**ある。
		Ookii biru ga aru.
		There is a large building.
Possessive	(d)	お金**が**ある。
		Okane ga aru.
		I have money.

が MARKS ELEMENTS OF PRIMARY PREDICATE FOCUS

As you may have already guessed, the subject in Japanese (not in a strict grammatical sense as in subject-verb agreement) refers to the element most prominent and focused upon, and it is directly associated with and predicated by the verb in active (not passive) sentences. These are elements of "primary predicate focus," and you mark them with が.

This category includes "reactive" description, where the noun represents the source for response and reaction.

    (e) アイスクリーム**が**好きだ。
        Aisukuriimu ga suki da.
        I like ice cream.

In the reactive description, the source that causes reaction or response is the subject. Only a limited number of verbal and adjectival predicates fall into this category (see Appendix 3).

ADDITIONAL GRAMMATICAL MARKERS

に 'in, at', locative marker, also a directional marker

    (f) お金はここ**に**ありますよ。
        Okane wa koko ni arimasu yo.
        There is money here.

に 'at', temporal marker specifying a certain time

    (g) 八時**に**オープンします。
        Hachiji ni oopunshimsu.
        This place opens at eight o'clock.

に 'from', marker of source

(h) 友だちに借りるよ。
Tomodachi ni kariru yo.
I borrow (it) from my friend.

へ 'to, toward', directional marker

(i) 明日図書館へ行く。
Ashita toshokan e iku.
I'll be going to the library tomorrow.

で 'in, at', locative marker, identifying a place of dynamic action

(j) ここで勉強するね。
Koko de benkyoosuru ne.
I study here.

で 'by, through', instrumental marker

(k) これで切る。
Kore de kiru.
I cut (it) with this.

と 'with', joint action

(l) 達也さんと食べます。
Tatsuya-san to tabemasu.
I'm going to eat with Tatsuya.

と 'and', enumerative
Note that the enumerative と connects only nouns and
noun phrases. Do not use と to connect verbs, adjectives, or
clauses.

(m) パスタとサラダを食べる。
Pasuta to sarada o taberu.
I eat pasta and salad.

か 'or', alternative

(n) カフェオレか紅茶を飲みます。
Kafe ore ka koocha o nomimasu.
I drink café au lait or tea.

から 'from', starting point

(o) あしたから夏休みですね。
Ashita kara natsuyasumi desu ne.
It is summer vacation from tomorrow, isn't it?

まで 'until, up to, to', ending point

(p) 五時まで待つよ。
Goji made matsu yo.
I'll wait until five o'clock.

LOCATIVE で AND に

You may be wondering about the difference between the two locatives で and に. Use で when describing the location where a dynamic action takes place. When using a stative verb, mark the location with に. The verbs that take this に are limited. Frequently used examples are いる, ある, 住 (す) む 'to live', and 置 (お) く 'to place (something)'.

DELETION OF PARTICLES

Some grammatical particles are deleted, especially in informal style. In (q), (r), and (s), the parenthesized particles are deleted without awkwardness.

(q) ビール (を) 飲んだ。
Biiru (o) nonda.
I drank beer.

(r) ここ (に) 置くよ。
Koko (ni) oku yo.
I'm placing it here.

(s) 学校 (へ) 行く？
Gakkoo (e) iku?
Are you going to school?

Graffiti

The locative particles introduced here may be followed by the topic markers は and も.

(t) 部屋には友だちがいる。
Heya ni wa tomodachi ga iru.
My friend is in the room.

(u) アメリカで勉強する。日本でもする。
Amerika de benkyoosuru. Nihon de mo suru.
I study in America. I also study in Japan.

8.7. Existential Sentences

Key Expressions

KE1   あそこにかわいいねこがいる。
        Asoko ni kawaii neko ga iru.
        A cute cat is there.

KE2   教室に子供たちがいます。
        Kyooshitsu ni kodomotachi ga imasu.
        Children are in the classroom.

KE3   マンガ本がたくさんあります。
        Mangabon ga takusan arimasu.
        There are many comic books.

Explanation

TWO EXISTENTIAL VERBS

There are two existential verbs, いる and ある. The meaning and the usage surrounding these two verbs differ from those of the comparable English existential verb, and they deserve special attention.

For expressing physical existence, if what exists is animate, use いる, as in KE1 and KE2. If inanimate, use ある, as in KE3.

POSSESSION

You can use いる and ある to express possession. Use いる for animate possession and ある for inanimate possession.

(a)   ガールフレンドが**いる**。
      Gaarufurendo ga iru.
      I have a girlfriend.

(b)   兄は車が**あります**。
      Ani wa kuruma ga arimasu.
      My (elder) brother has a car.

8.8. Basic Interactional Particles

Key Expressions

KE1   おいしいコーヒーですね。
        Oishii koohii desu ne.
        This is delicious coffee, isn't it?

KE2　もう三時だよ。

　　　　Moo sanji da yo.

　　　　It's already three o'clock.

KE3　今週は忙しかったなあ。

　　　　Konshuu wa isogashikatta naa.

　　　　I certainly was busy this week.

Explanation

In *Nihongo,* particularly when spoken, interactional particles frequently appear. They mark the speaker's emotions and attitude and are important in making the conversation go smoothly and comfortably. Here, I introduce ね and よ. A more detailed discussion of these and other interactional particles is given in sections 11.1 and 11.5.

Interactional particles generally convey a sense of familiarity and friendliness. So as a basic rule, you should avoid them toward a person with whom you want to maintain a certain distance. In formal and official situations, these particles appear less frequently.

CHOOSING BETWEEN ね AND よ

ね is a particle conveying your concern toward your partner's thoughts and feelings. ね (sometimes elongated to ねえ) usually signals or solicits agreement or confirmation. This is the case in KE1. You want to focus on or confirm how your partner is thinking and feeling. In contrast, as in KE2, よ is a particle requesting your partner's attention to the information.

Choose ね when you assume that your partner knows more than, or at least as much as, you do. In other words, you already think your partner understands or knows the issue at hand, and you seek confirmation. Choose よ when you assume that your partner knows less than you do.

In (a), the speaker knows that the partner knows that Ren wants to go to London. In (b), the speaker thinks the partner does not know about Ren's desire and wants to alert the partner to this fact.

(a)　連クン、ロンドンに行きたがっていますね。

　　　Ren-kun, Rondon ni ikitagatteimasu ne.

　　　Ren wants to go to London, right (as you know)?

(b) 連クン、ロンドンに行きたがっていますよ。
     Ren-kun, Rondon ni ikitagatteimasu yo.
     Ren wants to go to London (for sure, although you may
       not know).

なあ ATTACHED TO INFORMAL FORMS

The particle なあ is primarily used when recollecting a past event
with astonishment and amazement and making a sound of surprise to yourself. Because you are primarily addressing yourself,
this usage occurs only with informal verb forms. (See sections 3.4
and 12.5 for exceptions.)

(c) あの映画、感動した**なあ**。
     Ano eiga, kandooshita naa.
     I certainly was moved by that movie.

8.9. Questions

Key Expressions

KE1   行きますか。
         Ikimasu ka.
         Do you go? (Are you going?)

KE2   サンドイッチ、食べる？
         Sandoitchi, taberu?
         Do you (want to) eat sandwiches?

KE3   ねえ、カナちゃんて彼氏いる？
         Nee, Kana-chan te kareshi iru?
         Say, Kana, do you have a boyfriend?

KE4   試験は明日？
         Shiken wa ashita?
         Is the exam tomorrow?

KE5   この店はおいしいですか。
         Kono mise wa oishii desu ka.
         Is (the food served at) this place delicious?

KE6   ひとりでさびしかった？
         Hitori de sabishikatta?
         Were you lonely when left alone?

Explanation

FORMING QUESTIONS

For a formal question, as in KE1, add the question particle か at the end of the sentence. か may follow both formal and informal forms. But when か is attached to an informal ending, it is extremely blunt, and it is best to avoid it. For だ, only the [です + か] combination is possible (*だか). The particle か receives a slight rising intonation.

QUESTIONS IN CASUAL SPEECH

In conversation when you are asking a question, a rising intonation at the end of the utterance (without か) may suffice, as in KE2 and KE3. 食べる or 食べます with rising intonation (on the last mora only) means 'do you eat?' For sentences with だ, delete だ and just use rising intonation. Use KE4, 試験は明日? as an informal version of 試験は明日ですか. You must avoid *試験は明日だ? unless it is a repeated echo question (see section 13.13).

The above guidelines apply to adjective sentences as well, as shown in KE5 and KE6.

ANSWERING QUESTIONS

When answering yes/no questions, choose an appropriate phrase from the list below. Expressions are listed from more formal to less formal.

ええ	yes
はい	yes
うん	yes
いいえ	no
ううん	no

ACKNOWLEDGMENT か

When the question marker か appears with a falling intonation (□), it marks a statement acknowledging some fact unknown before. The acknowledgment か often occurs with のだ or んだ expressions, as in (b) and (c). (See section 9.12.)

(a) ああ、川原さんです**か**。(□)
Aa, Kawahara-san desu ka.
Oh, you are Ms. Kawahara, I see.

(b)　これでいいんですか。(□)
　　　Kore de ii n desu ka.
　　　This would do, I see.

(c)　武さん、もう帰ったんですか。(□)
　　　Takeru-san, moo kaetta n desu ka.
　　　Takeru, he already went home, I see.

8.10. Question Words

Key Expressions

KE1　　出発はいつ？
　　　　Shuppatsu wa itsu?
　　　　When is your departure?

KE2　　これ、いくら？
　　　　Kore, ikura?
　　　　How much is this?

KE3　　ケビンさんの電子辞書、どれですか。
　　　　Kebin-san no denshi jisho, dore desu ka.
　　　　Kevin's electronic dictionary, which one is it?

Explanation

A variety of question words (similar to English *what, when, where,* and so forth) is available. Unlike English, you insert these words in the place where their answers would normally appear. There is no need to start questions with interrogative words (as is the case in English).

LIST OF QUESTION WORDS

何 (なに)	what
いくつ	how many
いくら	how much (cost)
誰 (だれ)	who
どこ	which place, where
どれ	which one (among many)
どう	how
いかが	how [formal]
なぜ	why

8.11. Topic and Comment

Key Expressions

KE1 あしたは友達が来る。
Ashita wa tomodachi ga kuru.
Tomorrow my friend is coming.

KE2 手紙は読んだ。きみの気持ちはわかった。
Tegami wa yonda. Kimi no kimochi wa wakatta.
I read your letter. I understand how you feel.

KE3 このファミレスはパスタがおいしい。
Kono famiresu wa pasuta ga oishii.
At this diner, the pasta is delicious.

KE4 この事件には、なにか秘密がありますよ。
Kono jiken ni wa, nanika himitsu ga arimasu yo.
There is some secret about this incident.

KE5 このマンガ、超おもしろかった。
Kono manga, choo omoshirokatta.
This comic book, it was really enjoyable.

Explanation

WHAT ARE TOPIC AND COMMENT?

You must have been wondering about は as used in various sentences so far. Now we are ready to take this marker seriously.

は marks topic, that is, what is being talked about. It can be the subject, object, or any other grammatical element. Comment provides information regarding the topic.

Topic and comment themselves are not based on grammatical relations. Rather, the topic-comment relation is based on how information is structured in communication. It marks an overall umbrella-like system of distinguishing what is being talked about (topic) and what is being introduced as information added (comment) to the topic.

TOPIC-COMMENT IN ENGLISH

The topic-comment structure may roughly be translated into English 'as for X, it is Y' or 'speaking of X, it is Y'. In spoken English, the topic may appear at the beginning of the sentence or at the initial position of a stretch of an utterance.

(a) Fast-food restaurants...I go there only occasionally.

(b) John. I don't know about him.

TOPIC-COMMENT AND SUBJECT-PREDICATE STRUCTURES

Topic is marked by the topic marker は, among others. In KE1, あした は友達が来る, the topic chosen is the temporal phrase あした. The comment consists of subject and predicate, 友達 が来る.

What is introduced as topic (i.e., あした) defines the general framework into which the information described by comment is incorporated. The focus of information is placed on 友達, which is the subject of the sentence.

FROM NEW INFORMATION TO TOPIC

Imagine a situation where you are telling a story about カナ for the first time. First, you introduce her with が. No topic is yet assigned. Then you may use カナは to establish a topic. Once the topic is established, you may delete カナは altogether.

Although not all cases follow this sequence, this process occurs frequently when establishing a topic.

CHOOSING が INSTEAD OF は

Imagine a situation where you want to find out, among a group of people in a room, which one is the leader. You should ask as in (c).

(c) どの人がリーダーですか。
Dono hito ga riidaa desu ka.
Which person is the leader (of the group)?

In answer to (c), your friend would point to the leader and respond as in (d):

(d) あの人がリーダーです。
Ano hito ga riidaa desu.
That person is the leader.

This が provides new information and points out that that person (and that person alone) is the leader. This use of が, sometimes called exhaustive が, normally receives phonological prominence. A similar case follows.

(e) <conversation>

    A: あなた**が**書いたんですか。
       Anata ga kaita n desu ka.
       Did you write this?

    B: 私**が**書きました。
       Watashi ga kakimashita.
       I did write it.

QUESTIONS WITH は

Another possible way of asking a question is by making "the leader" the topic.

(f) リーダー**は**どの人ですか。
    Riidaa wa dono hito desu ka.
    The leader, which person is it?

An answer to this question may be something like (g). リーダー is the topic marked by は, and あの人です provides comment, a piece of new information.

(g) (リーダーは) あの人です。
    (Riidaa wa) ano hito desu.
    (The leader is) that person over there.

NEGATIVE は

In negative sentences (see section 8.12), you mark the negated element by は. In the following situation, the speaker first points out new information with が. Then, the speaker marks あなた with は in a negative sentence.

(h) あの人が悪い。あなた**は**悪くないよ。
    Ano hito ga warui. Anata wa warukunai yo.
    He is wrong. You are not wrong.

THE WHOLE-PART RELATIONSHIP

The topic-comment connection often represents the whole-part relationship. This is shown in KE3, このファミレスはパスタがおいしい. Here the topic is このファミレス, and the comment is パスタがおいしい. The topic refers to the whole (the diner), while the comment explains one part (the pasta) of that whole. Another similar example follows.

(i)　あのホテル**は**窓からの景色**が**すばらしかったなあ。
　　Ano hoteru wa mado kara no keshiki ga subarashikatta
　　　naa.
　　That hotel's view from the window was magnificent.
　　['As for that hotel, the view from the window was
　　　magnificent.']

The topic あのホテル offers the framework, and 窓からの景色が
すばらしかった is the comment. This, in turn, consists of the subject 窓からの景色 and the predicate すばらしかった. The topic defines the whole (the hotel), and the subject focuses on one part of it
(the view from the window).

MULTIPLE TOPICS

Topics may appear more than once in a sentence. In (j), the topic
framework is a combination of 渡辺さん and the temporal phrase
きのう.

(j)　渡辺さん**は**きのう**は**仕事を休みました。
　　Watanabe-san wa kinoo wa shigoto o yasumimashita.
　　Ms. Watanabe was absent from work yesterday.

OTHER TOPIC MARKERS

At this point, I should introduce additional topic markers. も signals topic with the meaning of 'also' and 'in addition'. って marks
topic in casual speech. The phrase といえば also introduces a topic,
and it literally means 'speaking of'.

(k)　佐々木さん**も**休みました。
　　Sasaki-san mo yasumimashita.
　　Ms. Sasaki was also absent.

(l)　買い物**って**、渋谷で？
　　Kaimono tte, Shibuya de?
　　You say shopping, are you going to Shibuya?

(m)　<conversation>
　　A:　ゆりさん**って**、高校生？
　　　　Yuri-san tte, kookoosei?
　　　　Yuri, are you a high school student?

B: うん。あなた**も**？
　　Un. Anata mo?
　　Yes. Are you also?

(n) 海外旅行**といえば**やはりハワイですね。
　　Kaigai ryokoo to ieba yahari hawai desu ne.
　　Speaking of travel abroad, as expected, Hawai'i is the
　　　best.

TOPIC MARKERS OVERRIDE GRAMMATICAL PARTICLES

As evidenced by the sentences introduced above, topic markers
trump the grammatical particles が and を. This takeover also applies to the element of primary predicate focus. So it is possible to
say, for example, アイスクリームは好 (す) きです, in which case アイ
スクリーム is the topic.

TOPIC IN SUBORDINATE CLAUSES

Since the topic is what is being talked about, it does not normally
occur in a subordinate clause. This is because a subordinate clause
is less important than the main clause in terms of its contribution
to the overall information presented. When a noun appears in a
subordinate clause, instead of は, you mark it with the appropriate
grammatical particle.

CONTRASTIVE は

There is a special use of は, often called "contrastive は." When the
は-marked phrase together with は is prominently pronounced, it
implies contrast, regardless of whether or not the contrasted item
is specified. When there are multiple topics within an utterance or
a sentence, more often than not, some carry a contrastive meaning.

　　In (o), ボストンへは is pronounced prominently (in a higher tone
and with more volume than normal), and it carries the contrastive
meaning. Jun goes at least to Boston, although he may not go to
the implicitly contrasted location (for example, New York City).

(o) 潤はボストンへ**は**行きます。
　　Jun wa Bosuton e wa ikimasu.
　　Jun goes at least to Boston.

TOPIC WITHOUT A MARKER

You can present a topic just by placing it at the initial position and
pausing for a moment. In written discourse, a mere 読点 (とうてん)

may suffice, as in KE5. This is similar to English topic presentation in *That guy, he loves baseball.* Similarly, the phrase あいつ in (p) marks a topic.

(p) あいつ、野球が好きだよ。
     Aitsu, yakyuu ga suki da yo.
     That guy, he loves baseball.

8.12. Negation

Key Expressions

KE1   タバコは吸いません。
        Tabako wa suimasen.
        I don't smoke.

KE2   誰もいなかった。
        Dare mo inakatta.
        No one was there. [lit. 'There wasn't anyone.']

KE3   そんなんじゃねえよ。 [blunt style]
        Sonna n janee yo.
        That's not it.

KE4   好きな子？いねえよ。 [blunt style]
        Sukina ko? Inee yo.
        Someone I like? I don't have anyone.

Explanation

To form negative sentences in *Nihongo*, change the verb endings into negative forms (see section 7.12). The topic marker は defines what is negated, a case of negative は, as shown in KE1. Negative は also implies contrast.

NEGATION WITHOUT は

If the relevant phrase does not constitute a topic, it is negated without は. You would use other appropriate case markers. For example, (a) is appropriate when answering the question, "Who isn't coming?"

(a) 山田さんが来ません。
     Yamada-san ga kimasen.
     Mr. Yamada is not coming.

NEGATION WORDS

As in KE2, negative statements take interrogative words followed by も. Additional examples are なにも and どこへも.

(b) **なにも**ありません。
Nani mo arimasen.
There isn't anything.

(c) **どこへも**行きません。
Doko e mo ikimasen.
I don't go anywhere.

NEGATION IN DIFFERENT STYLES

In rapid casual speech, ら in らない and らなかった becomes ん, creating わかんない (instead of わからない) and わかんなかった (instead of わからなかった).

In blunt masculine (youth) style, ない changes to ねえ. This creates forms such as 行かねえ instead of 行かない, and 食べねえ instead of 食べない. じゃねえ in KE3 and いねえ in KE4 are such examples. These expressions are considered blunt and often rude, although coming from a male speaker, they may simply mark masculinity. You should avoid them under normal circumstances.

(d) それ、全然、**わかんねえ**。[blunt style]
Sore, zenzen, wannee.
I don't get it at all.

(e) おまえ**じゃねえ**。あいつが悪いんだ。[blunt style]
Omae janee. Aitsu ga warui n da.
It's not you. He's wrong.

NEGATION OF ADJECTIVES

To negate adjectives, use the conjugation presented in section 7.13.

(f) この映画はあまり**おもしろくない**。
Kono eega wa amari omoshirokunai.
This movie isn't that interesting.

(g) あの駅弁、**あまりおいしくなかった**ですね。
Ano ekiben, amari oishikunakatta desu ne.
That box lunch (purchased) at that station wasn't very
good, was it?

(h) 私はあの先生、**好きじゃなかった**なあ。
Watashi wa ano sensei, suki janakatta naa.
I sure didn't like that teacher.

8.13. Negative Questions

Key Expressions

KE1   土曜日、原宿に行きませんでしたか。
Doyoobi, Harajuku ni ikimasendeshita ka.
On Saturday, didn't you go to Harajuku?

KE2   それ、関係なくない？
Sore, kankeinakunai?
That isn't related, right?

KE3   いっしょに行かない？
Isshoni ikanai?
Won't you come along?

KE4   それ、ひどくない？
Sore, hidokunai?
Isn't that awful?

Explanation

FORMING NEGATIVE QUESTIONS

Placing the question marker か immediately after a negative verb ending creates a negative question. You can also make a negative question without か by slightly raising the tone at the end of the negative sentence. You can do the same for adjective negative questions.

NEGATIVE QUESTIONS FOR INVITATION

You can use non-past negative questions directed to your partner when offering an invitation or making a suggestion. For example, in KE3, the speaker makes a suggestion to come along.

(a) じゃ、あとで、みんなで**会いませんか**？
Ja, atode, minna de aimasen ka?
Then how about getting together later?

(b) ラーメンとか**食べない**？ (See sections 12.13 and 13.5 for と
か.)
Raamen toka tabenai?
Want to eat *raamen* noodles?

NEGATION FOR POLITENESS

Negative questions also function to express politeness and indirectness. For example, by using (c), rather than (d), your request for a favor becomes more polite. Here, although the construction is negative, your assumption is not.

(c) 何か書くもの**ありませんか**。
Nanika kaku mono arimasen ka.
Would you have something to write with? [lit. 'Isn't there anything to write with?']

(d) 何か書くもの**ありますか**。
Nanika kaku mono arimasu ka.
Do you have something to write with? [lit. 'Is there anything to write with?']

In this way, negative questions are used in casual speech as a softening device. Instead of saying それ、ひどい, you may say それ、ひどくない？ as in KE4. These ない endings are frequently observed in conversation, although somewhat limited among older speakers.

NEGATION IN BLUNT SPEECH

In blunt speech, それ、すごくねー？ 'Isn't that great?' instead of それ、すごくない？ is used. Although this is blunt, by using a negative question, the utterance becomes somewhat softened. These seemingly contradictory strategies are useful to express various attitudes.

RESPONDING TO NEGATIVE QUESTIONS

When you respond to a negative question, what the questioner assumes plays a major role. So an affirmative response marks your agreement with the questioner's assumption(s). ええ, はい or うん signals a "yes," although the content of the answer itself is negative.

(e) <conversation>
    A: 妹に会わなかった？
        Imooto ni awanakatta?
        You didn't see my younger sister, did you?
    B: うん、会わなかったよ。
        Un, awanakatta yo.
        No [lit. 'yes'], I didn't.

Graffiti

The double negation なくない？ in conversation offers politeness and vagueness. But なくない can sometimes be confusing.
For example, when someone says このバッグ、かわいくなくない？,
whether the speaker's assumption is positive (i.e., indeed cute) or
negative (actually not cute) remains unclear. In such cases, use
contextual cues to come up with the correct interpretation.

8.14. Preferred Word Order

Key Expressions

KE1   ゆうべバイト先の店で大学の友達と七時からビールを飲んだ。
        Yuube baitosaki no mise de daigaku no tomodachi to
          shichiji kara biiru o nonda.
        Last night I drank beer from seven o'clock with my col-
          lege friends at a place where I work part time.

KE2   それ、彼がやったんじゃないよ。
        Sore, kare ga yatta n janai yo.
        That isn't something he did.

KE3   サキはボーイフレンドと車で大阪へ行ってしまった。
        Saki wa booifurendo to kuruma de Oosaka e
          itte-shimatta.
        Saki drove off to Osaka with her boyfriend.

Explanation

SOV AND THE VERB-FINAL PRINCIPLE

When considering the structure of a Japanese sentence, the key to
remember is that it basically follows the S(ubject)-O(bject)-V(erb)
order. In addition, remember that the most important part of the

sentence is the verbal element, with all other elements appearing before it.

TOPIC APPEARS FIRST

Although the grammatical word order is relatively free, there is a preferred order of elements within the sentence. First, topics, if they appear, come in the initial position. This is because by identifying a topic, both you and your partner share a common starting point.

WORD ORDER

The preferred word order is schematized below. Numbers under column II show the preferred order of elements within that slot.

I	II	III	IV
Topic	1. temporal	Verbal/	Interactional particles
	2. locative	Adjectival	
	3. subject	Predicate	
	4. joint action (と)		
	5. method (で)		
	6. starting point (から)		
	7. direction (に、 へ)		
	8. object (を)		

Graffiti

When describing the order of things, Japanese and English exhibit a clear contrast. In specifying addresses, Japanese starts from a larger area to a specific area, while in English the reverse is true. For example, Tookyoo no Bunkyoo-ku 'Tokyo's Bunkyoo Ward' versus Los Angeles, California. Likewise, addresses written on envelopes and cards follow this basic principle. In Japanese, the larger area designation precedes the smaller area designation. This principle is also followed in the presentation of personal names. The family name comes first, followed by the first name.

CHAPTER 9

Simple Sentences—Enhanced

9.1. Progressive Forms

Key Expressions

KE1 歌を歌っています。
Uta o utatteimasu.
(He) is singing a song.

KE2 電車が止まっている。
Densha ga tomatteiru.
The train is stopped.

KE3 川上さん、結婚してる？
Kawakami-san, kekkonshiteru?
Kawakami, is he married?

Explanation

Recall the gerundive て form of the verb discussed in section 7.12. The [て form + いる] combination offers the progressive ている form. This is somewhat similar to the English progressive tense, the combination of the *be*-verb and the verb gerundive *(-ing)* form.

In casual speech, ている is contracted to てる.

FUNCTIONS OF ている

1. For active durative verbs, ている expresses the progression of an action. KE1 is such an example.

    (a) スージーは今バーでワインを飲んでいる。
    Suujii wa ima baa de wain o nondeiru.
    Susie is now drinking wine at the bar.

(b) 和也？今、テレビ**見てる**よ。
　　Kazuya? Ima, terebi miteru yo.
　　Kazuya? He's watching television now.

2. For active non-durative verbs, ている refers to the continuation of a present state resulting from an already completed action, as in KE2 and KE3. For example, the verb 結婚する 'to get married' describes non-durative action (getting married is achieved in an instant). 結婚している means 'to be married' (as the result of getting married).

　　The negation of this ている points out an unachieved result.

(c) まだ**結婚していません**。
　　Mada kekkonshiteimasen.
　　She isn't married yet.

(d) 私、それ、**聞いてない**よ。
　　Watashi, sore, kiitenai yo.
　　I haven't heard that. (Nobody told me about that.)

3. For some active verbs, ている refers to an action repeated for a certain duration of time. When using (e), you mean the habitual, repeated action of commuting, not that you are in the middle of commuting.

(e) 姉は大学に**通っています**。
　　Ane wa daigaku ni kayotteimasu.
　　My (elder) sister commutes to the university.

4. For a stative verb, ている describes a continuing state. In the case of the *be*-verb, でいる is possible.

(f) いい子**でいます**。
　　Ii ko de imasu.
　　I continue to be a good kid.

Graffiti

There are two additional extended uses of ている.

1. Reference to an experience

(g) あの人はよく外国へ**行っている**。
　　Ano hito wa yoku gaikoku e itteiru.
　　He has traveled to foreign countries often.

2. Progressive form only verbs
    Certain verbs are used only in the ている form, and they
    merely describe the state or quality of things.

    (h) 目の前に高い山が**そびえていた**。
        Me no mae ni takai yama ga sobieteita.
        In front of my eyes, the tall mountain rose.

9.2. Verbs of Giving and Receiving

Key Expressions

KE1   これは友達にもらいました。
       Kore wa tomodachi ni moraimashita.
       I received this from my friend.

KE2   これ、あげるよ。
       Kore, ageru yo.
       l give this to you. (You can take it.)

KE3   先生が弟に本をくださった。
       Sensei ga otooto ni hon o kudasatta.
       The teacher gave my younger brother a book.

KE4   たくさんの方から励ましの言葉をいただきました。
       Takusan no kata kara hagemashi no kotoba o
           itadakimashita.
       I received words of encouragement from many people.

Explanation

Consider that the transference of an object or service can be described in two ways. We can say that A "gives" it to B. The same
incident can be reported from the receiver's point of view, that is, B
"receives" something from A. But in *Nihongo,* there is an additional
dimension.

THE *UCHI* AND *SOTO* RELATIONSHIP

Japanese verbs of giving and receiving involve a third dimension,
an aspect not necessarily significant in English. Depending on who
receives, two different types of verbs of giving are used. If the receiver is you or someone in your *uchi* group, you choose くれる.
Someone くれる 'gives' something to you or to a member of your

uchi group. If you or a member of your group are not the receiver, you choose あげる, someone 'gives' something to someone.

For the verb of receiving, use もらう regardless of whether you or someone else receives.

SOCIAL STATUS

Depending on the relative social status of the participants and the persons described in the giving-receiving event, you must choose different verb forms. Depending on *meue* or *meshita* relationships, each of the くれる, あげる, and もらう take the following additional forms.

Verb	Social status of the giver and receiver
くれる	
くださる	giver is *meue*
くれる	giver is equal
くれる	giver is *meshita*
あげる	
さしあげる	giver is *meshita*
あげる	giver is equal
やる	giver is *meue*
もらう	
いただく	receiver is *meshita*
もらう	receiver is equal
もらう	receiver is *meue*

CASE MARKERS ASSOCIATED WITH GIVING AND RECEIVING

For describing the giver (G), receiver (R), and things exchanged (T), the following case markers are used.

[G が R に T を	くださる / くれる]
[G が R に T を	さしあげる / あげる / やる]
[R が G に / から T を	いただく / もらう]

The particle に is preferred when the receiver has direct personal contact with the giver, whereas the particle から is preferred when the source is somewhat impersonal.

See the particles used in the Key Expressions, that is, もらう in KE1, くださる in KE3, and いただく in KE4.

9.3. Giving and Receiving Actions

Key Expressions

KE1   友達が来てくれた。
Tomodachi ga kite-kureta.
My friend (kindly) came for a visit.

KE2   あとで電話してくれない？
Atode denwashite-kurenai?
Will you please call me later?

KE3   ２０分待ってもらいました。
Nijuppun matte-moraimashita.
I had him wait for me for twenty minutes.

KE4   これ貸してあげるよ。
Kore kashite-ageru yo.
I'll lend this to you.

KE5   先生にお話していただきました。
Sensei ni ohanashishite-itadakimashita.
We had the teacher give a talk.

Explanation

When actions are performed for the benefit of someone (or occasionally to damage someone), you must communicate the benefit (or damage) by using the verbs of giving and receiving. For this pattern, use the て form of the verb in combination with くれる, あげる, and もらう.

For example, 来てくれる means someone came and that action was favorably received. If you simply describe it as 来る, the description remains neutral.

The specific verb of giving or receiving chosen for this structure depends on the relative social status of the giver and the receiver. The appropriate verb should be chosen from the group we learned in section 9.2.

MEANINGS OF てくれる

As in KE1, てくれる describes a beneficial action taken for (thus given to) you or a member of your *uchi* group. KE1 expresses the feeling of gratitude (for the friend's kind visit).

However, てくれる occasionally refers to an unfavorable or damaging action. It expresses a feeling of regret as in (a):

(a) 弱ったなあ、また、あいつ、ミスして**くれた**。
    Yowatta naa, mata, aitsu, misushite-kureta.
    What a bother, he made a mistake again.

MEANINGS OF てあげる

As in KE4, use てあげる to describe an action that you or someone take(s) (thus give[s]) to benefit the receiver. It also describes your strong will as in (b). As an extended use, you can also express a feeling of abandonment, as in (c).

(b) いつかきっとピアノのコンクールで一等をとって**やる**。
    Itsuka kitto piano no konkuuru de ittoo o totte-yaru.
    Some day I will win the first prize in the piano contest.

(c) 結婚を許してくれない。死ん**でやる**！
    Kekkon o yurushite-kurenai. Shinde-yaru!
    They don't approve of my marriage. I'm going to die!

AVOIDING てあげる QUESTIONS

Special consideration is required when using てあげる. When you make an offer, the question, such as in (d), may make your partner feel resentful. It gives an impression that since your partner is helpless, he or she must receive charity from you. A thoughtful speaker will use (e) or (f) instead.

(d) あ、それ、持って**あげましょう**か。
    A, sore, motte-agemashoo ka.
    Shall I carry (it) for you?

(e) あ、それ、持ちましょうか。
    A, sore, mochimashoo ka.
    Shall I carry (it)?

(f) あ、それ、持ちます。
    A, sore mochimasu.
    Let me carry (it).

MEANINGS OF てもらう

As in KE3, てもらう describes a beneficial action you or another receive. This action is usually something desired or specifically requested. KE5 describes the beneficial action of the teacher (*meue* person) giving a talk. Accordingly, the word ていただく is chosen.

Graffiti

てもらう appears in てもらって (も) いいですか as an expression of request. This form is widely used (not among seniors) as a polite request, but you should avoid it toward your *meue* person. Instead, use ていただけませんでしょうか.

(g) ここに書いてもらって (も) いいですか。
     Koko ni kaite-moratte (mo) ii desu ka.
     Can you write it here?

(h) 写真とってもらって (も) いいですか。
     Shashin totte-moratte (mo) ii desu ka?
     Can you take our picture?

9.4. Expressions of Desire

Key Expressions

KE1   お金が欲しいなあ。
        Okane ga hoshii naa.
        I want money.

KE2   もうちょっと食べたい！
        Moo chotto tabetai!
        I want to eat a bit more!

KE3   あの人、新しいデジカメを欲しがっていたよ。
        Ano hito, atarashii dejikame o hoshigatteita yo.
        He wants a new digital camera.

KE4   彼、渋谷のカラオケボックスに行きたがってた。
        Kare, Shibuya no karaoke bokkusu ni ikitagatteta.
        He wanted to go to the karaoke bar in Shibuya.

Explanation

欲しい AND たい

Two patterns are used for expressing desire. If what you desire takes a grammatical noun, use 欲しい 'to want, to desire', as in

KE1. If you want some action performed and it is expressed by a verb, use the [stem of the verb + たい] structure, as in KE2. When the verb is だ, you must use である or でいる. The verbs used in this pattern are limited to those expressing controllable actions only.

YOUR OWN OR SOMEONE ELSE'S DESIRE

Note that 欲しい and たい are used only for the first person and in question forms for the second person. For describing third-person desire, you must use がっている, which marks that the desire is someone else's. Use がる attached to the stems of adjectives 欲しい and たい. We have 欲しがっている 'someone wants something' and 会 (あ) いたがっている 'someone wants to meet'.

This shift is required in *Nihongo* because a distinction is made between what a person directly experiences or feels and information to which a person has only indirect access.

PARTICLES INVOLVED IN EXPRESSIONS OF DESIRE

The object of desire is the source that causes someone to desire. In reference to the element of primary predicate focus (see section 8.6), we understand that the source causing desire is the information of central focus. So when using 欲しい, as in KE1, mark the object of desire by が. When it constitutes a topic, mark it by は or other topic markers.

When たい is used, you mark the object of desire by が or を, as in (a) or (b):

(a) ワインが飲みたい。
    Wain ga nomitai.
    I want to drink wine.

(b) ワインを飲みたい。
    Wain o nimitai.
    I want to drink wine.

When you use 欲しがっている (as in KE3) and たがっている, the object of desire is marked by を. Needless to mention, as in KE4, certain case markers do not take を. For example, in the case of 駅 (えき) へ行 (い) く 'to go to the station', へ remains unchanged.

9.5. Potential and Ability

Key Expressions

KE1   日本語を話すことができます。
       Nihongo o hanasu koto ga dekimasu.
       I can speak Japanese.

KE2   日本語が少し話せます。
       Nihongo ga sukoshi hanasemasu.
       I can speak Japanese a little.

KE3   一時間以内にそっちに行ける。
       Ichijikan inai ni sotchi ni ikeru.
       I can get there within an hour.

KE4   こんなもの、食べられないよ。
       Konna mono, taberarenai yo.
       This kind of thing, I can't eat it.

KE5   あなたにうそはつけない。
       Anata ni uso wa tsukenai.
       I can't lie to you.

Explanation

TWO WAYS TO EXPRESS ABILITY

There are two ways to express potential and ability, that is, こと
ができる, as in KE1, and the potential form of the verb, as in KE2
through KE5.

ことができる

The ことができる pattern is attached immediately after the basic
form of the verb. If you are negating, use ことはできない, as given
in (a).

   (a) 今すぐ出かけることはできないよ。
        Ima sugu dekakeru koto wa dekinai yo.
        I can't leave right away.

Potential Forms

Potential verb endings are formed as shown below.

U-verbs: Replace the final *-u* with *-eru.*

書く	kaku	to write	書ける
遊ぶ	asobu	to play	遊べる

RU-verbs: Replace the final *-ru* with *-rareru.*

食べる	taberu	to eat	食べられる
起きる	okiru	to get up	起きられる

Irregular verbs

する	suru	to do	できる
来る	kuru	to come	来 (こ) られる、来 (こ) れる

PARTICLES ASSOCIATED WITH THE POTENTIAL FORM

When using a potential expression, as in KE2, the particle が marks the object of what a person can do. For ことができる, use を to mark what a person can do. If the thing that a person can do is a topic, the topic marker takes over, as in KE5.

(b) 難しい漢字が読めますか。
Muzukashii kanji ga yomemasu ka.
Can you read difficult *kanji* (characters)?

(c) 難しい漢字を読むことができますか。
Muzukashii kanji o yomu koto ga dekimasu ka.
Can you read difficult *kanji* (characters)?

(d) 簡単な漢字は読めます。
Kantanna kanji wa yomemasu.
Simple *kanji* (characters), I can read them.

(e) 簡単な漢字は読むことができます。
Kantanna kanji wa yomu koto ga dekimasu.
Simple *kanji* (characters), I can read them.

SHORTER POTENTIAL FORM

There is an alternative shorter potential form for RU-verbs. Replace the final *-rareru* with *-reru.* This is called ら抜きことば (ら-deletion version), and it is often thought to be irregular or incorrect. However, in casual speech, especially among youth, 食べれる is used without awkwardness.

食べる	taberu	to eat	食べれる
捨てる	suteru	to throw away	捨てれる

(f)   何でも**食べれる**。
     Nan demo tabereru.
     I can eat anything.

(g)   こんなもの、**食べれない**よ。
     Konna mono, taberenai yo.
     This kind of thing, I can't eat it.

(h)   なかなか、物が**捨てれなく**てね。
     Nakanaka, mono ga suterenakute ne.
     I can't throw away things easily.

Graffiti

Although we have translated Japanese potential expressions into English 'can', you must avoid equating *can* with Japanese potential forms. *Can* is used not only for potential expressions but also for many other purposes, such as expressing permission and possibility. Expressions such as *Can I borrow this?* or *It can happen* cannot be translated into the Japanese potential forms studied here.

9.6. Modal Verbs

Explanation

A wide range of modal verbs is available. They follow different verb and adjective forms.

1.   To convey doubt; used when you express uncertainty, 'perhaps will'

     [verb informal form + だろう (or でしょう)]
     [noun + だろう (or でしょう)]
     [い adjective informal form + だろう (or でしょう)]
     [な adjective stem (i.e., delete the final な) + だろう (or でしょう)]

     (a)   あしたは雨が降る**だろう**。
          Ashita wa ame ga furu daroo.
          Perhaps it will rain tomorrow.

     (b)   子供たちは五人ぐらい来る**でしょう**。
          Kodomotachi wa gonin gurai kuru deshoo.
          Maybe about five children will come.

(c) それはちょっと、無理でしょう。
Sore wa chotto muri deshoo.
Perhaps that would be difficult.

2. To guess with doubt; used when you don't know all the facts but may conclude with reasonable likelihood that something is so, 'may be so'

[verb informal form + かもしれない (or かもしれません)]
[noun + かもしれない (or かもしれません)]
[い adjective informal form + かもしれない (or かもしれません)]
[な adjective stem + かもしれない (or かもしれません)]

In casual speech, this expression can be shortened to かも.

(d) あしたは雨が降る**かもしれない**なあ。
Ashita wa ame ga furu kamoshirenai naa.
Tomorrow it may rain.

(e) そこは危険**かもしれません**。
Soko wa kiken kamoshiremasen.
That place may be dangerous.

(f) <conversation>
A: あした行けない**かも**。
Ashita ikenai kamo.
I may not be able to go tomorrow.
B: えっ？
Ett?
What?
A: ちょっと用事があって。
Chotto yooji ga atte.
I have some chores.

3. To convey social responsibility; used when pointing out that a certain action is an obligation that should be followed as a rule and that it is naturally expected of a person, 'ought to'
[verb informal non-past form + べきだ (or べきです)]

(g) 大事な行事には参加する**べきだ**。
Daijina gyooji ni wa sankasuru beki da.
One ought to participate in important events.

4. To express a natural course of events; used when expecting and anticipating events and facts as a natural outcome; based on the objective conditions to which you have direct

access, you have every reason to believe that things will turn
out just as expected, 'is supposed to'

[verb informal form + はずだ (or はずです)]
[noun + のはずだ (or のはずです)]
[い adjective informal form + はずだ (or はずです)]
[な adjective modifying form + はずだ (or はずです)]

(h) あの人は、もう来ている**はずです**。
　　Ano hito wa, moo kiteiru hazu desu.
　　She should be here already.

(i) 新鮮なくだものはおいしい**はずです**。
　　Shinsenna kudamono wa oishii hazu desu.
　　Fresh fruit should be delicious.

(j) それは簡単な**はず**。
　　Sore wa kantanna hazu.
　　That should be simple.

5. To speculate; used when conveying a likeliness of something
   being so, but little commitment is made as to whether you believe its certainty; speculation based on information primarily
   obtained from sources other than yourself, 'seem'

[verb informal form + らしい (or らしいです)]
[noun + らしい (or らしいです)]
[い adjective informal form + らしい (or らしいです)]
[な adjective stem + らしい (or らしいです)]

(k) あの人は、大阪へ行った**らしいです**。
　　Ano hito wa, Oosaka e itta rashii desu.
　　He seems to have gone to Osaka.

(l) そこはちょっと危険**らしいよ**。
　　Soko wa chotto kiken rashii yo.
　　That place seems to be a little dangerous.

6. To convey likelihood; used when pointing out likelihood based
   on a resemblance of things and situations, 'be likely, be
   under the impression, seem'

[verb informal form + ようだ (or ようです)]
[noun + のようだ (or のようです)]
[い adjective informal form + ようだ (or ようです)]
[な adjective modifying form + ようだ (or ようです)]

(m) あの人は、大阪へ行った**ようです**。
Ano hito wa, Oosaka e itta yoo desu.
It is likely that he went to Osaka.

(n) 彼は学生の**ようだ**。
Kare wa gakusei no yoo da.
I'm under the impression that he is a student.

(o) 最近彼は元気になった**ようだ**。
Saikin kare wa genkini natta yoo da.
I'm under the impression that recently he has gotten well.

7. To guess with confidence; used when you are quite certain of your assumptions, conveying more confidence than だろう and かもしれない, 'must'

[verb informal form + にちがいない (or にちがいありません)]
[noun + にちがいない (or にちがいありません)]
[い adjective informal form + にちがいない (or にちがいありません)]
[な adjective stem + にちがいない (or にちがいありません)]

(p) あの絵は値段も高い**にちがいありません**。
Ano e wa nedan mo takai ni chigaiarimasen.
The price of that painting must be high.

(q) 犯人はあいつ**にちがいない**。
Hannin wa aitsu ni chigainai.
The perpetrator must be that guy.

8. To make an eyewitness conjecture; used when conjecturing the likelihood of a future event or the current condition of something, based on what you have personally perceived, 'it looks (as if)'

[verb stem ＋そうだ (or そうです)]
[い adjective stem (i.e., delete the final い)＋そうだ (or そうです)]
[な adjective stem＋そうだ (or そうです)]

(r) あしたは、雨になり**そうだ**。
Ashita wa ame ni narisoo da.
It looks like it will rain tomorrow.

(s) そのくだもの、おいし**そうです**ね。
Sono kudamono, oishisoo desu ne.
That fruit looks delicious.

(t) このセーター、暖か**そう**。
Kono seetaa, atatakasoo.
This sweater looks warm.

NEGATION USING MODAL VERBS

When using modal verbs, you must negate the verb and the adjective preceding the modal verb. For example, あしたは、雨は降らないだろう 'It won't rain tomorrow'.

(u) あの人には**会えないかもしれない**なあ。
Ano hito ni wa aenai kamoshirenai naa.
I may not be able to see him.

(v) ユキは、試験だから、パーティーには**来ないはず**だけど。
Yuki wa, shiken da kara, paatii ni wa konai hazu da
kedo.
Because there is an exam, Yuki should not be coming to
the party.

(w) きのうから、何も**食べていない**らしい。
Kinoo kara, nanimo tateteinai rashii.
It seems that he hasn't eaten anything since yesterday.

(x) それはあまり**簡単じゃない**でしょう。
Sore wa amari kantan janai deshoo.
Probably that isn't so simple.

9.7. Prohibition and Obligation

Key Expressions

KE1   授業中は英語を話してはいけません。
Jugyoochuu wa eigo o hanashite wa ikemasen.
You must not speak English during the class.

KE2   そんなにお酒飲んじゃだめよ。
Sonnani osake nonja dame yo.
You shouldn't drink that much sake.

KE3   あしたまでにこの本を読まなければなりません。
Ashita made ni kono hon o yomanakereba narimasen.
I must read this book by tomorrow.

Explanation

In addition to the modal verbs we studied in section 9.6, we should pay special attention to the use of two modal expressions that show prohibition and obligation.

PROHIBITION

To express prohibition or a strong negative command, [v/adj て + は + いけない] is available, as in KE1. ては and では used in prohibition expressions are contracted to ちゃ and じゃ respectively in casual speech. This and additional forms used for this purpose are listed below. KE2 is an example of じゃだめ.

てはいけない	てはいけません	(いけない lit. 'it is wrong')
ては困る	ては困ります	(困る lit. 'it is problematic')
てはだめだ	てはだめです	(だめだ lit. 'it is bad')

All these are translated into the English 'must not' or 'should not'.

   (a) ここで大声を**あげては困ります**。
       Koko de oogoe o agete wa komarimasu.
       You must not speak loudly here [lit. 'Speaking loudly here
         is problematic'].

   (b) あそこで**遊んじゃだめ**！
       Asoko de ason ja dame!
       You must not play over there.

Toward your *meue* person, the prohibition expressions introduced here should be avoided. Instead, negative request forms such as ないでくださいませんか or ないでいただけませんか are recommended.

OBLIGATION

Duty and obligation are expressed indirectly by using the negative ば conditional, that is, なければ. なければ is then followed by ならない or いけない. See KE3 for an example of なければならない.

These expressions mean 'if you do not do this, it is not good' (or 'it bothers me'), and they are normally translated with the English auxiliary verb 'must'.

なければならない describes absolute obligation.

(c) この建物に入るには、許可を**得なければならない**。

Kono tatemono ni hairu ni wa kyoka o **enakereba
   naranai**.

You must obtain permission to enter this building.

(d) いっしょうけんめい**働かなければなりません**。

Isshookenmei **hatarakanakereba narimasen**.

I must work hard.

(e) 八時までに東京駅へ**行かなければなりません**。

Hachiji made ni Tookyoo-eki e **ikanakereba narimasen**.

I must get to the Tokyo station by eight o'clock.

なければいけない is often used to offer advice to, give orders to, or make an emphatic request of your *meshita* person. It is addressed directly to the listener.

(f) <conversation>

A: 大切な手紙だから字をきちんと**書かなければいけません**よ。

Taisetsuna tegami da kara ji o kichinto **kakanakereba
   ikemasen** yo.

Since this is an important letter, you must write the
   characters neatly.

B: はい、わかりました。

Hai, wakarimashita.

Yes, I will.

The obligation pattern may also take だめだ.

(g) 早く**起きなければだめ**よ。

Hayaku **okinakereba dame** yo.

You must get up early.

なければ can be contracted to なけりゃ and なきゃ.

(h) すぐ**帰ってこなけりゃだめ**よ。

Sugu **kaette-konakerya dame** yo.

You must come back right away.

(i) **勉強しなきゃだめ**よ。

Benkyooshinakya dame yo.

You must study.

9.8. Modal Suffixes

Key Expressions

KE1　パーティーの準備ですか。もうしてありますよ。
Paatii no junbi desu ka. Moo shite-arimasu yo.
The preparations for the party? They're already
completed.

KE2　ビールもたくさん買っておいたよ。
Biiru mo takusan katte-oita yo.
I bought a lot of beer (for future use).

KE3　そんな昔のこと、もう忘れてしまったなあ。
Sonna mukashi no koto, moo wasurete-shimatta naa.
I had forgotten, it was so long ago.

KE4　えっ、私の分も食べちゃったの？
Ett, watashi no bun mo tabe-chatta no?
What, you ate up my portion, did you?

Explanation

Among Japanese modal suffixes, the following three forms are
most useful. They all take the て form of the verb.

てある EXPRESSION

The てある structure indicates that a certain state was created as a
result of someone's special action. Use it when you are conscious
of someone having done something, and its result is useful for the
next step. KE1 is such an example.

　The verbs appearing in this and the next pattern are volitional
in nature. What you cannot control cannot be performed with a
specific intent.

　Let's assume that you specifically bought some nice wine for
a party. Now you want to describe the current situation resulting
from that wine purchase. You would say something like おいしいワ
インが買ってあるよ 'Delicious wine is already bought'.

　The negation of the てある expression produces ワインは買って
ない 'The wine is not bought yet', pointing out that something is yet
to be completed.

ておく EXPRESSION

The ておく structure describes a state achieved intentionally for some future purpose, as in KE2. Unlike てある、ておく focuses more on the action itself. For example, you bought delicious wine for the party, and you want to refer to the action itself. You are likely to say something like おいしいワインを買っておいたよ 'I bought delicious wine'. ておく is contracted to とく in casual speech as in おいしいワイン買っといたよ.

てしまう EXPRESSION

てしまう indicates completion and finality. As in KE3 and KE4, you emphasize that the action is complete and irrevocable. It adds a note of fatalism in that what has been done once cannot be undone. It is similar to the English *end up doing* and *finish doing*. てしまう is contracted to ちゃう in casual speech.

Graffiti

てしまう may sometimes indicate positiveness as well, as shown in (a):

(a) 彼にプレゼントもらっちゃった。
     Kare ni purezento morat-chatta.
     I received a gift from my boyfriend.

9.9. Passives

Key Expressions

KE1   この家は、1930 年代に建てられました。
        Kono ie wa, senkyuuhyaku sanjuunen dai ni
            tateraremashita.
        This house was built in the 1930s.

KE2   この雑誌には、おもしろい記事がたくさん掲載されている。
        Kono zasshi ni wa, omoshiroi kiji ga takusan
            keisaisareteiru.
        In this magazine, many interesting articles are
            presented.

KE3   へんな男に追いかけられた。

             Henna otoko ni oikakerareta.

             I was chased by a creepy guy.

KE4   雨に降られちゃってねえ。

             Ame ni furare-chatte nee.

             I got caught in the rain.

Explanation

The passive in *Nihongo* takes the れる and られる forms of the verb. The particle に marks the element that causes the action in question.

PASSIVE CONJUGATION

U-verbs and RU-verbs: Replace the final *-u* with *-areru.*

| 書く | kaku | to write | 書かれる |
| 食べる | taberu | to eat | 食べられる |

Irregular verbs

| する | suru | to do | される |
| 来る | kuru | to come | 来 (こ) られる |

Existential verb

| いる | iru | to exist | いられる |

FUNCTIONS OF THE PASSIVE

There are two primary motivations for using the passive.

1. When the need to refer to the agent of an action is weak or nonexistent. Good examples are KE1 and KE2. This use is similar to English, where passives are used without the agent indicated with the *by* phrase, as in *His book was published.*
2. When pointing out inconveniences and suffering. This function is important in Japanese, and, as in KE3, it indicates that the speaker is suffering from someone else's action or is experiencing something unpleasant. For this pattern, both transitive and intransitive verbs may be used. For example, 降る is intransitive, but it can be used to convey inconvenience, as in KE4. Here, the passive conveys negative consequences similar to the English expression *I got caught in the rain.*

DIRECT AND INDIRECT PASSIVES

In terms of grammatical structure, there are two types of passives, that is, direct and indirect. In direct passives, the object of the related active sentence is the subject of the passive sentence. In indirect passives, you do not find such a correlation.

1. Direct passive

    Active   (a) 佐々木さんは山田さんをだました。
                   Sasaki-san wa Yamada-san o damashita.
                   Ms. Sasaki deceived Ms. Yamada.

    Passive   (b) 山田さんは佐々木さんに**だまされた**。
                   Yamada-san wa Sasaki-san ni damasareta.
                   Ms. Yamada was deceived by Ms. Sasaki.

2. Indirect passive

    Active   (c) 妹が私のケータイを使った。
                   Imooto ga watashi no keetai o tsukatta.
                   My younger sister used my cell phone.

    Passive   (d) 妹に私のケータイを**使われた**。
                   Imooto ni watashi no keetai o tsukawareta.
                   My younger sister used my cell phone (and I
                       suffered from the consequence).

    Active   (e) ペットの犬が死んだ。
                   Petto no inu ga shinda.
                   My pet dog died.

    Passive   (f) ペットの犬に**死なれた**。
                   Petto no inu ni shinareta.
                   My pet dog died on me.

It should be added that sometimes indirect passives imply a positive influence, but overwhelmingly the implication is negative. In fact when positive indirectness is stressed, normally the verbs of giving and receiving are used.

9.10. Causatives and Permissives

Key Expressions

KE1   弟をコンビニに行かせた。
Otooto o konbini ni ikaseta.
I made my (younger) brother go to the convenience store.

KE2   カラオケで最初に私に歌わせてくれた。
Karaoke de saishoni watashi ni utawasete-kureta.
They kindly let me sing first at karaoke.

KE3   そんなこと、あの人にさせられないよ。
Sonna koto, ano hito ni saserarenai yo.
I can't make him do such a thing.

KE4   強いカクテル、あんまり飲ませないで。
Tsuyoi kakuteru, anmari nomasenaide.
Don't make me drink a strong cocktail.

Explanation

CAUSATIVES

The causative expresses the idea that someone or something causes, influences, or allows someone else to do something. Causative expressions normally do not use stative verbs, the existential verb ある, or the *be*-verb. To use causatives, you must use せる and させる forms as given below.

CAUSATIVE CONJUGATIONS

U-verbs: Replace the final *-u* with *-aseru*. When the final *-u* is
   not preceded by a consonant, replace *-u* with *-waseru*)

| 書く | kaku | to write | 書かせる |
| 買う | kau | to buy | 買わせる |

RU-verbs: Replace the final *-ru* with *-saseru.*

| 食べる | taberu | to eat | 食べさせる |

Irregular verbs

| する | suru | to do | させる |
| 来る | kuru | to come | 来 (こ) させる |

Existential verb

| いる | iru | to stay | いさせる |

CAUSATIVES AS PERMISSIVES

Causative forms are used as permissives when the causee does not oppose the action and he or she is likely to willingly engage in the action, as in KE2.

SHORTER CAUSATIVE AND PERMISSIVE FORMS

Causatives and permissives have alternative shorter forms. They are obtained by changing the final せる to す. The shortened forms tend to express more direct and forceful causation than the standard forms.

書く	書かせる	書かす
買う	買わせる	買わす
食べる	食べさせる	食べさす

PARTICLES FOR CAUSATIVES AND PERMISSIVES

Mark the causee by を, as in KE1, or by に, as in KE2 and KE3. For the selection of either を or に, follow the guideline given below.

1. When the verb is transitive and the direct object marker を appears, in order to avoid its double appearance, use に to mark the causee.

    (a) 弟に部屋をそうじさせた。
        Otooto ni heya o soojisaseta.
        I made my (younger) brother clean the room.

2. When the verb expresses instant change and response, use を.

    (b) お客さんを怒らせてしまった。
        Okyakusan o okorasete-shimatta.
        I caused the customer to get angry.

3. When the causative expression conveys that the causer is responsible for the event that happens or has happened, use only を.

    (c) 息子を交通事故で死なせたんです。(See section 9.12 for んで
        す.)
        Musuko o kootsuujiko de shinaseta n desu.
        (I am to be blamed that) I caused my son's death due to a
            traffic accident.

CAUSATIVE PASSIVES

Causatives may be combined with passives to form causative passives. The causative ending せる goes through the passive ending changes. 書かせる takes 書かせられる 'to be forced to write' and 食べ させる takes 食べさせられる 'to be forced to eat'. The irregular verbs する and 来る take させられる and 来させられる.

For U-verbs, shortened causative passive endings are also available. For example, 書かす takes 書かされる, as in (f).

(d) 子供たちはきらいな食べものを**食べさせられた**。
Kodomotachi wa kiraina tabemono o tabesaserareta.
The children were forced to eat the food they disliked.

(e) 長い間いやな仕事を**させられました**。
Nagai aida iyana shigoto o saseraremashita.
For a long time I was forced to do a job I hated.

(f) たくさん漢字を**書かされました**。
Takusan kanji o kakasaremashita.
I was forced to write many *kanji*.

9.11. Volitional Forms

Key Expressions

KE1 今日は、一生懸命仕事をしよう。
Kyoo wa, isshookenmei shigoto o shiyoo.
I'm going to work hard today.

KE2 今は、何も考えないでいよう。
Ima wa, nanimo kangaenaide iyoo.
I won't think about anything for now.

KE3 パーティー、行こうよ。
Paatii, ikoo yo.
Let's go to the party.

KE4 いっしょに暮らそう。ね、そうしようよ。
Isshoni kurasoo. Ne, soo shiyoo yo.
Let's live together. Let's do that.

KE5 これからは、遅刻しないようにしましょうね。
Korekara wa, chikokushinai yooni shimashoo ne.
Let's make sure not to be late from now on.

Explanation

Volitional forms communicate one's volition, as in KE1 and KE2. You also use them when making invitations and suggestions, as in KE3, KE4, and KE5. Volitional forms are available for only those verbs describing humanly controllable actions.

VOLITIONAL CONJUGATION

For formal volitional forms, change ます of the formal non-past verb form to ましょう. For informal volitional forms, the following rules apply.

U-verbs: Replace the final *-u* with *-oo.*

| 書く | kaku | to write | 書こう |
| 買う | kau | to buy | 買おう |

RU-verbs: Replace the final -る with -よう.

| 食べる | taberu | to eat | 食べよう |
| 考える | kangaeru | to think | 考えよう |

Irregular verbs

| する | suru | to do | しよう |
| 来る | kuru | to come | 来 (こ) よう |

Existential verb

| いる | iru | to stay | いよう |

EXPRESSING YOUR OWN VOLITION

When the subject of the volitional forms is the first-person singular, it expresses the speaker's will and intention. Use this expression in the informal form only. It often appears with the form ようと思う [lit. 'to think to do'], or ようと思っている [lit. 'to be thinking about doing'].

(a) いやなことは忘れ**ようと思う**。
     Iyana koto wa wasureyoo to omou.
     I think I'll forget those unpleasant things.

(b) 自分の気持ちをはっきり伝え**ようと思っている**。
     Jibun no kimochi o hakkiri tsutaeyoo to omotteiru.
     I'm thinking about clearly communicating my feelings.

VOLITIONAL FORMS FOR INVITATIONS

Invitations by volitional forms are direct, and you should not use them toward your *meue* person. Inviting and suggesting by using volitional forms is similar to the English expressions of *let's...* or *let's not....* You may also use volitional forms with the interrogative particle か, as shown below.

(c) じゃ、そろそろ出かけようか。
Ja, sorosoro dekakeyoo ka.
Shall we go out now?

(d) どうですか、コーヒーでも飲みましょうか。(See section 12.13 for でも.)
Doo desu ka, koohii demo nomimashoo ka.
How about... shall we have coffee or something?

9.12. *No Da* Sentences

Key Expressions

KE1　銀行へ行ってきたのです。
Ginkoo e itte-kita no desu.
(It's that) I went to the bank.

KE2　だから行ったんです。
Dakara itta n desu.
That's why I went.

KE3　<conversation>
A: すみません。今日はお休みなんですけど。
Sumimasen. Kyoo wa oyasumi na n desu kedo.
Sorry, we are closed today.
B: そうなんですか。
Soo na n desu ka.
Is that right? I see.

KE4　俺行く。どうしても行くんだ! [masculine speech]
Ore iku. Dooshitemo iku n da!
I'm going. No matter what, I'm going!

KE5　いつ旅行から帰ってきたんですか。
Itsu ryokoo kara kaette-kita n desu ka.
When was it that you returned from your trip?

KE6　やっぱり行くの？
Yappari iku no?
Are you going anyway?

Explanation

のだ SENTENCES

Ending a sentence with のだ offers an explanation as to why a situation is the way it is, as in KE1. It is a frequently used clause- and sentence-final form. In casual speech, instead of のだ, んだ is used, as in KE2 and KE3. You can shorten のだ as の, as well. Using の is more prevalent in feminine speech.

Since there is already a main verb, adding these phrases extends the predicate, and they are similar to English *it is (the case) that* or *it is for the reason that.*

FUNCTIONS OF のだ

The basic function of のだ and んだ is to appeal to the assumed common understanding or knowledge between you and your partner. When such common knowledge does not exist, のだ is used to describe the information as if the knowledge were shared. It encourages empathy. There are at least five related but distinct functions of のだ, as listed below.

1. To signal that what precedes のだ offers the reason or cause related to the issue at hand, as in KE2

    (a) ごめん、時間がなかった**んだ**。
         Gomen, jikan ga nakatta n da.
         Sorry, it's that I didn't have time.

2. To emphasize what precedes のだ, as in KE4

    (b) どうしてもあなたのことが忘れられない**んです**。
         Dooshitemo anata no koto ga wasurerarenai n desu.
         No matter what, I cannot forget you.

3. To present information or to make a request in a milder tone, as in A's utterance in KE3

    (c) お聞きしたいことがある**んですが**。
         Okikishitai koto ga aru n desu ga.
         I have something I would like to ask you.

4. To offer confirmatory recognition of information, as in B's utterance in KE3

(d) それで行ったんだ。
Sorede itta n da.
I see; that's why she went.

(e) そうなんだ。
Soo na n da.
I see, that's what it is. (Often used as a listener response when you are convinced of what is being said.)

5. To communicate one's discovery

(f) こんなところにあったんだ 。
Konna tokoro ni atta n da.
It was here. (I found it.)

のだ USED FOR ASSERTION

As in KE4, you may demonstrate firm determination by using のだ for assertion.

(g) 絶対、試験に合格するんだ。
Zettai, shiken ni gookakusuru n da.
No matter what, I'm going to pass the examination.

The assertive のだ may also be used when you strongly demand that your partner do something.

(h) すぐ行くんだ！
Sugu iku n da!
(You) go right away.

のだ IN QUESTIONS

When you ask a question using のですか (or んですか), rather than the information itself, you focus on your will and feelings associated with the content of the の clause. As in KE5, when adding のですか, you assume that what is being questioned is already shared among the participants, more so than questions without のですか. のですか may appear with の only, as shown in KE6 in conversation.

When you ask a question using のだ, as in どこへ行けばいいの？ (instead of どこへ行けばいい？), you are asking for more than information. You are communicating your desire to appeal to your partner, something along the lines of "I really want to know where to go." The second sentence in (i) conveys such urgency.

(i)   どうすればいい？どうすればいいの？
      Doo sureba ii? Doo sureba ii no?
      What should I do? What should I really do?

UBIQUITOUS のだ

Observe how many times のだ is used in (j).

(j)   <conversation>
      A: これどうしたの？
          Kore doo shita no?
          How did you get this?
      B: 弟にもらった**んだ**。
          Otooto ni moratta n da.
          I got it from my (younger) brother.
      A: へえ、弟さんいる**んだ**。
          Hee, otooto-san iru n da.
          I see; you have a (younger) brother.

9.13. Order of Sentence-Final Elements

Explanation

Sentence-final elements include verbs, various types of verb endings, modal verbs, modal suffixes, and final particles. The general principle is that the more personal and emotional the statement, the more likely those elements will appear toward the very end. Thus starting with the verb that carries the referential meaning, other elements such as causatives, passives, and negative forms follow, and interactional particles are attached at the final position.

LIST OF SENTENCE-FINAL ELEMENTS

Here is a list specifying the order of sentence-final elements. Obviously, not all elements are required.

Verbs
Causatives
Passives
Negative form
Modal verbs
Modal suffixes

Past tense
Interactional particles

Examples

(a) なんか変なことをさせられそう。
Nanka henna koto o saseraresoo.
I'm about to be forced to do something strange.

(b) 行きたくないらしいです。
Ikitakunai rashii desu.
It seems that he doesn't want to go.

(c) なぐられたようだね。
Nagurareta yoo da ne.
It seems like you were beaten.

(d) 難しそうだったそうですよ。
Muzukashisoo datta soo desu yo.
I hear that it looked difficult.

CHAPTER 10

Complex Sentences

10.1. Conjunctions

Key Expressions

KE1   映画を見た。それから食事をした。
       Eiga o mita. Sorekara shokuji o shita.
       We saw a movie. And then we had dinner.

KE2   早く行った。だから、欲しいものが買えた。
       Hayaku itta. Dakara, hoshii mono ga kaeta.
       I went early. So I could buy what I wanted.

KE3   何度も本を読みました。けれどもわかりませんでした。
       Nando mo hon o yomimashita. Keredomo
           wararimasendeshita.
       I read the book many times. But I didn't understand it.

Explanation

CONNECTING SENTENCES AND CLAUSES

Japanese conjunctions are used to connect both sentences and clauses. This section introduces basic conjunctions as given below.

1. Addition
    そして and それから, among others, to add a related statement to the first sentence
2. Expansion
    それで and だから, among others, to add an expansion to the first sentence

3. Opposition

しかし, でも, and けれども, among others, when the second sentence expresses a view opposing the first

Some of these basic conjunctions also connect clauses, but they do so under certain restrictions. For から, [て form of the verb + から] means 'after', and the [verb + から] means 'because'. Study (a) and (b) for these examples. In addition, けれども can connect clauses, as given in (c), to mean 'although'.

(a) 映画を見**てから**、食事をした。
Eiga o mite kara, shokuji o shita.
After we saw the movie, we had dinner.

(b) 早く行っ**たから**、欲しいものが買えた。
Hayaku itta kara, hoshii mono ga kaeta.
Because I went early, I could buy what I wanted.

(c) 何度も本を読んだ**けれども**、わかりませんでした。
Nando mo hon o yonda keredomo, wakarimasendeshita.
Although I read the book many times, I didn't understand it.

Note that although けれども can connect clauses, しかし and でも cannot. See the next section for a variety of connecting forms used in complex sentences.

Graffiti

In casual speech, で may appear instead of それで. で can encourage the continuation of talk, as shown below.

(d) <conversation>
A: デートしたんだ。駅前で会ってね。
Deetoshita n da. Ekimae de atte ne.
We had a date. We met in front of the station.
B: で？
De?
And?
A: で、近くのカフェに入ったんだけど。(See section 13.6 for けど.)
De, chikaku no kafe ni haitta n da kedo.
And we went into a café nearby.

10.2. Connecting Clauses

Key Expressions

KE1 用事ができて行けませんでした。
Yooji ga dekite ikemasendeshita.
I couldn't go because I had a chore.

KE2 あなたが好きな物だから、買ってきたんですけど。
Anata ga sukina mono da kara, katte-kita n desu kedo.
Because this is something you like, I bought it.

KE3 朝から何も食べてないんで、お腹がすいちゃってね。
Asa kara nani mo tabetenai nde, onaka ga sui-chatte
ne.
Since I haven't eaten anything this morning, I'm
hungry.

KE4 春になると桜が咲く。
Haru ni naru to sakura ga saku.
When spring comes, cherry blossoms bloom.

KE5 このカード、使うとき注意しなきゃ。
Kono kaado, tsukau toki chuuishinakya.
I must be careful when I use this card.

KE6 忙しいんだ。試験があるし。
Isogashi n da. Shiken ga aru shi.
I'm busy. I have an exam, so....

Explanation

て FORM AS A CONNECTOR

The most basic way to connect clauses is to use the て form of
verbs and adjectives. The semantic relationship between the two
connected clauses depends on the specific context. In KE1, 用事が
できて offers a reason or cause for 行けませんでした。

(a) 今朝は早く起きて犬の散歩に行った。
Kesa wa hayaku okite inu no sanpo ni itta.
I got up early and took my dog for a walk.

(b) 傘を持たないで出かけてしまった。
Kasa o motanaide dekakete-shimatta.
Not taking an umbrella, he went out.

(c) この魚安くておいしいね。

Kono sakana yasukute oishii ne.

This fish is inexpensive and delicious, isn't it?

から AND ので

から and ので are frequently used to connect a cause or reason and the resulting effect, as in KE2 and KE3. Be warned that the order of clauses is the reverse of English. Just like particles, you attach conjunctions to the clause-final position whose clause is conjoined with another. から and ので are attached to both formal and informal forms. There is one exception. When you use ので after だ, change it to な to produce なので.

(d) これは便利なので、よく売れます。

Kore wa benrina node, yoku uremasu.

Because this is convenient, it sells well.

It should be noted that in casual speech, ので is shortened to んで, as in KE3.

STYLE IN SUBORDINATE CLAUSES

When two clauses are connected, the predicate in the subordinate clause normally, but not exclusively, takes the informal style. As a basic rule, the style of the sentence appears in the main verb. When you use a formal ending in a subordinate clause along with the formal ending in the main clause, the utterance becomes supra-polite (e.g., これは便利ですので、よく売れますね).

CHOOSING から OR ので

As in KE2, から focuses more on the reason or cause, while, as in KE3, ので focuses strongly on the resulting effect. The から clause provides a personally interpreted cause or reason. When you express a personal judgment such as speculation, opinion, intention, command, suggestion, question, or request, you should use から. Use ので when presenting the cause more objectively without projecting the speaker's opinion.

An independent から clause is often used as an answer to a question.

(e) <conversation>

A: どうして買わないの？
Dooshite kawanai no?
Why don't you buy (it)?

B: お金がない**から**。
Okane ga nai kara.
Because I don't have any money.

Another marker, もの (もん in casual speech), is used in a similar way, especially in feminine and children's speech. For example, お金がないもん.

CONNECTING WITH と

The conjunction と 'whenever' connects clauses in the following situations. Use the basic forms of verbs before と.

1. When one action triggers another

(f) おまえ、酒を飲む**と**陽気になるよなあ。 [masculine speech]
Omae, sake o nomu to yookini naru yo naa.
When [whenever] you drink, you become cheerful.

2. When reporting the natural and obvious consequence of an action or procedure, as in KE4

(g) ３と５を足す**と**８になる。
San to go o tasu to hachi ni naru.
When you add three and five, you get eight.

3. When reporting the immediate reaction to an action

(h) ドアが開く**と**子犬が飛び出してきた。
Doa ga aku to koinu ga tobidashite-kita.
When the door opened, a puppy jumped out.

CONNECTING WITH とき

As in KE5, you can use the temporal phrase とき to connect clauses. If the tense of the verb in the とき clause is past, the action referred to is already completed.

(i) 買い物をする**とき**注意しましょう。
Kaimono o suru toki chuuishimashoo.
When (before) we shop, let's be careful.

(j) 買い物をした**とき**注意しましょう。
Kaimono o shita **toki** chuuishimashoo.
After we've bought something, let's be careful.

CONNECTING WITH し

Use し when connecting a series of acts or states that together lead to a summary judgment or conclusion.

(k) ロンドンへ行った**し**、パリへ行った**し**、今年の夏は楽しかった。
Rondon e itta shi, Pari e itta shi, kotoshi no natsu wa tanoshikatta.
I went to London and also to Paris; this summer was really fun.

(l) この辺は寒い**し**、暗い**し**、危険だ**し**、ちょっとねえ。
Kono hen wa samui shi, kurai shi, kiken da shi, chotto nee.
This area is cold, dark, and dangerous, and I wonder about it.

Graffiti

You may use the て form and し to weaken a statement or to obscure the cause or reason, especially in conversation. They often appear at the utterance-final position, leaving the impression that the statement is incomplete and thus less imposing. KE6 is such an example.

(m) 今週はちょっと忙しいんですよ。出張がある**し**。
Konshuu wa chotto isogashii n desu yo. Shutchoo ga aru shi.
This week I'm a bit busy. There is a business trip, so....

(n) 会えなかった。忙しく**て**。
Aenakatta. Isogashikute.
I couldn't see him. I was busy.

10.3. Conditionals

Key Expressions

KE1   これを読めばわかりますよ。
      Kore o yomeba wakarimasu yo.
      If you read this, you will understand.

KE2   時間があれば行きます。
      Jikan ga areba ikimasu.
      If I have time, I'll go.

KE3   お金持ってるなら少し貸して。
      Okane motteru nara sukoshi kashite.
      If you have money, will you lend me some?

KE4   あなたも日本人ならわかるでしょ。
      Anata mo nihonjin nara wakaru desho.
      If you are Japanese, you should understand it.

KE5   時間があったら、おみやげ買ってくるね。
      Jikan ga attara, omiyage katte-kuru ne.
      If I have time, I'll buy you a souvenir.

Explanation

ば CONDITIONAL

The ば conditional is the most straightforward conditional expression in Japanese. As in KE1 and KE2 above, in the ば conditional, the condition specified in the clause must be satisfied first; then on that condition, the event described in the main clause is expected to occur.

ば CONDITIONAL CONJUGATION

For all verbs except the *be*-verb, replace the final *-u* with *-eba*.

書く	kaku	to write	書けば
食べる	taberu	to eat	食べれば
来る	kuru	to come	来れば
いる	iru	to stay	いれば

For the *be*-verb, replace the verb with なら. なら may be followed
   by ば, although ば is frequently deleted.

| だ | da | to be | なら (ば) |

For い adjectives, replace the final い with ければ.

おいしい	oishii	delicious	おいしければ

For な adjectives, change な to なら (ば).

便利な	benrina	convenient	便利なら (ば)

なら CONDITIONAL

The なら conditional is used when the condition is based on information traced not to the speaker but to someone else, often to the speaker's partner. KE3 is such an example. In KE3, the speaker's partner gave the impression that he had money. Based on that information, the speaker presents the condition, that is, "if you have money."

なら *Conditional Conjugation*

To form the なら conditional, attach なら to verb informal forms.

書く	kaku	to write	書くなら
食べる	taberu	to eat	食べるなら
来る	kuru	to come	来るなら
いる	iru	to be	いるなら

For the *be*-verb and adjective なら forms, the following changes occur.

だ	da	to be	なら (ば)
おいしい	oishii	delicious	おいしいなら (ば)
便利な	benrina	convenient	便利なら (ば)

CHOOSING ば OR なら

As stated earlier, while the ば conditional originates with the speaker, the なら conditional is preferred when the condition is suggested by the partner. Study the following sentences.

(a) お金があれ**ば**、それ買うんだけど。
    Okane ga areba, sore kau n da kedo.
    If I have money, I'll buy that.

(b) お金持ってる**なら**少し貸して。
    Okane motteru nara sukoshi kashite.
    If (you say that) you have money, loan me some.

たら CONDITIONAL

たら functions as both temporal and conditional. KE5 takes the conditional reading.

To form the たら conditional, attach ら to the verb and adjective informal past tense form. You have forms such as 書いたら, 食べたら, 来 (き) たら, いたら, だったら, おいしかったら, and べんりだったら.

Meanings of the たら Conditional

The たら conditional offers several interpretations, depending on the type and tense of the verb.

1. When the situation expressed in the たら clause is certain to occur, the temporal interpretation is appropriate.

    (c) 六時になっ**たら**帰りましょう。
         Rokuji ni nattara kaerimashoo.
         When six o'clock comes, let's go back.

2. When the situation expressed in the たら clause is uncertain, the conditional interpretation is appropriate.

    (d) 時間があっ**たら**飲みに行きません？
         Jikan ga attara nomi ni ikimasen?
         If you have time, let's go out drinking.

3. When the action in the main clause refers to something that has already happened, the temporal reading is appropriate.

    (e) 家につい**たら**すぐ友達が来た。
         Uchi ni tsuitara sugu tomodachi ga kita.
         When I arrived home, my friend soon came for a visit.

4. When the verb in the たら clause is stative or たら occurs with an adjective, only the conditional reading is appropriate.

    (f) いい本があっ**たら**、買う。
         Ii hon ga attara, kau.
         If there is a good book, I'll buy it.

    (g) 高かっ**たら**買わない。
         Takakattara kawanai.
         If it is expensive, I won't buy it.

たら *for Expressing Desire*

The たら conditional can be used independently to express desire. It describes a situation contrary to the facts (i.e., subjunctive).

(h) あの人に会え**たら**なあ。
Ano hito ni aetara naa.
I wish I could see her.

CHOOSING たら OR ば

The たら conditional and ば conditional differ in the degree of likelihood that the condition will become reality. In (i), the speaker feels that the condition (of Hikaru's returning) is likely to be met. In (j), the speaker is less committed and communicates the doubt (i.e., whether Hikaru will come here at all). It expresses a greater sense of doubt.

(i) 光君が帰ってき**たら**知らせてください。(See section 12.7 for てくだ さい.)
Hikaru-kun ga kaette-kitara shirasete-kudasai.
If and when Hikaru returns, please let me know.

(j) 光君が来れ**ば**はっきりするんですが。
Hikaru-kun ga kureba hakkiri suru n desu ga.
If Hikaru comes here, things will be clarified, but....

10.4. Clausal Modification

Key Expressions

KE1　　きのう買ったケータイ、すごいよ。
Kinoo katta keetai, sugoi yo.
The cell phone I bought yesterday is awesome.

KE2　　友だちにあげるプレゼントを忘れてしまった。
Tomodachi ni ageru purezento o wasurete-shimatta.
I forgot the present I was going to give to my friend.

Explanation

Clausal modification is a structure where modification is achieved not by an adjective but by a clause. Unlike in English, in *Nihongo* the clausal modifier precedes the noun modified. The modifying clause normally takes informal forms, as in KE1 and KE2. There are no relative pronouns comparable to *what, which,* or *that* (as in *the cell phone [that] I bought*).

TWO TYPES OF CLAUSAL MODIFIERS

There are two types of clausal modifiers. With the first, the basic, the modified noun constitutes a part of the propositional content of the modifying clause. See きのう買ったケータイ 'the cell phone I bought yesterday' in KE1.

With the second, the clausal explanation, the modified noun is semantically associated with the modifying clause but the noun itself does not constitute a grammatical element within it. Think of the example ガラスを割 (わ)る音 (おと) 'the sound of someone breaking glass' as a case of clausal explanation.

Of these two types, only the first functions similarly to the so-called clausal modifiers (with relative pronouns) in English. Here we will focus on the first basic type. We will study the second type in the next section.

TOPIC MARKER AND MODIFYING CLAUSE

Because the modifying clause is a subordinate clause and since topic identifies the topic of the whole sentence, avoid using topic marker は (and other topic markers) within the modifying clause. Rather, use whatever case marker is appropriate within the modifying clause. However, this does not apply when は conveys strong contrast.

の INSTEAD OF が

が in the modifying clause is often changeable with の, as in (b).

   (a) 雨が降る日はうっとうしい。
       Ame ga furu hi wa uttooshii.
       Rainy days are annoying.

   (b) 雨の降る日はうっとうしい。
       Ame no furu hi wa uttooshii.
       Rainy days are annoying.

の emphasizes modification (rather than being a subject), and as a result, when the modified element is less concrete, の becomes inappropriate. 私たちが毎日食べているようなもの 'the kinds of things we eat every day' is preferred to *私たちの毎日食べているようなもの.

Graffiti

Clausal modification is used to give context to the modified noun. For example, if you think your partner may not remember you, you might remind him or her by saying that you have met before.

(c) この前、ピクニックでいっしょだった佐久間です。
Kono mae, pikunikku de issho datta Sakuma desu.
I'm Sakuma, who met you at the picnic the other day.

10.5. Clausal Explanation

Key Expressions

KE1 あれ、どこかでガラスを割る音がするよ。
Are, dokoka de garasu o waru oto ga suru yo.
Listen! I hear the sound of someone breaking glass somewhere.

KE2 泣ける映画が見たいなあ。
Nakeru eiga ga mitai naa.
I want to see a movie that would make me cry.

KE3 DVDを買ったおつりはここに置きますよ。
Diiviidii o katta otsuri wa koko ni okimasu yo.
I'm leaving here the change I got when I bought the DVD.

KE4 佐々木さんが結婚したっていううわさ聞いた？
Sasaki-san ga kekkonshita tte yuu uwasa kiita?
Did you hear the rumor that Ms. Sasaki got married?

Explanation

Clausal explanation provides a general explanation about a noun that does not constitute a grammatical element within the clause. To understand the clausal explanation, you must consider an extended meaning. Sometimes you must add appropriate phrases. Compare the two expressions below.

(a) きのう買ったケータイ
kinoo katta keetai
the cell phone I bought yesterday

(b) ガラスを割る音
garasu o waru oto
the sound of someone breaking glass

As explained in section 10.4, in きのう買ったケータイ、ケータイ constitutes the grammatical object, an essential element of the clause ケータイを買った. In the glass-breaking example, the sound is something closely associated with the breaking of the glass, but it is not a part of the ガラスを割る clause.

Study KE2 and KE3, where English translations with added phrases explain the circumstances.

CLAUSAL EXPLANATION AND という

Some clausal explanations must take the quotation phrase という while for others it is optional. Follow the guideline given below. Note that, as in KE4, in casual speech っていう is used, although when it is preceded by ん, ていう appears instead.

1. For the clausal explanation semantically associated with reporting or representing, you must use という.

    (c) 台風が東北地方を襲った**という**ニュースが流れた。
    Taifuu ga toohoku chihoo o osotta to yuu nyuusu ga
        nagareta.
    The news that a typhoon attacked northeastern Japan
        was reported.

2. For a clause that directly explains sensory information, you cannot use という.

    (d) その時、誰かが助けを求める声が聞こえた。
    Sono toki, dareka ga tasuke o motomeru koe ga kikoeta.
    I heard then the voice of someone seeking help. (*助けを
        求めるという声)

3. When という is used but is optional, the speaker creates a somewhat abstract or distant impression.

(e) 風邪が治る薬が欲しい。

　　Kaze ga naoru kusuri ga hoshii.

　　I want some medicine that would cure a cold.

(f) 風邪が二日で治る**という**薬を試してみたんだけど。

　　Kaze ga futsuka de naoru to yuu kusuri o tameshite-mita
　　n da kedo.

　　I tried this medicine, which they say should cure my cold
　　in two days.

10.6. *Koto* and *No* Clauses

Key Expressions

KE1　　約束は守ることが大切です。

　　　　Yakusoku wa mamoru koto ga taisetsu-desu.

　　　　It is important to keep promises.

KE2　　いつも笑顔でいることはむずかしい。

　　　　Itsumo egao de iru koto wa muzukashii.

　　　　It is difficult to be smiling all the time.

KE3　　安田さんが手を振っているのが見えます。

　　　　Yasuda-san ga te o futteiru no ga miemasu.

　　　　I can see Yasuda waving.

KE4　　勉強するのもしないのも君次第。

　　　　Benkyoosuru no mo shinai no mo kimi shidai.

　　　　Whether you study or not is up to you.

Explanation

こと AND の AS NOMINALIZERS

こと and の are nominalizers that make clauses into noun phrases. English is provided with three ways of making a clause into a grammatical noun. The first is to use *that* in forming a clause, as in *that I keep promises*. The second is to attach *to* to a verb, as in *to keep promises*. The third is to make a verb into a gerundive form, as in *keeping promises*.

こと *Nominalizer*

こと nominalizes a clause that refers to actions or events in abstract, indirect, or general ways. You use the こと clause to express a formal and more distant feeling, pointing out facts reached after some thought. Study KE1 and KE2.

の Nominalizer

Use の for nominalizing concrete actions or events. You use the の clause to point out directly and immediately perceived facts. If the main verb requires concrete, immediate action such as 見える 'to be seen', or 聞こえる 'to be heard', you must use の. KE3 is such an example.

CHOOSING こと OR の

As mentioned above, こと describes a general fact, while の refers to a specific action or behavior. In KE4, 勉強するの and しないの refer to specific actions.

To clarify this point further, contrast (a) and (b) below. 見るの refers to the specific behavior of someone viewing, while 見ること refers to the general meaning of viewing. こと is often used with verbs connoting a deductive or abstract thinking process.

(a) テレビで野球を見る**の**が好きだ。
Terebi de yakyuu o miru no ga suki da.
I like to watch baseball games on television.

(b) テレビで野球を見る**こと**はあまりない。
Terebi de yakyuu o miru koto wa amari nai.
I rarely do things such as watching baseball games on television.

USE OF THE こと CLAUSE

The verb informal form followed byことがある can function in two ways. The [verb informal non-past + ことがある] pattern refers to the occasional occurrence of an event. The [verb informal past + ことがある] pattern describes a past experience.

(c) 日本へ**行くことがある**。
Nihon e iku koto ga aru.
I occasionally go to Japan.

(d) 日本へ**行ったことがある**。
Nihon e itta koto ga aru.
I have been to Japan.

Another pattern, [verb informal non-past + ことになる], de-scribes an event as something that happens beyond your control, as in (e).

(e) 日本へ行くことになりました。
Nihon e iku koto ni narimashita.
It has been decided [lit. 'it has become'] that I would go to Japan.

USE OF こと AS A NOUN

こと may be used as a regular noun to mean (intangible) things or facts.

(f) 君が言ったことは、忘れないよ。
Kimi ga itta koto wa, wasurenai yo.
I won't forget what you said.

(g) 言いたいことがあるんなら、言えば？
Iitai koto ga aru n nara, ieba?
If you have something you want to say, why don't you say it?

(h) いやなことは忘れちゃった。
Iyana koto wa wasure-chatta.
I forgot those unpleasant things.

Graffiti

Adding こと to a noun renders the noun more abstract. As a result, the statement becomes less direct. When referring to feelings and attitudes about エリカ, use エリカのこと instead of エリカ. In that way the statement becomes more general and adds the feeling that it is not just Erika but things about Erika.

(i) エリカのことが好き。
Erika no koto ga suki.
I like (things about) Erika.

(j) 私のこと、どう思う？
Watashi no koto, doo omou?
What do you think about (things about) me?

10.7. Quotation

Key Expressions

KE1 　鈴木さんは「ごめんなさい」と言いました。
Suzuki-san wa "Gomennasai" to iimashita.
Ms. Suzuki said, "I'm sorry."

KE2 　高橋さんも行くって言ってたよ。
Takahashi-san mo iku tte itteta yo.
Mr. Takahashi also said that he was going.

KE3 　あした、彼といっしょに、ドライブ行く、みたいな。
Ashita, kare to isshoni, doraibu iku, mitaina.
Tomorrow, I'm going driving with him, like....

KE4 　もう、結婚しちゃおうかな、なんてね。
Moo, kekkonshi-chaoo ka na, nante ne.
I'll get married; I shouldn't say so, but....

Explanation

QUOTATION MARKERS

The quoted portion of direct quotations is graphologically marked by quotation marks 「　」, as in KE1. There are cases where direct quotations are not marked in written Japanese, however. The use of quotation marks is less orderly in comparison to that of English.

In spoken Japanese, the quoted portion is marked by intonation and voice quality.

QUOTATIVE と

Direct quotation reflects the style of the quoted person and carries features similar to spoken Japanese. Attach と after the quoted portion, and add the verb 言う. In the casual style と changes to っ て, as in KE2. Note that って changes to て when it is preceded by ん. This applies to all cases of って when it is linked to a quotation.

ように言う FOR QUOTING COMMAND

When quoted speech is in command form, you can use ように言う for indirect quotation.

(a) よく注意する**ように言われた**。
Yoku chuuisuru yooni iwareta.
I was told to be very careful.

WHEN ASKING FOR JAPANESE WORDS

A quotative expression may be particularly useful when you want to learn the equivalents of foreign words.

(b) <conversation>
A: 「advertising」は日本語で何**と言います**か。
Advertising wa nihongo de nan to iimasu ka.
How do you say "advertising" in Japanese?
B: 「広告」**と言います**。
Kookoku to iimasu.
It is "kookoku."

Instead of と言う, you may use the *be*-verb, as in 「advertising」は日本語で何ですか.

HEARSAY という

The expression という can also end an utterance to indicate hearsay.

(c) 山奥のその村には今でも熊が出る**という**。
Yamaoku no sono mura ni wa ima demo kuma ga deru to yuu.
They say that in that village deep in the mountains, bears appear even now.

と MARKING VARIOUS QUOTATIVE EXPRESSIONS

A number of verbs may take the quotative と.

1. と書（か）く 'to write'

(d) その手紙には、母が入院した**と書いてありました**。
Sono tegami ni wa, haha ga nyuuinshita to kaite-arimashita.
In the letter it was written that my mother was hospitalized.

2. と考（かんが）える 'to think, to consider'
3. と思（おも）う 'to think'
4. と聞（き）く 'to hear'

    (e)　エリックって、ニューヨークへ帰った**って聞いた**けど。
        Erikku tte, Nyuu Yooku e kaetta tte kiita kedo.
        About Eric, I heard that he went back to New York.

みたいな

As a kind of quotation, you may add みたいな at the utterance-final position, as in KE3. This is often used in casual conversation, and it adds a distancing and softening effect. By adding みたいな, you avoid a strong commitment to what you are saying. Since みたいな describes someone else's state, it gives the impression that you are revealing your own thoughts as if they were observed as someone else's. What precedes the みたいな utterance may take a rising intonation (□), increasing the non-committal sense.

    (f)　あの人のこと、愛してる(□)、**みたいな**。
        Ano hito no koto, aishiteru, mitaina.
        I love him, like....

なんて AND なんちゃって

Quotation in conversation may be marked by なんて instead of と, as in KE4. Also you may use なんちゃって, a shortened version of なんて言ってしまって 'to have said such a thing'. Use these quotative expressions to qualify what you just said, often with a softening effect, to diminish the impact of the statement.

    (g)　俺が一番、**なんちゃって**。
        Ore ga ichiban, nan chatte.
        I'm the best; uh, I shouldn't say so, but....

Graffiti

Sometimes you may reveal your *honne,* your true thoughts and feelings. But then you might regret it immediately afterward. This is particularly so when you realize you have revealed too much and it seems a bit difficult for the partner to take. Expressions such as なんて, なんて言ってしまって, なんて言っちゃって, and なんちゃって are useful, since you can add them to make light of your remarks. It is as if you said something in quotation and qualified it afterward. This kind of self-quotation makes use of two different voices and attitudes coming from the same person.

CHAPTER 11

Emotive Expressions

11.1. Interactional Particles *Ne* and *Yo*

Key Expressions

KE1　向こうに着いたらね、電話して。すぐにね。
Mukoo ni tsuitara ne, denwashite. Suguni ne.
When you get there, please call me, will you? Right away.

KE2　残念ですねえ。
Zannen desu nee.
Too bad, isn't it?

KE3　行きますよ、行けばいいんでしょ。
Ikimasu yo, ikeba ii n desho.
I'm going, and that's what you want, right?

KE4　会いたい、会いたいよ。
Aitai, aitai yo.
I want to, I really want to see you.

KE5　もう終りかよ。
Moo owari ka yo.
Is it over already, really?

Explanation

In spoken *Nihongo*, interactional particles frequently appear. They are important for making a conversation go smoothly and comfortably. We studied the basics of ね and よ in sections 7.10 and 8.8. Here we will focus on additional information critical to their effective use.

ね FOR EMPATHY AND FRIENDLINESS

When the speaker uses ね to give information the partner does not know, ironically because ね assumes the partner's knowledge, it adds to the sense of empathy and intimacy. For example, when asked a question that requires some thought, you may answer そうですねえ。やっぱり子供 (こども) の頃 (ころ) が一番 (いちばん) なつかしいですねえ 'Let me think. After all, to me, childhood is the sweetest time of all'.

ね is also used simply to add a tone of friendliness, both at phrase-final and sentence-final positions. Some utterances may be accompanied with multiple ね, でね, or ですね, the last of which adds a tone of formality. The high frequency of ね is generally a sign of familiarity and friendliness. When you are being reserved or when you are talking impersonally (in a public speech, for example), you seldom use ね.

ねえ

A long ねえ uttered slowly at the end of a sentence emphasizes the speaker's commitment to deep thoughts, including highest admiration and most moving feelings. It also conveys sympathy, as in KE2.

You may use the utterance-initial ねえ to attract attention from someone in an empathy-soliciting way, for example, ねえ、お父さん 'Say, Dad'.

ATTENTION-GETTING よ

よ marks information directly addressed to the partner. For example, you can catch the attention of a passerby who has accidentally dropped something by saying なにか落 (お) としましたよ 'You dropped something'.

Partly because of this request for attention, よ often elicits a highly emotional appeal. Obviously, one can express feelings without よ. But when added, よ conveys urgency and expresses the feeling of "I'm telling you; can't you understand?" or "I'm telling you; please understand me."

If you respond to a request by saying 行 (い) きますよ 'I'm going', it can mean a strong understanding-seeking reply, bordering on a defiant attitude, that is, "I'm going; don't you get it?" Study key expression KE3, where よ conveys such an attitude. For this reason, よ may be used to pass judgment and to strongly vent one's opinion on some issue.

よ WITH STRONG AND WEAK STRESS

It is important to note the strong versus weak stress accompanying よ. The strongly pronounced よ (accompanied by high tone), because it focuses on information, may imply an excessive eagerness and a sense of admonishment. For example, 気 (き) を付 (つ) けて運転 (うんてん) してよ (with stress) 'Please drive carefully, OK?' borders on giving an order with admonishment. よ pronounced without stress does not add this sense of admonishment, as in そろそろ帰 (かえ) りましょうよ 'Let's go back soon'.

会 (あ) いたい。会いたいよ。

よ also signals a strong desire to reach the partner's heart. In this case よ is interpreted with a feeling of "Please understand me; please understand how I feel." This is particularly so when two similar utterances are repeated, once without and once with よ, as illustrated in KE4. By first saying 会いたい 'I want to see you' and repeating 会いたいよ 'I really want to see you', the speaker expresses a desperate desire to emotionally reach the partner.

When the talk consists of multiple sentences, よ is added to those sentences containing the main points. よ sentences aim to directly appeal to the partner, and that intention is normally associated with sentences that carry the main points. Obviously, you should not overuse よ, and avoid tacking it onto everything.

RESTRICTIONS ON ね AND よ

When you have exclusive information, something the partner does not know, you cannot use ね. For example, *頭 (あたま) がいたいですね 'I have a headache, right?' is inappropriate.

Because よ demands attention, you should avoid using it toward your *meue* person. To assume a lack of knowledge on the part of your *meue* person is disrespectful. It is important to remind your boss by saying ミーティング、二時からですね 'The meeting is from two o'clock, isn't it?', instead of ミーティング、二時からですよ 'The meeting is from two o'clock, OK?'

よね

The combination of よ and ね exists as よね but not *ねよ. As a general rule, the closer the expression is placed to the end of a sentence, the less is its focus on information. Since よ has more to do with information than ね, よ appears before ね. The reverse is inappropriate. The meaning of よね is a combination of (1) a focus on the content of what you are saying (information), and (2) your overriding concern toward the partner's thoughts and feelings.

かよ

The かよ combination is used in casual speech to express surprise, doubt, and disappointment, as in KE5. Consider a situation where you are surprised that your partner left the restaurant without paying for the meal. Then you might say to yourself 食い逃げかよ 'Just eating and running away, is he?'

11.2. Primary Feelings

Key Expressions

KE1 　　わあ、うれしい！
　　　　Waa, ureshii!
　　　　Wow, I'm happy!

KE2 　　やったー！
　　　　Yattaa!
　　　　Yes, I did it!

KE3 　　それ、ひどいよ。
　　　　Sore, hidoi yo.
　　　　That's just awful.

KE4 　　なんだか、寂しい。
　　　　Nandaka, sabishii.
　　　　Somehow I feel lonesome.

Explanation

EXPRESSING YOUR FEELINGS

Japanese speakers show their emotions quite readily, especially among *uchi* members in casual and intimate situations. When expressing your own emotions, you have descriptive adjectives as well as a variety of other expressions at your disposal. Since emotion is frequently expressed straightforwardly without regard to the speech style, an informal style is widely used.

JOY AND HAPPINESS

うれしい！	Wow, I'm delighted.
ラッキー！	Lucky!
やったー！	Success. I did it!

(a) すてきなクリスマスプレゼントもらっちゃった。**ラッキー**！
Sutekina Kurisumasu purezento morat-chatta. Rakkii!
I got a wonderful Christmas present. Lucky me!

SADNESS, PAIN, AND DIFFICULTIES

悲 (かな) しい	(I'm) sad.
つらい	(unbearably) painful and difficult
ひどい	nasty, hurtful, awful, destructive, devastating

(b) 彼女にフラれた。マジ**悲しい**よ。
Kanojo ni furareta. Maji kanashii yo.
She dumped me. I'm really sad.

LONELINESS

寂 (さび) しい	lonely
ひとりぼっち	feeling totally alone

(c) ひとりで旅行したんだけど、**寂しかった**。
Hitori de ryokooshita n da kedo, sabishikatta.
I traveled alone, but I was lonely.

DISLIKE AND HATRED

いやな	disagreeable, offensive, nasty
にくらしい	hateful, detestable

(d) あいつは人の悪口を言う**にくらしい**ヤツなんだ。
Aitsu wa hito no waruguchi o yuu nikurashii yatsu na n
da.
He speaks ill of others, a detestable guy.

ANGER AND FRUSTRATION

腹 (はら) が立 (た) つ	to get angry, to be furious
ムカつく	to get disgustedly mad
頭 (あたま) にくる	to get really mad, to lose one's cool

(e) あいつの態度**ムカ**つく。
Aitsu no taido mukatsuku.
His attitude is really disgusting.

(f) **頭にくる**ようなことばかりでいやになる。
Atama ni kuru yoona koto bakari de iyani naru.
I hate it; I have to face so many things that make me re-
ally mad.

DESCRIBING SOMEONE ELSE'S EMOTIONS

When describing someone else's emotions, a different strategy must be used. This is because someone else's emotions are only indirectly describable. You have access to someone's internal feelings only through outward signs. You only indirectly recognize that someone is actually feeling an emotion. When such signs are evident, you may use そうだ 'seem, look like' or the がる structure.

(g) となりの林さんは奥さんをなくして**寂しそうだ**。
     Tonari no Hayashi-san wa okusan o nakushite sabishisoo da.
     Mr. Hayashi, my neighbor, seems lonely since his wife passed away.

(h) 妹さんはとても**悲しがっています**よ。
     Imooto-san wa totemo kanashigatteimasu yo.
     His sister is very sad. [lit. His sister shows that she is very sad.]

11.3. Exclamatory Phrases

Key Expressions

KE1   きれいな空！
        Kireina sora!
        (What a) beautiful sky!

KE2   いやなヤツ。
        Iyana yatsu.
        (What a) nasty guy!

KE3   見上げると、美しい満月。
        Miageru to, utsukushii mangetsu.
        Looking up, (I see) the beautiful full moon.

KE4   一回で成功！
        Ikkai de seikoo!
        Success in one try!

Explanation

The [adjective + noun] structure may be used as it is. These independent phrases are uttered to identify the source of an emotion, as in KE1 and KE2.

Sentences without predicates result in KE3 and KE4. We can assume that が見えた is deleted from KE3, and in KE4, した is deleted. Avoiding a full-sentence description adds to the immediacy and dramatic effect. These independent expressions function as exclamatory phrases.

SHARING FEELINGS

The emotive meanings that independent exclamatory phrases express originate in the psychological support shared by participants. Specifically, by presenting the object by which you are deeply moved, you expect your partner to share the same feeling toward the object. By sharing an identical perspective toward the same object and by appreciating that you and your partner are sharing this intimate experience, you two feel empathy toward each other.

11.4. Attitudinal Adverbs

Key Expressions

KE1　どうせ間に合わないだろう。
Doose maniawanai daroo.
You won't be in time anyway.

KE2　やっぱり、無理だった。
Yappari, muri datta.
As expected, it was impossible.

KE3　せめて声だけでも、聞きたい。
Semete koe dake demo, kikitai.
At least his voice I want to hear.

KE4　まさか、あの人が万引きするなんてね。
Masaka, ano hito ga manbikisuru nante ne.
Impossible to believe that he shoplifted.

KE5　<conversation>
A:　神崎が自殺した。
Kanzaki ga jisatsushita.
Kanzaki committed suicide.
B:　まさか。
Masaka.
No way. Impossible.

Explanation

A number of attitudinal adverbs (or sentential adverbs) express the speaker's emotional attitude. These adverbs differ from ordinary adverbs that qualify the verb, for example, 速 (はや) く 'fast', qualifying the verb 走 (はし) る 'to run'. Instead, they reveal how the speaker feels.

どうせ

どうせ expresses your it-can't-happen-anyway attitude of resignation toward a certain state or event, as in KE1. Regardless of how you tackle the situation, it seems that the conclusion is predetermined and is inevitable. When using どうせ, you are abandoning the idea that you can personally make a difference.

どうせ can communicate a negative attitude, as shown below.

(a) <conversation>
A: その人仕事やってるの？
Sono hito shigoto yatteru no?
Does he have a job?
B: **どうせ**マイナーな仕事でしょ。
Doose mainaana shigoto desho.
It's probably a dead-end job at best.

やっぱり

やっぱり (or formal やはり or very casual やっぱ) is used when an action turns out to be as you expected, as in KE2. The expectation can be something personal. For example, you see someone in the distance, and she looks like your friend. When she comes closer, it turns out you were right. You may say to yourself やっぱり勇貴 (ゆうき) くんだ 'It's Yuuki, as I thought'.

Compare (b) and (c).

(b) **どうせ**つまんないよ、そんなパーティー。
Doose tsumannai yo, sonna paatii.
You won't enjoy such a party anyway.

(c) あのパーティーさ、**やっぱり**つまんなかった。
Ano paatii sa, yappari tsumannakatta.
That party wasn't fun after all.

せめて

せめて expresses the attitude that although the ideal result cannot be achieved, at least some results are expected. Sentence KE3 is such an example. As another example, you may say せめて日曜日 (にちようび) はゆっくりしたい 'At least on Sundays I want to relax', with a sense that you have given up any hope on relaxing on other days.

せっかく

せっかく expresses your attitude that although an intended result is not achieved, something has purposely been done anyway. For example, you purchased some wine and cheese for a party only to learn that the party was canceled. You might say something like せっかくワインとチーズ買ったのに 'I bought wine and cheese especially for the party, but'.

まさか

まさか is a strong negative response, emphatically rejecting a proposition. For example, if we know that the man in question is virtuous, then we know that it is impossible for him to shoplift. KE4 conveys such a feeling.

In KE5, speaker B knows that Kanzaki would never commit suicide, and he confesses that attitude by まさか. This sentiment can be expressed in a full sentence まさかあの人がそんなことするはずはない 'Absolutely, no way (to believe) that he would do such a thing!'

11.5. Interactional Particles and Markers

Key Expressions

KE1	おまえ、バカだな。	
	Omae, baka da na.	
	You're a real fool.	
KE2	がんばろうぜ。	
	Ganbaroo ze.	
	Let's do our best.	
KE3	そろそろ行くぞ。	
	Sorosoro iku zo.	
	We are leaving now.	

KE4　　　そんなことするわけないじゃん。
　　　　　Sonna koto suru wake nai jan.
　　　　　There's no way I would do such a thing.

KE5　　　<conversation>
　　　　　A:　行きたい？
　　　　　　　Ikitai?
　　　　　　　Want to go?
　　　　　B:　行きたいッス。
　　　　　　　Ikitai ssu.
　　　　　　　I want to go.

Explanation

な

な seeks confirmation, including self-confirmation, as in KE1. Use this in casual situations only, and mostly in masculine speech, toward your *meshita* person.

ぜ

ぜ expresses strong insistence, mostly in masculine speech among *uchi* members. KE2 is such an example.

ぞ

ぞ is used primarily in masculine speech, and it communicates the speaker's strong will. ぜ and ぞ occur almost exclusively with informal verb forms.

じゃん

じゃん is added at the end of an utterance in a way similar to ね, but its use is restricted to casual speech. It carries with it a strong casual attitude and is more frequently used in youth speech. KE4 is a good example.

ッス

Instead of using the formal ending, adding ッス to the verb and adjective informal form (except the *be*-verb) makes the speech semiformal. For the *be*-verb, delete it totally and add ッス, as in (a). This style maintains formality while it at the same time conveys a casual tone. This style, frequently written in カタカナ, is used by youth, primarily in masculine speech (especially among members of athletic associations).

(a) <conversation>

    A: 今日、何時まで？

       Kyoo nanji made?

       Today, until what time (are you here)?

    B: 三時までッス.

       Sanji made ssu.

       Until three o'clock.

11.6. Emphatic Markers

Key Expressions

KE1   あの映画、すごく感動した。

        Ano eiga, sugoku kandooshita.

        That movie, I was really moved by it.

KE2   俺ら、メチャクメチャ怒られたよ。[masculine speech]

        Orera, mechakucha okorareta yo.

        We were scolded like crazy.

KE3   めちゃかわいい！

        Mecha kawaii!

        Crazily cute!

KE4   あ、使い方、超かんたんだよ。

        A, tsukai kata, choo kantan da yo.

        Oh, the way to use this is super simple.

KE5   えっ、1200円？　超安いじゃん。買っちゃおう。買っちゃ
        おう。

        Ett, sennihyaku-en? Choo yasui jan. Kat-chaoo.
          Kat-chaoo.

        What? It's only twelve hundred yen? Super cheap. I'm
          going to buy this for sure.

KE6   はいはい、よーくわかりました。

        Hai hai, yooku wakarimashita.

        Yes, sure, I really got it.

KE7   そんなこと言うなっ。[blunt style]

        Sonna koto yuu natt.

        Don't ever say such a thing.

Explanation

すごく

When emphasizing your views and feelings, use emphatic adverbs such as すごく and とても. In casual conversation, すごい may function as an adverb, for example, すごい感動した 'I was really moved'. In blunt masculine speech, you are likely to use スゲー, めちゃ, メチャクチャ and the like.

In casual situations, you may use メチャクチャ for emphasis, as in KE2. めちゃ, a shortened version of メチャクチャ, can be affixed to all parts of speech, although most frequently you use it with adverbs and adjectives. For example, as in KE3, めちゃかわいい means 'crazily cute'. Other variations include メッチャ, ムチャ, and メチャメチャ. Emphatic めちゃ and other similar expressions are often written in カタカナ.

Mature adult speakers use these expressions less frequently.

超

超 (ちょう) 'super, extremely, exceedingly' can be affixed to all parts of speech, making it quite versatile. For example, 超カッコいい 'extremely cool', and 超勉強 (ちょうべんきょう) する 'to study really hard'. Study KE4 and KE5, where 超 is affixed to adjectives.

Although originally limited to youth, these emphatic prefixes have spread to the general public, at least in casual conversation. メチャクチャ, めちゃ, and 超 obviously carry a casual tone, and you should avoid them in formal situations.

SOUND CHANGES

You express emotion not only through phrasing and sentence structure but also by sound. As discussed earlier in section 4.10, usually an increase in volume and length indicates emphasis. The elongation of vowels brings an emphatic effect. よーく, instead of よく 'well', means 'really well', as shown in KE6.

As you may recall, another sound change is the insertion of a glottal stop. A glottal stop is the sound usually transcribed as a small っ, which creates a more emphatic emotive effect. For example, ぜんっぜん, instead of ぜんぜん '(not) at all', means 'absolutely not'. As in KE7, the glottal stop may appear at the end of an utterance. It expresses an extraordinarily strong assertive attitude.

(a) うれしいっ！
Ureshiitt!
I'm so glad!

(b) いっただっきまーす！
Ittadakkimaasu!
Thank you for the meal (I'm going to eat now).

Graffiti

Other emphatic expressions may prove useful. The affixes ど, バカ, and ま are non-productive. Do not add these affixes freely to words unless you check with a dictionary.

1. ど is affixed to nouns, adding the meaning of 'in the middle or center of'.

ど真 (ま) ん中 (なか)	smack in the middle
ど素人 (しろうと)	complete lay person

2. バカうま, consisting of the word バカ 'fool' and うまい 'delicious', means 'extraordinarily delicious'.
3. ま is added to a limited number of adjectives, as in まっ黒 (くろ) 'pure black' and まっ白 (しろ) 'pure white'.
4. You may be familiar with マンガ Japanese, where another kind of emphatic strategy is observed. I'm referring to the use of unusual 濁点 (だくてん) added to *hiragana*. 濁点 refers to two side strokes added to た to produce だ. When 濁点 are added to vowels, they signal extraordinary scream-like cries. Your *Nihongo* teacher is likely to mark these wrong, but I've found some examples in マンガ, short stories, and novels. I have found the following examples, all of which are used for interjectional cries of shock and surprise. While it is difficult to pronounce these sounds, each conveys emphasis.

   う" え (instead of the usual うえ)
   あ" ― (instead of the usual あー)
   え" ― (instead of the usual えー)

11.7. Repetition

Key Expressions

KE1   会いたくて、会いたくて、もうほんとに会いたくて。
        Aitakute, aitakute, moo hontoni aitakute.
        Want to see him, want to see him, I really want to see
        him.

KE2   さあ、すわって、すわって。
        Saa, suwatte, suwatte.
        Here, sit, sit here.

KE3   <conversation>
        A: お祭り行く？
              Omatsuri iku?
              Want to go to the festival?
        B: 行く、行く。
              Iku, iku.
              Yes, I'll go, I'll go.

KE4   やろう、やろう。今すぐやろう。
        Yaroo, yaroo. Ima sugu yaroo.
        Let's do it, let's do it. Let's do it right away.

Explanation

REPETITION FOR EMPHASIS

When you are overwhelmed, repetition offers a means to convey
that emotion. Your emotional state can be conveyed by repeating a
phrase twice, three times, or even more. Although this is achieved
in English as well, repetition occurs rather frequently in *Nihongo*.
Study all the Key Expressions where verbs are repeated multiple
times.

   Repetition may also occur across speakers. Your partner may
repeat your very words, which enhances empathy. See B's utterance in KE3.

REPETITION FOR RHYTHM

The repetition of short phrases creates and maintains a rhythm. The
repetition in B's utterance in KE3 and in KE4 are such examples.

   You may hear a Japanese speaker say そうそう 'right, right', or
even そうそうそうそうそう 'right, right, right, right, right'.

11.8. Interjections for Surprise, Disbelief, and Relief

Key Expressions

KE1 　ええっ、五万円？
　　　Eett, goman-en?
　　　What? Fifty thousand yen?

KE2 　うそ！そんなことないでしょ。
　　　Uso! Sonna koto nai desho.
　　　You're kidding! That can't be.

KE3 　うそだあ。それ絶対うそ。
　　　Uso daa. Sore zettai uso.
　　　That's a lie. Absolutely, that's a lie.

KE4 　ほんと？
　　　Honto?
　　　Really?

KE5 　へえ。
　　　Hee.
　　　Really, I see.

KE6 　なにそれ。
　　　Nani sore.
　　　What (the heck) is that! What do you mean by that!

KE7 　やだ、そんなことも知らないの？
　　　Yada, sonna koto mo shiranai no?
　　　Oh no, you don't even know that?

KE8 　なんだ、そんなこと？大事件かと思っちゃった。
　　　Nan da, sonna koto? Daijiken ka to omot-chatta.
　　　What a relief; that's it? I thought it was a major
　　　　disaster.

Explanation

えっ AND うそ

Surprise and disbelief are expressed through interjections such as えっ, ええっ, and うそ！ You use えっ when you are simply surprised at your partner's unexpected comment. Use うそ！ as a challenge to the veracity of what you are hearing. You may also hear people scream うっそうー！ 'No kidding!' as an emotional version of うそ.

ほんと？ AND へえ

You can also use ほんと？ 'Really?' (or 本当 (ほんとう) ですか？) to communicate a sense of doubt. A certain use of なに (or なん) also conveys disbelief. You may utter なんだって？ (or なんですって？) in response to a surprising piece of information.

へえ conveys a sense of being reluctantly persuaded. New information is beginning to convince you, but you are not completely convinced as yet. へえ signals a casual tone, so you should avoid it when talking to your *meue* person. Instead, choose an expression such as そうなんですか、知りませんでした 'Is that right? I didn't know'.

なにそれ

Another commonly used expression is なにそれ, which is not really a question but an expression of disbelief. This is often spoken in a tone of disgust. In certain contexts, this expression conveys the speaker's criticism. The blunt version, なんだそれ, is used in a similar way.

Although an ordinary question takes the form それなに？or それはなんですか？, in the disbelief exclamation, the order is usually inverted as above. It also takes on a rising intonation on the word なに, as shown in (b).

(a) それ、なに。
     Sore, na¬ni.
     What is it?

(b) なに、それ。
     Na□ni, sore.
     What is that!

いやだ AND なんだ AS INTERJECTIONS

いやだ (or casual やだ) expresses, as in KE7, surprise when you discover your partner does not live up to what you think is appropriate. You say なんだ when you are relieved at some news, as in KE8. You expected worse, but things turned out to be less serious. いやだ, やだ, and なんだ are interjections and occur only in the informal style.

Graffiti

When you are surprised or upset, repetition of the initial mora may occur. In fact, this stuttering shows up in マンガ as a means to illustrate the excitement.

(c) <conversation>
    A: いくら？
       Ikura?
       How much is it?
    B: 五千円。
       Gosen-en.
       Five thousand yen.
    A: ご、五千円？
       Go, gosen-en?
       Fi-five thousand yen?

(d) <conversation>
    A: ご、ごめん。おれ、バカだよな。
       Go, gomen. Ore, baka da yo na.
       So-sorry. I'm a fool, aren't I?
    B: うん、知ってる。
       Un, shitteru.
       Yes, I know.

11.9. Whispered Confession and Comment

Explanation

In certain genres, you may find the speaker's inner dialogue and a third-person's comments explicitly presented. Although these are not actually uttered by anyone, they present emotion-rich communication.

CONFESSIONAL WHISPER

Example (a) illustrates a case where the speaker reveals her inner thoughts. This represents a scene familiar in マンガ. B's expressions in parentheses are confessional whispers and are not actually spoken. Still, マンガ creators present these pseudo-utterances to make them available to the reader. They often appear in different fonts (often handwritten scripts) and sizes that separate them from the dialogue presented in speech balloons.

(a)   <conversation in マンガ>
    A: 新入生？
        Shinnyuusei?
        A new student?
    B: はい。上田です。よろしくお願いします。
        Hai. Ueda desu. Yoroshiku onegaishimasu.
        Yes. I'm Ueda. How do you do?
    A: かわいいね。
        Kawaii ne.
        Cute.
    （B: **かわいいって言われた。**）
        Kawaii tte iwareta.
        Boy, he said I am cute.
    A: その帽子。
        Sono booshi.
        That hat of yours.
    （B: **なんだ、帽子か。**）
        Nan da, booshi ka.
        Woops, he means my hat.
    A: あ、君も。
        A, kimi mo.
        Oh, you, too.
    B: えっ？
        Ett?
        What?

The whispers in parentheses express B's inner feelings. They reveal B's *honne* and expose her otherwise privately held thoughts.

THIRD-PERSON COMMENT

Instead of a whispered confessional, sometimes a third-party commentary is offered. Often these comments guide the reader toward the perspective endorsed by the third-party participant. In マンガ, sometimes the comment actually carries the narrator's voice.

In a television variety show, sometimes the producer's comments pop up on the screen.

(b)   <conversation on a variety show>
    A: あの人、若いから。
        Ano hito, wakai kara.
        He is young, so....

B: や、一番年長だけど。
　　Ya, ichiban nenchoo da kedo.
　　Actually, he is the oldest one.
A: 年長だけど、若いみたいな。
　　Nenchoo da kedo, wakai mitai na.
　　Well, he is the oldest, but he is young, like. . . .
Pop-up caption
　　（適当！？）
　　Tekitoo!?
　　Just going along!?

To make them easier to comprehend, Japanese television variety shows often contain captions (or subtitles) of key phrases and pop-up commentary. The commentary provides clues as to how the viewer should understand the verbal exchanges.

Here, the comment 適当！？ 'just going along' guides the viewer to take A's statement 年長だけど、若いみたいな with a grain of salt.

11.10. Interjectional Sound Effects

Key Expressions

KE1　　ジャーン、私が焼いたクッキーです！
　　　　Jaan, watashi ga yaita kukkii desu!
　　　　Here they are! Cookies I baked!

KE2　　ブー、そんなのダメ、ダメ。
　　　　Buu, sonna no dame, dame.
　　　　Boo, that's no good, at all.

KE3　　ガーン。ショック！
　　　　Gaan. Shokku!
　　　　Gaan. What a shock!

Explanation

SOUND EFFECTS WHEN TALKING

To effectively communicate emotion, Japanese speakers (primarily young speakers) sometimes use sound effects. These sound effects, similar to the phrases used in マンガ, are produced by the speakers themselves. It has been pointed out that this tendency in casual speech is influenced by マンガ, which a majority of Japanese people enjoy reading.

Because interjectional sounds are direct expressions of yourself and are made in informal situations only, you should avoid them in formal situations.

KINDS OF SOUND EFFECTS

1. When surprised, imitating the English interjection *wow*

    (a) ワオ、スゲー！
        Wao, sugee!
        Wow, that's terrific.

2. When presenting something in a dramatic flourish, as in KE1

    (b) ジャーン！私の新しいケータイです。
        Jaan! Watashi no atarashii keetai desu.
        Here it is! This is my new cell phone.

3. When disagreeing and disapproving, as in KE2; related to the English word *booing*

    (c) ブー。そんなのうまくいくはずない。反対、反対。
        Buu. Sonna no umaku iku hazu nai. Hantai. Hantai.
        No. There's no way that would work. I'm opposed to it.

4. When disgusted, with a sense of surprise

    (d) ゲッ、ちょっときびしくない？
        Gett, chotto kibishikunai?
        What! Isn't that a bit too severe?

5. When shocked at hearing bad news, as in KE3

    (e) <conversation>
        A: どうしたの？
           Doo shita no?
           What's wrong?
        B: 彼、彼女いたんだ。
           Kare, kanojo ita n da.
           He has a girlfriend.
        A: えっ。
           Ett.
           What!
        B: ガーン。もうだめ。
           Gaan. Moo dame.
           Gaan. It's over.

11.11. Exclamations

Key Expressions

KE1　なんとあの人が来るとは！
　　　Nanto ano hito ga kuru to wa!
　　　Boy, what a surprise that he came!

KE2　なんてやさしい人！
　　　Nante yasashii hito!
　　　What a kind person!

KE3　なんて素晴らしいんだろう。
　　　Nante subarashii n daroo.
　　　How wonderful it is!

KE4　あの事件からずっと、どれほど苦しんだことか。
　　　Ano jiken kara zutto, dorehodo kurushinda koto ka.
　　　Since that incident, how much I've suffered!

Explanation

なんと

The interjection なんと is an emotive phrase added as a preface to an exclamative expression of surprise. It is similar to English expressions such as *Surprise!*, *Believe it or not!*, or *Guess what!* You use なんと when you, in amazement, break unexpected and extraordinary news. In turn, your partner anticipates surprising news to follow. This way, you successfully communicate your amazement while inviting your partner's curiosity.

なんて

なんて appears in combination with adverbs and adjectives to convey extraordinariness. It is often followed by だ, だろう, のだ, んだ, のだろう, or んだろう. Study KE2 and KE3.

こと EXCLAMATION

It is also possible to express an exclamatory attitude by making a nominal phrase with こと. For example, まあ、がんばること！ 'Wow, how hard he tries!' The こと nominal exclamative is stereotypically associated with feminine speech. It should be noted that this expression is rarely used among youth.

どれほど AND どんなに

In written style, another kind of exclamation is used. Here you use the degree words どれほど 'to what extent' or どんなに 'how much'. Attach these phrases before verbs and adjectives, followed by こと か. KE4 is a good example.

(a) **どれほど**うれしかったことか。
Dorehodo ureshikatta koto ka.
How pleased I was!

(b) **どんなに**勉強したことか。
Donnani benkyooshita koto ka.
How much he has studied!

11.12. Rhetorical Questions

Key Expressions

KE1   そんなことできる？できるわけないでしょ。
Sonna koto dekiru? Dekiru wake nai desho.
How can I do such a thing? No way.

KE2   なにやってんだ！ [blunt style]
Nani yatte n da!
What (in the world) are you doing!

KE3   なに言ってんの！
Nani itte n no!
What are you talking about!

KE4   君になにができる！
Kimi ni nani ga dekiru!
What can you do!

KE5   そんなところに行けるものか。
Sonna tokoro ni ikeru mono ka.
How can I go to such a place!

Explanation

Rhetorical questions are questions in form only. Although questions such as そんなことできる？ take the form of a question, you are not expecting an answer. By posing these unanswerable questions, you are conveying extreme emotion. Rhetorical questions are interpreted as a strong negation of what has been stated. No one would supply an answer to a rhetorical question such as "What kind of fool do you think I am?"

なに RHETORICAL QUESTIONS

Rhetorical questions often appear with question words, most often with なに, as in KE2, KE3, and KE4. なに rhetorical questions often end with the のだ or んだ form.

ものか RHETORICAL QUESTIONS

Another strategy often used in rhetorical questions is the utterance-final ものか (or casual もんか), as shown in KE5. Again, a non-literal interpretation is required. For example, as a strong negative response to a request, you may answer そんなことができるものか, meaning '(Of course not.) How can I do such a thing!'

PART V

Use

CHAPTER 12

Interaction Strategies

12.1. Choosing Formal and Informal Styles

Key Expressions

KE1　行きます。行く。
Ikimasu. Iku.
I'm going.

KE2　かわいいです。かわいい。
Kawaii desu. Kawaii.
It's cute.

KE3　鎌倉に着く時間をおしえていただきたいんですが。
Kamakura ni tsuku jikan o oshiete-itadakitai n desu ga.
I'd like you to tell me the time you arrive at Kamakura.

Explanation

For the selection of speech styles, a number of situational, personal, and linguistic factors play a role.

SITUATIONAL FACTORS

1. Familiarity

   The degree of informal style increases with the degree of familiarity you have with your partner. When speaking to a child, even when you don't know the child, casual and friendly speech is appropriate.

2. Relative social status

   Toward your *meue* person, it is best to maintain a formal style, sometimes with supra-polite expressions (see the next section). Toward your *meshita* person, there is less reason to

193

use a formal style, although formality and politeness are often maintained for expressing courtesy and distance.

3. Situation

Communication situations can be divided into public and private. Public situations include official, professional, or ritualistic events, typically taking place in public institutions, hospitals, stores, banks, libraries, educational facilities, and so on.

A public situation can be either with an audience (as in formal business meetings) or without an audience (as in informal two-person talks). In public situations with an audience, the formal speech style is used unless there are reasons to do otherwise. In public situations without an audience, a certain level of formality is sustained, although if the relationship is based on familiarity and *amae,* there is a tendency to use the informal style. Also, if a personal relationship is established, a casual and frank communication style is preferred. It should be noted that an educational context often takes on an informal atmosphere. In grade schools and junior high schools, schoolchildren tend to use the casual style toward the teacher. In many cases, intimacy is emphasized over formality.

Private situations include interactions with family members, informal gatherings, and unofficial meetings. In private situations, there is more of a tendency to choose the casual or blunt styles, although other factors can play a significant role in determining the appropriate speech style.

4. Method of communication

Indirect communication (e.g., letters) tends to take on formality. Direct communication (e.g., face-to-face conversation) tends to reflect the speaker-partner relationship more immediately. The style used in e-mail tends to be casual in general, although formal letters can be transferred electronically. Cellphone text messaging requires short and simple sentences, and the informal style is dominant.

5. Type of encounter

Prearranged purposeful encounters tend to take on formal and polite features. Ordinary casual encounters tend to be less formal.

6. Topic of conversation

A technical topic tends to take on the formal style, whereas a personal topic encourages casual speech.

PERSONAL FACTORS

The speaker's personal feelings influence the ultimate outcome. Mixing formal and informal styles offers a means for you and your partner to constantly adjust the sense of distance or closeness. If your friend suddenly uses an unusually polite expression, you should pay attention. He or she is likely to be upset and wants to insist on and maintain an emotional distance. By inserting the formal style, you communicate distance. By downshifting the formal ending to the informal and adding friendly features, you express a desire to be closer to your partner.

FAMILIARITY AND FORMALITY

A shift from formality to familiarity occurs when the interpersonal relationship changes. For example, a young man who is in love with his female boss may shift from formal to informal style as their intimacy increases. When two people are romantically involved, emotional closeness overrides expected formality.

In recent years, Japanese speakers have tended to place more importance on familiarity than formality. For example, at a store, instead of maintaining the formal style throughout, a salesperson may include informal speech. Doing so, the salesperson conveys warmth and support.

Here is another example. When college students talk to professors, if they are intimate, the casual style is tolerated and perhaps even welcomed. A male student may say something like 先生、メシ食いに行きませんか 'Professor, won't you go out for supper with us?' This friendly invitation is preferred to the more formal (and distant) expression using honorifics such as 先生、お食事ご一緒にいかがですか 'Professor, would you like to have supper with us?' It is not that the student is incapable of using honorifics. Rather, emphasizing familiarity and closeness trumps the ritual of maintaining formality. In general, particularly in communication involving young people, familiarity is becoming more prevalent than formality.

LINGUISTIC FACTORS

When you address your partner, stylistic features primarily accompany the main clause only. While the choice between formal and informal is based on situational and personal factors, the linguistic factor discourages stylistic marking for subordinate clauses.

Likewise, in a discourse, among multiple sentences, you would mark main sentences with the appropriate style. So if you use the formal style, sentences conveying key information are the ones marked accordingly, while sentences offering supplementary information may take the informal style.

12.2. Politeness and Honorifics

Key Expressions

KE1 先生はもうお帰りになりました。
Sensei wa moo okaerininarimashita.
The professor has already gone home.

KE2 お客さまは帰られましたが。
Okyakusama wa kaeraremashita ga.
The guest has already left.

KE3 すぐお電話いたしますので。
Sugu odenwaitashimasu node.
I will call right away.

KE4 父は今外出しておりますが。
Chichi wa ima gaishutsushiteorimasu ga.
My father isn't here now [lit. 'has gone out'].

Explanation

POLITENESS

All utterances in *Nihongo* appear with a certain level of politeness. Politeness is expressed through a variety of linguistic devices and related strategies. We recognize two levels of politeness, that is, polite and supra-polite. The informal style is not "polite" in this narrow sense. (However, remember that the informal style is perfectly polite when it is appropriate. Excess formality can be "impolite.")

The polite style uses formal verb forms and other polite expressions. Supra-polite expressions include formal verb forms plus respectful and humble forms. The prefixes ご and お (see section 7.3) and other very polite strategies are a part of the supra-polite style.

HONORIFICS (RESPECTFUL AND HUMBLE FORMS)

Honorifics refer to respectful and humble forms that generate clearly marked politeness levels.

You use respectful forms when addressing or talking about your *meue* person. Examples are KE1 and KE2. In the same situation, humble forms are used in reference to your own or your *uchi* member's action or state, as in KE3 and KE4. By humbling your or your *uchi* member's action, you signal social differentiation. The use of respectful and humble forms is not optional. Appropriate forms must be chosen in each social situation, except when social equals interact or when the *uchi* relationship is firmly established.

Two Types of Respectful Forms

There are two distinct respectful forms. First is the use of the respectful form of the verb. Respectful forms are identical to passive forms. Therefore, 書 (か) く takes 書かれる, and 起 (お) きる takes 起きられる. Irregular verbs take される and 来 (こ)られる. KE2 takes 帰られる as a respectful form of 帰る.

The second is the pattern [お + stem of the verb + になる], a slightly more formal type than the first. The prefix お is normally attached to 和語 (わご), as in KE1. Similarly, ご is attached to 漢語 (かんご) in the [ご + noun + になる] pattern.

Humble Forms

Humble forms are generated by the pattern [お + stem of the verb + する], as shown in KE3. If you are telling your boss that you will 'deliver' 届 (とど) ける the file later, you should say お届けします. Note that する takes いたす as a humble form (see the chart below). お届けいたします is used for a very humble style. Again, the prefix お is normally attached to 和語 (わご), as in KE3. ご is attached to 漢語 (かんご) in the [ご + noun + する] or the [ご + noun + いたす] structure.

You can use all humble and respectful forms introduced here in either the informal or formal style. It depends on the situation, although it is more likely that you would choose the formal style.

Special Forms

The verbs listed below have special respectful and humble forms. These forms must be learned one by one. KE4 uses the humble form おる in the [て form + いる] structure.

			Respectful	*Humble*
会う	au	to meet	お会 (あ) いになる	お目 (め) にかかる
いる	iru	to be	いらっしゃる	おる
行く	iku	to go	いらっしゃる	参 (まい) る
する	suru	to do	なさる	いたす
食べる	taberu	to eat	めしあがる	いただく
飲む	nomu	to drink	めしあがる	いただく
見る	miru	to see	ごらんになる	拝見 (はいけん)する
言う	yuu	to say	おっしゃる	申 (もう) す

Examples

(a) 先生いらっしゃいますか。[respectful form]
Sensei irasshaimasu ka.
Is the professor in?

(b) お手紙拝見いたしました。[humble form]
Otegami haiken'itashimashita.
I read your letter.

(c) あしたいらっしゃる？[respectful form]
Ashita irassharu?
Are you going tomorrow?

(d) では、ご訪問になりますか。[respectful form]
Dewa, gohoomon ni narimasu ka.
Well then, will you be visiting?

(e) ご返送いたします。[humble form]
Gohensooitashimasu.
I am sending this back.

お AND ご AS NOUN PREFIXES

As we studied in section 7.3, お and ご are prefixes attached to limited nouns to mark politeness. Use お for certain 和語 and ご for certain 漢語.

(f) お買い物ですか。
Okaimono desu ka.
Are you going shopping?

(g) ご出発はいつですか。
Goshuppatsu wa itsu desu ka.
When are you leaving?

12.3. Masculine and Feminine Speech

Key Expressions

KE1 うまい飯、食いてえな。[masculine speech]
Umai meshi, kuitee na.
I want to eat a delicious meal.

KE2 おいしいもの、食べたいね。
Oishii mono, tabetai ne.
I want to eat something delicious.

Explanation

As we studied earlier in sections 3.2 and 3.3, we must keep in mind that masculine and feminine speech styles are not mutually exclusive, and Japanese speakers may use both styles across genders. It is discriminatory to associate certain features of feminine speech as being essentially a reflection of biological gender.

Gender differences in language are in decline, and only limited cases of blunt speech exhibit a marked masculine feature.

DIFFERENCES

The following lists summarize the primary differences between masculine and feminine speech.

Masculine Speech

1. だろ (う) is frequently preferred.
2. Abrupt negative commands are used, as in するな 'Don't do that'.
3. Certain expressions are strongly associated with masculine speech (e.g., the particles ぞ, ぜ, and な, certain slang and cursing words, and so on).
4. The prefixes お and ご are used but not as extensively as in feminine speech.
5. Certain phrases are considered masculine, such as めしを食う (in feminine speech, ごはんを食べる).

Feminine Speech

1. でしょ(う) is frequently preferred.
2. Abrupt negative commands are avoided. Instead, しないで (ください) 'Please don't do that' is preferred.

3. Certain expressions are limited to feminine speech (e.g., the interjection あらまあ 'wow', sentence-final わ [pronounced in a higher tone] and かしら 'I wonder', the personal pronouns あたし and あたくし 'I', and so on). These expressions are used among older women in a limited way, and they are disappearing from the ordinary speech of the majority of Japanese speakers.
4. The prefixes お and ご are more extensively used.
5. Certain phrases are considered feminine, such as すてき 'nice'.
6. In general, older women tend to speak politely, sometimes extremely politely.

SITUATIONAL FACTORS

Although blunt masculine speech is primarily used among male friends, it is sometimes used toward familiar and intimate females. For example, a man may highlight the masculine speech style and speak in a blunt style when he wants to emphasize his intimacy through masculine identity (e.g., toward his girlfriend). The same speaker would avoid blunt speech toward another woman. Likewise, a woman may choose a feminine style to express femininity toward a specific person or under certain circumstances (e.g., when femininity is favorably evaluated). The same speaker may avoid feminine speech when her professional authority is at stake.

PERSONAL FACTORS

The use of feminine and masculine styles may be motivated by playing out certain personal characteristics or by role playing. The feminine speech style may be used by a male who emphasizes femininity, or the masculine speech style may be preferred when a boyish girl speaks. Given that speech style is closely associated with our sense of self-identity regardless of biological gender, the speaker makes use of gender-related styles to his or her advantage.

12.4. Youth Language

Key Expressions

KE1   メッチャかわいい。
         Metcha kawaii.
         Super cute.

KE2   <conversation>
       A: テストの勉強、俺、もうバッチリ。
           Tesuto no benkyoo, ore, moo batchiri.
           Studying for the exam, I've done perfectly.
       B: えっ。あ、忘れてた。チーン。
           Ett. A, wasureteta. Chiin.
           What? Oh, I forgot.

KE3   もうどうでもいい、みたいな。
          Moo doo de mo ii, mitaina.
          Nothing matters any more, like....

Explanation

WHEN AND WHEN NOT TO USE YOUTH LANGUAGE

Young people tend to use youth language among themselves more frequently than toward people of other generations. Particularly in formal situations, young people are expected to speak in a variety of the dominant adult speech. Under such circumstances, speaking in youth language reflects a lack of education, humbleness, or grace.

CHARACTERISTICS OF YOUTH LANGUAGE

1. Shortening of existing phrases

    あけおめ 'Happy New Year' (from 明 (あ) けましておめでとうござ います)
    メリクリ 'Merry Christmas' (from メリークリスマス)

2. Change of meanings

    ヤバイ 'extremely good, overwhelmingly excellent' (from the original meaning of 'in danger, risky')

3. Emphatic expressions

    A variety of emphatic words has originated among young people. Some of them are now in use among the general public as well (see section 11.6).

(a) メッチャむずかしい。
     Metcha muzukashii.
     Super difficult.

(b) 超元気だよ。
     Choo genki da yo.
     I'm extremely well.

    (c) マジむかつく。
        Maji mukatsuku.
        It really makes me mad.

4. Onomatopoeic words inserted in conversation

    Influenced by comics, young speakers may use ono-
matopoeic and interjectional words found in comics (see
sections 6.9 and 11.10). They voice those sound effect words
themselves.

    (d) 彼女、彼氏いたんだ。**ガーン**。
        Kanojo, kareshi ita n da. Gaan.
        It turned out that she has a boyfriend.

5. Invention and use of *ru-kotoba* (new verbs created by adding
ru to nouns)

    コクる 'to confess (love)' (from 告白 (こくはく) する)
    コビる 'to go to convenience stores' (from コンビニに行 (い)く)

OBJECTIFYING AND SELF-ALIENATING EXPRESSIONS

As touched upon in section 3.5, objectifying and self-alienating expressions give the impression that you are being solicitous of and
considerate to your partner. They also work as a strategy to deflect
potential disagreement or possible criticism. Overall, these expressions give the impression that the speech has been "softened." The
softening strategy functions to lessen the potentially negative impact a statement may make.

1. Self-alienating expressions

    (e) 私って、ホントは、**結構飲めたりして**······
        Watashi tte, honto wa, kekkoo nometari shite....
        But, in truth, maybe I can drink a lot?

2. Objectified expressions

    (f) 今朝、起きたら頭も痛いし、もう人生どうでもいいや、**みたい**
        な。
        Kesa, okitara atama mo itai shi, moo jinsei doo demo ii
          ya, mitaina.
        This morning when I got up, I had a headache and felt
          like I didn't care about my life any more, like....

3. Overly self-conscious expressions

(g) あたしって**意外と**シャイなんです。
Atashi tte igaito shai na n desu.
(You may not think so, but) surprisingly, I am shy.

WHY YOUTH LANGUAGE?

There are a number of reasons for speaking in youth language, the following among others.

1. To relish a sense of camaraderie
2. To convey humor and friendliness
3. To frankly communicate your feelings
4. To communicate feelings as felt through your senses
5. To be playful and entertaining

12.5. Borrowing *Nihongo* Varieties

Explanation

Borrowing the variation or style typically associated with someone else is a creative tool. Here we focus on borrowing gendered styles and generational styles.

BORROWING GENDERED STYLES

Taking advantage of the features associated with masculine and feminine speech, you might borrow the style atypical of your own. For example, suppose you are a male speaker commenting on a woman who is wondering about a cheap (actually fake) gemstone. Although you yourself are not likely to say これほんものかしら 'is this real?', by imitating stereotypical feminine speech, you vividly express what you want to say. You may incorporate this speech in the following expression.

(a) これほんものかしら、な、バカさが、かわいい。
Kore honmono kashira, na, bakasa ga, kawaii.
She is cute in her foolishness to even think "Is this real?"

BORROWING GENERATIONAL STYLES

Another borrowing occurs when a speaker borrows from a variation associated with a certain generation. One variation is called オ

ジサン言葉 (ことば), a style used by male speakers over fifty years old or so. It features なあ placed after the formal style, producing ですなあ and ますなあ。If a female speaker all of a sudden uses this style, it gives the air of a middle-aged man making comments and giving advice. For example, by saying そういうことですなあ 'I think that is the case' instead of そういうことです, you add that authoritative attitude associated with mature male speakers.

BORROWING VOICES CREATIVELY

Obviously, whatever you say is your own. Even when you "borrow" someone else's style, you are the one who borrowed it. In this sense, it is your creativity that makes borrowing happen.

By introducing styles stereotypically associated with someone else, you introduce different voices into your speech. This strategy becomes useful when you want to say something against social expectations. Breaking the rules and overriding the expected are tools for your linguistic creativity.

One way to incorporate a socially unacceptable style into your speech is to use quotations, as shown below.

(b)   「ふざけんな、バカ」とか思っちゃった。
      "Fuzaken na, baka" toka omot-chatta.
      I thought, "Cut it out, you idiot."

12.6. Greetings and Introductions

Key Expressions

KE1   おはようございます。
          Ohayoo gozaimasu.
          Good morning.

KE2   こんにちは。
          Konnichiwa.
          Good afternoon.

KE3   こんばんは。
          Konbanwa.
          Good evening.

KE4   はじめまして。岡田美佐です。
          Hajimemashite. Okada Misa desu.
          How do you do? I'm Misa Okada.

Explanation

GREETINGS

ございます makes おはよう formal and polite. Use this when greeting your *meue* person. When using こんにちは, remember that ん is one mora, and the phrase contains five morae, pronounced as ko-n-ni-chi-wa. Don't forget that は in こんにちは and こんばんは is read "wa."

Responding to Greetings

As in English, when greeted with these expressions, responding in kind with the same phrase will suffice. If you bow (even slightly) when answering, you are adding a greater degree of politeness. After the greeting, innocuous comments on the weather (small talk) offer a useful strategy for establishing rapport.

When to Greet

Although at least in some parts of the United States it is common to acknowledge or greet complete strangers in an elevator or elsewhere, such exchanges are not customary in Japan.

Restrictions on Greetings

こんにちは and こんばんは are not used among family members. Likewise, when familiar company employees meet each other at the company, instead of こんにちは, they use other brief greetings such as あ、どうも, or nod to acknowledge each other.

Regardless of the time of day, when people are simply acknowledging each other, どうも (or the casual ども) is sufficient. In casual masculine speech, おいッス and おっ are also used.

Many Americans greet each other by saying *How are you?* Although it is possible to literally translate this phrase into いかがですか 'how are you?', this expression is not normally used unless you are specifically concerned about the physical condition of your partner. Only when you meet your friend after an absence of some time, and you are concerned about how he or she has been, do you use お元気 (げんき) ですか and other expressions in different formality levels, such as 元気ですか and 元気?

INTRODUCTIONS

When introducing yourself, first use はじめまして 'how do you do', followed by your name, as in KE4. Then add どうぞよろしく or よろ

しく [lit. 'please be good to me'], something similar to the English *I'm pleased to meet you.* You are expected to bow as you utter these phrases.

(a) <conversation>
    A: はじめまして。田中健と申します。どうぞよろしく。
        Hajimemashite. Tanaka Ken to mooshimasu. Doozo yoroshiku.
        How do you do? I'm Ken Tanaka. Nice to meet you.
    B: 堤です。こちらこそよろしく。
        Tsutsumi desu. Kochira koso yoroshiku.
        I'm Tsutsumi. Nice to meet you, too.

(b) <conversation>
    Aya: お母さん、こちら美恵さん。
           Okaasan, kochira Mie-san.
           Mother, this is Mie.
    Mie: はじめまして。美恵です。
           Hajimemashite. Mie desu.
           How do you do? I'm Mie.
    Mother: はじめまして。娘がお世話になってます。よろしくね。
           Hajimemashite. Musume ga osewa ni nattemasu. Yoroshiku ne.
           How do you do? Thanks for being kind to my daughter. Nice to meet you.

12.7. Making Requests

Key Expressions

KE1   じゃ、電話してください。
          Ja, denwashite-kudasai.
          Call me, then.

KE2   何ですか。ちゃんと言ってくださいよ。
          Nan desu ka. Chanto itte-kudasai yo.
          What is it? Please give it to me straight.

KE3   お願いだからすぐ来て。
          Onegai da kara sugu kite.
          Please, please come right away!

KE4　オレの気持ちもわかってくれよ。[masculine speech]
　　　Ore no kimochi mo wakatte-kure yo.
　　　You should understand my feelings.

KE5　結果がわかったら、知らせてくれない？
　　　Kekka ga wakattara, shirasete-kurenai?
　　　Will you please let me know the result when you find
　　　　out?

KE6　お電話していただけませんでしょうか。
　　　Odenwashite-itadakemasen deshoo ka.
　　　Would you please call me?

KE7　電話してもらっていいですか。
　　　Denwashite-moratte ii desu ka.
　　　Will you call me?

KE8　<conversation>
　　　A:　ねえ。
　　　　　Nee.
　　　　　Say. . . .
　　　B:　何？
　　　　　Nani?
　　　　　What is it?
　　　A:　ひとつだけお願いしてもいい？
　　　　　Hitotsu dake onegaishite mo ii?
　　　　　Can I make just one request?

Explanation

There are several ways to make requests in Japanese, all of which involve verbs of giving and receiving. When making a request, use the て form of the verb followed by ください, as in KE1 and KE2, with a casual alternative using the て form only, as in KE3. A blunt version takes てくれ, as in KE4. KE5 offers a softening effect by the use of てくれない？ Use these expressions only toward your social equals or *meshita* persons.

When making a request to your *meue* person, use the suprapolite version, such as ていただけませんでしょうか, as in KE6.

てもらっていいですか, as in KE7, is frequently used, particularly among youth, as a formal request (see section 9.3). However, among older speakers, ていただけませんでしょうか is preferred.

DEGREES OF POLITENESS

Here is a list of different kinds of request forms for the verb 書(か) く 'to write', arranged from the most direct to the most polite.

書いてくれ。 Write this.
書いてください。 Please write this.
書いてくれますか。 Could you write this?
書いてくれませんか。 Couldn't you write this?
書いてもらっていいですか。 Would you write this for me?
書いてもらってもいいでしょうか。 Would you please write this for me?
書いていただけますか。 Could you kindly write this?
書いていただけませんか。 Could you please kindly write this?

Informal versions are useful as well.

書いてくれる？ Will you write this?
書いてくれない？ Won't you write this?
書いてもらっていい？ Can you write this for me?
書いていただける？ Will you kindly write this?

URGENT PLEAS

When you make an urgent plea, お願 (ねが) いだから 'I'm pleading with you' may be added prior to your request. This is a request addressed to *amae* partners. You should avoid using it toward a partner with whom you show your respect or maintain distance.

RESPONDING TO REQUESTS

1. Granting requests

(a) はい。
Hai.
Yes, I will.

(b) オッケー。
Okkee.
Okay.

(c) はい、承知しました。
Hai, shoochishimashita.
Yes, certainly.

(d) はい、わかりました。
　　Hai, wakarimashita.
　　Yes, I'll take care of it.

(e) 了解。
　　Ryookai.
　　All right.

2. Refusing requests

(f) そう言われましてもねえ‥‥‥
　　Soo iwaremashite mo nee....
　　Well, my apologies, but I cannot....

(g) ごめん。ちょっとむずかしいなあ、それは。
　　Gomen. Chotto muzukashii naa, sore wa.
　　Sorry. It's a bit difficult, I'm afraid.

(h) <conversation>
　　A: お願いします。
　　　　Onegaishimasu.
　　　　Please, please, I beg you.
　　B: 悪いけど無理だよ。
　　　　Warui kedo muri da yo.
　　　　Sorry, but it's impossible.
　　A: なんとかお願いします。
　　　　Nantoka onegaishimasu.
　　　　Will you please, I beg you.
　　B: 勘弁してくれよ。
　　　　Kanbenshite-kure yo.
　　　　Stop it, will you?

12.8. Asking for and Granting Permission

Key Expressions

KE1　　<conversation>
　　A: 部屋に入ってもいいですか。
　　　　Heya ni haitte mo ii desu ka.
　　　　May I enter the room?
　　B: ええ、どうぞ。
　　　　Ee. Doozo.
　　　　Yes, please.

KE2   <conversation>
           A: ねえ、今日、君の車借りていい？
                Nee, kyoo, kimi no kuruma karite ii?
                Can I borrow your car today?
           B: いや、ちょっと。
                Iya, chotto.
                Uh, that's a bit of a problem.

Explanation

ASKING FOR PERMISSION

Use the て form of the verbs and adjectives followed by (も)いいです
か to ask for permission, as in A's utterance in KE1. In the casual
style, ていい？ suffices, as in A's utterance in KE2.

The negative forms are also used, either as なくて or the more
casual ないで.

(a) 急いでいるんで、片付け**なくて**もいいですか。
    Isoideiru nde katazukenakute mo ii desu ka.
    Because I'm in a rush, is it okay not to put things back in
        their proper place?

(b) これ、食べ**ないで**いいよね。
    Kore, tabenaide ii yo ne.
    It's all right not to eat this, right?

GRANTING PERMISSION

(c) はい、いいです。
    Hai, ii desu.
    Yes, it is fine.

(d) ええ、かまいません。
    Ee, kamaimasen.
    Yes, that's no trouble at all.

(e) はい、どうぞ。
    Hai, doozo.
    Yes, go ahead.

(f) <conversation>
    A: 確認したいと思いますが、よろしいでしょうか。
         Kakuninshitai to omoimasu ga, yoroshii deshoo ka.
         Just to confirm, is it all right?

B: はい、お願いします。
Hai, onegaishimasu.
Sure, please.

NOT GRANTING PERMISSION

1. Prohibition

   (g) <conversation>
   A: 食べてもいいですか。
   Tabete mo ii desu ka.
   May I eat now?
   B: (まだ食べては) だめですよ。
   Mada tabete wa dame desu yo.
   No, not yet.

   (h) <conversation>
   A: これ買っていい？
   Kore katte ii?
   Can I buy this?
   B: だめよ。
   Dame yo.
   No, you may not.

2. Softer denial of permission
   You should use softer strategies when addressing your *meue* person.

   (i) <conversation>
   A: ここでお酒を飲んでもいいですか。
   Koko de osake o nonde mo ii desu ka.
   Can we drink sake here?
   B: いやあ、ちょっと。
   Iyaa, chotto.
   Well...I'm afraid not.

   (j) <conversation>
   A: もう、帰ってもいいですか。
   Moo, kaette mo ii desu ka.
   May I leave now?
   B: ああ、それが、すみませんが、もう少し待ってくださいま
   せんか。
   Aa, sore ga, sumimasen ga, moo sukoshi matte-ku-
   dasaimasen ka.
   Sorry, but could you wait a bit longer?

12.9. Apologizing

Key Expressions

KE1 すみません、ちょっと先約があるので。
   Sumimasen, chotto sen'yaku ga aru node.
   I'm sorry, but I have another appointment.

KE2 ごめんなさい。
   Gomennasai.
   I'm sorry.

KE3 <conversation>
   A: ごめん、何だっけ？
     Gomen, nan dakke?
     Sorry, what was it?
   B: えっ？覚えてないの？
     Ett? Oboetenai no?
     What? You don't remember?

Explanation

FREQUENT APOLOGIZING

Typically Japanese speakers apologize far more frequently than Americans. Apologies convey that you recognize your failure to meet others' expectations. This in turn negates placing the blame on others and thus shows your thoughtfulness. Apologizing is considered a virtue in Japan. When you apologize and show remorse, Japanese are often emotionally moved and are more willing to forgive.

EXPRESSIONS OF APOLOGY AND POLITENESS

Here are examples of expressions of apology from less to more polite.

ワリー。 [blunt] Sorry.
わるい。 Sorry. [lit. 'I was bad.']
コメン。 Sorry, excuse me.
ごめんなさい。 I'm sorry. Please excuse me.
失礼 (しつれい) 。 Sorry, excuse me. [frequently used in masculine speech]
ごめんなさい。 I'm sorry, please forgive me.
すみません。 I'm sorry.

申 (もう) しわけありません。 I'm sorry.
申しわけございません。 I'm very sorry. [supra-polite]

APOLOGY OR GRATITUDE

すみません and 申しわけありません, under discussion here, are used to express gratitude as well (see the next section). Depending on the circumstances, it is important to interpret some of these as expressions of gratitude and not as apologies.

BOWING FOR APOLOGY

When apologizing, it is important to bow. The more deeply felt your apology, the more slowly and deeply you bow. During the apology, you are normally expected to cast your eyes downward and assume an apologetic and humble stance.

12.10. Expressing Gratitude

Key Expressions

KE1　　ありがと。
　　　　Arigato.
　　　　Thank you.

KE2　　サンキュ。
　　　　Sankyu.
　　　　Thank you.

KE3　　どうもありがとうございます。
　　　　Doomo arigatoo gozaimasu.
　　　　Thank you very much.

KE4　　どうもすみませんでした。
　　　　Doomo sumimasendeshita.
　　　　Thanks.

Explanation

Varied styles for saying thanks are available.

ありがとう。 Thanks.
ありがとうございます。 Thank you.
ありがとうございました。 Thank you. (often after the favor is done)
どうも（どうも）。 Thanks.

どうもすみません。 Thank you for your trouble.
どうもすみませんでした。 Thank you. (after the favor is done)
サンキュでした。 Thanks. (after the favor is done)

SPECIAL THANKS

The expression お世話 (せわ) になりました [lit. 'thanks for taking care of me'] is used when you part from someone who took care of you. For example, when parting from a host family (for good), use this expression to mean 'thank you for taking care of me.' It is advisable to bow as these words are uttered.

RESPONDING TO THANKS

When you are thanked, appropriate responses include the following:

いいえ、どういたしまして。 You are welcome; it's my pleasure.
いいえ。 Welcome.

Later Thanks

In Japan, it is customary for a person who received a favor earlier to again express gratitude the next time the giver and recipient meet. Let's assume that your teacher took you and your friend out for coffee a week ago. What follows is a typical interaction when you run into the teacher again.

(a) 先生、この間はどうもありがとうございました。
Sensei, kono aida wa doomo arigatoo gozaimashita.
Thank you very much for [your favor] the other day.

12.11. Offering Advice and Suggestions

Key Expressions

KE1   すぐあやまる方がいいんじゃない？
Sugu ayamaru hoo ga ii n janai?
Wouldn't it be better to apologize right away?

KE2   もっと早く行った方がいいでしょう。
Motto hayaku itta hoo ga ii deshoo.
It would be better if you went a bit earlier.

KE3   そろそろ始めたらどうでしょう。
Sorosoro hajimetara doo deshoo.
How about starting soon?

KE4   そんなバカなこと、もういいかげんにしたら？

Sonna bakana koto, moo iikagen ni shitara?

Why don't you stop such a foolish thing already?

Explanation

方 (ほう) がいい

The 方がいい pattern takes informal endings of the verbs and adjectives. As in KE2, the past tense gives a slightly politer impression. The use of 方がいい is generally for your *meshita* person or close friends.

たら

The たら conditional, followed by the optional formulaic clauses of どう, どうだろう, and どうでしょう, provides another strategy for offering advice and suggestions. KE3 is such an example, and KE4 is a shortened version using only たら.

SUGGESTIONS TOWARD SOCIAL SUPERIORS

When suggesting and advising your *meue* person or those to whom you wish to extend politeness, you must use a politer version. One option is to use respectful forms and 方がいい. Instead of いい, you can also use よろしい to make the statement formal. Endings such as かと and かと存 (ぞん) じますが increase the level of politeness.

(a) もう少し早くいらっしゃった方がよろしいかと。[supra-polite style]

Moo sukoshi hayaku irasshatta hoo ga yoroshii ka to.

I wonder if it is better for you to go a bit earlier.

OTHER EXPRESSIONS FOR ADVICE AND SUGGESTIONS

The following expressions are listed from the most direct to the most indirect. As you can see, in general, the more elaborate the expression, the more polite it becomes, which is also true in English.

行 (い) け。 Go now!

行きなさい。 Go.

行くほうがいい（です）。 You should go.

行ったほうがいい（です）。 I think you should go.

行ったほうがいいでしょう。 Perhaps it's better if you go.

行ったらどうですか。 How about going?

行ったほうがよろしいかと思いますが。 I think it's better for you to
　　go.
いらっしゃったら？ Won't you go?
いらっしゃった方がよろしいんじゃないかと思いますが。 I wonder if
　　it is better for you to go.
いらっしゃった方がよろしいんじゃないかと存じますが。 I wonder if
　　it would be better for you to go.

12.12. Giving Orders and Commands

Key Expressions

KE1　　勉強しなさい！
　　　　Benkyooshinasai!
　　　　Study now!

KE2　　気を付けなさいよ。
　　　　Kiotsukenasai yo.
　　　　You better be careful.

KE3　　黙れ！ [blunt style]
　　　　Damare!
　　　　Shut up!

KE4　　おれの話を聞け！ [blunt masculine style]
　　　　Ore no hanashi o kike!
　　　　Hey, listen to my story.

KE5　　来るな！ [blunt style]
　　　　Kuru na!
　　　　Don't come!

Explanation

なさい

For giving orders, [stem of the verb + なさい] and the abrupt command form of the verb are available. Study KE1 and KE2. These
are used strictly by a *meue* person toward a *meshita* person. The
reverse, a command toward your *meue,* is considered extremely
rude.

なさい AND てください

You may use two levels of command forms when addressing your
meshita person. The [stem of the verb + なさい] form is used in both

masculine and feminine speech, and the abrupt command form is used predominantly in masculine speech. Use the [stem of the verb + なさい] when addressing children or subordinates. In general, however, even when a *meue* person issues a command, if it is addressed to an adult, the [て form of the verb + ください] pattern is recommended. It shows consideration for others and is more pleasantly accepted.

ABRUPT COMMAND FORMS

U-verbs: Replace the final -*u* with -*e.*

書く	kaku	to write	書け

RU-verbs: Replace the final るwith ろ.

食べる	taberu	to eat	食べろ

Irregular verbs

する	suru	to do	しろ
来る	kuru	to come	来 (こ) い

Be-*verb*

だ	da	to be, to stay	でいろ

NEGATIVE ABRUPT COMMAND FORMS

Adding な to the basic form of the verb results in a negative abrupt command form.

書く	kaku	to write	書くな
起きる	okiru	to get up	起きるな
来る	kuru	to come	来るな

(a) **帰ってくれ**。迷惑なんだ。
Kaette-kure. Meiwakuna n da.
Leave. You're being a bother.

(b) <conversation>
A: おい、これ**持て**よ。[blunt style]
Oi, kore mote yo.
Hey, carry this.
B: えっ。
Ett.
What?
A: 俺だけに荷物**持たせるな**よ。[masculine speech]
Ore dake ni nimotsu motaseru na yo.
Don't make only me carry the luggage.

(c)   <conversation>
   A:　あんまり悪いこと**すんな**よ。
     Anmari warui koto sun na yo.
     Don't do bad things.
   B:　わかってるよ。
     Wakatteru yo.
     I know, I know.

12.13. Inviting and Responding to Invitations

Key Expressions

KE1　　コーヒーでもいかがですか。
      Koohii demo ikaga desu ka.
      How about some coffee?

KE2　　冷たい飲み物とかどう？
      Tsumetai nomimono toka doo?
      How about something cold to drink?

KE3　　あした映画行かない？
      Ashita eiga ikanai?
      Want to go see a movie tomorrow?

KE4　　<conversation>
      A:　今日の夜とか会わない？
         Kyoo no yoru toka awanai?
         Can we get together tonight?
      B:　うん。会いたい。どこがいい？
         Un. Aitai. Doko ga ii?
         Yes. I want to see you. Where?

Explanation

いかがですか AND どう？

いかがですか 'how about it' or its informal version どう（ですか）
are useful for making suggestions and offering invitations by specifying items, as given in KE1. You can also use いかがでしょうか, a
politer version, for people toward whom you must be polite. In casual situations, the shortened expression どう is used, as in KE2.

USING でも OR とか

When suggesting or inviting, the items you specify are often followed by でも or とか, as in KE1 and KE2 respectively. Both でも

and とか suggest other choices, similar to English *or something*. This makes the suggestion less specific and therefore less demanding (see section 13.5).

As we studied in section 8.13, the negative non-past addressed to your partner functions as invitation, as in KE3 and A's utterance in KE4.

RESPONDING TO INVITATIONS AND SUGGESTIONS

1. Positive

    ええ、いいですねえ。 Yes, that will be nice.
    うん、そうしよう。 Yes, let's do so.
    はい、よろこんで。 With pleasure.
    ええ、ぜひ。 Yes, by all means.
    では、お願 (ねが) いします。 Yes, thank you.

2. Negative

    そうですねえ。ちょっと。 Let me see. Uhh....
    今夜 (こんや) はちょっと。 Tonight isn't the best time.
    いえ、結構 (けっこう) です。 No, thank you.
    無理 (むり)。 Impossible.

3. Undecided

    そうですねえ‥‥‥ Well....
    そうだなあ‥‥‥ Well....

Graffiti

Among youth, when refusing an offer, the expression 大丈夫 (だいじょうぶ) (です) is used. 大丈夫 (です) literally means 'I'm fine as I am' and suggests that you are fine without accepting the offer. This is a way of saying that there is no need for what is being offered. Although this refusal is a facade of indirectness, it functions as a direct refusal.

(a) <conversation>
    A: 上がってコーヒーでも飲んでって。
       Agatte koohii demo nondette.
       Come in and have some coffee.
    B: あ、ボク、**大丈夫です**から。 [masculine speech]
       A, boku, daijoobu desu kara.
       No thanks.

12.14. Being Serious and Nervous

Key Expressions

KE1   マジですか？
        Maji desu ka.
        Are you serious?

KE2   まじめな話。
        Majimena hanashi.
        It's serious.

KE3   ほんとマジごめん。
        Honto maji gomen.
        Really, seriously, I'm sorry.

KE4   すみません。緊張しちゃって。
        Sumimasen. Kinchooshi-chatte.
        Sorry. I'm nervous.

Explanation

まじ AND マジ

The frequency and various ways まじ is used deserve our special attention. まじ, often written in カタカナ, is a shortened casual form of まじめな and まじめに. Use まじですか 'Are you serious?' as a formal version.

まじ and まじで？ are frequently used in casual conversation as a device to confirm your partner's seriousness and genuine intentions. It is similar to *Do you really mean it?* These phrases are also used as interjections to mean something like *Really?* They show you are surprised or are in a state of disbelief. マジ is particularly prevalent in youth speech, although its use has extended to speakers in their thirties and forties.

INTERACTION USING マジ AND マジで

(a) <conversation>
     A: あの人、結婚するんだってよ、来月。
         Ano hito, kekkonsuru n datte yo, raigetsu.
         I hear she's getting married next month.
     B: うそ。**マジ？**
         Uso. Maji?
         No kidding. Seriously?

A:　うん、**マジで**。うちの会社の人と。
　　Un, maji de. Uchi no kaisha no hito to.
　　Yeah, seriously. To a man in our company.

マジ AS EMPHATIC MARKER

マジ is used as an emphatic adverb, as in K3. This use is generally restricted to youth speech.

マジダサい。 Really not cool
マジこわい。 Really scary.
マジうるせえ。 Really bothersome. [blunt style]
マジ狂 (くる) ってる。Really crazy.
超マジごめん。I'm really, really sorry.

WHEN NERVOUS

When nervous, you may describe yourself as 緊張する. This confession-like expression, as in KE4, often disarms your partner, and thus you may receive warm support as well.

Graffiti

When doubting the seriousness of your partner, you can also use (b) or (c). The utterance in (b) strongly challenges the truthfulness of your partner's feelings, and (c) strongly tells your partner to be serious.

(b)　それ本気で言ってます？
　　Sore honki de ittemasu?
　　Are you saying that to really mean it?

(c)　ふざけないで。
　　Fuzakenai de.
　　Don't be silly. Be serious.

12.15. Fighting and Cursing

Key Expressions

KE1　　なんだと！
　　　Nan da to!
　　　What (are you talking about)!

KE2	なに！
	Nani!
	What!
KE3	ばか。
	Baka.
	You fool.
KE4	くそ！
	Kuso!
	Shit!
KE5	ちくしょう！
	Chikushoo!
	Hell. Damn! Fuck! [lit. 'beast']

Explanation

In general, words for fighting and cursing are used frequently in the more assertive masculine style, but female speakers use them if the situation necessitates or allows for them. These straightforward expressions are blunt and more likely to be tolerated among *uchi* members.

As expected, curse or swear words are generally forbidden in formal situations, and using them would result in almost an irrevocably unpleasant and confrontational relationship.

FIGHTING WITH なに

The interjection なに, associated with the word 何 (なに) 'what', appears in conflict situations. It signals the speaker's anger and resentment. If you use them, pronounce them clearly and strongly, to show strong opposition. なに！ (as a conflict interjection) is often pronounced as na□ni with the higher tone placed on に instead of on the question word na¬ni, which takes the higher tone on な.

NO ANSWERS EXPECTED

Although なに is a question word, under this circumstance, you do not expect an answer from your partner. Interjections such as なんだと！ 'what (are you talking about)!' and なにを！ 'What (the hell)!' convey accusatory, challenging, defiant, and fighting attitudes. Your partner may offer no response or may fight back with other defiant expressions, including なに expressions.

(a) <conversation>

A: いい加減にしろよ。
Ii kagen ni shiro yo.
Behave yourself.

B: **なんだと！**
Nan da to!
What are you talking about!

A: **なに！**
Nani!
What are YOU saying!

CURSE AND SWEAR WORDS

1. ばか

ばか [lit. 'fool'] is an interjection that expresses the speaker's anger and frustration. When used with a specific pronoun or a name, のばか is added, as in 隼人 (はやと) のばか 'Hayato, you idiot'. ばかやろう, more derogatory than ばか, combines ばか and やろう 'idiot' (in derogatory speech) and expresses a maddening hatred and anger.

2. くそ

くそ [lit. 'shit'] is uttered as a curse word when the speaker is very upset and frustrated. くそ is also used in combination with other phrases, such as くそむずかしい [lit. 'shit difficult']. Also available is くそったれ 'shithead, shitty one'. In all cases, くそ signals the speaker's derogatory attitude combined with anger, strong dislike, and frustration.

3. ちくしょう

ちくしょう refers to beasts in a derogatory way, and when used as a curse word, it emphasizes that someone or something is below human dignity.

MORE FIGHTING WORDS

You may not encounter too many occasions to use fighting words, but it is important that you know what they mean. And you ought to have some ability to fight back verbally. The following examples are possible.

(b) 死ねっ！
Shinett!
Die, you die!

(c) ほっとけ。[blunt style]
Hottoke.
Leave me alone.

(d) 知らねえよ。[blunt style]
Shiranee yo.
I don't give a damn.

BEING DEFIANT

When being defiant, you can make use of a number of interjectional sounds. A few of the more frequently used interjections are the following:

1. In defiance

(e) ふん、生意気な。
Fun, namaiki na.
Humph, you've got a lot of nerve.

2. In disgust

(f) ちぇっ，ケチだなあ。
Chett, kechi da naa.
Ugh, boy, are you stingy.

3. When dismissively criticizing

(g) なにさ、子供のくせに。
Nani sa, kodomo no kuseni.
What the hell, you're just a child.

Graffiti

Although these fighting and curse words rarely appear in your Japanese language textbooks, they are an important part of your *Nihongo* project. If you are a *manga* fan, you will find these words frequently in various fight scenes and conflict situations. More important, even if you may not use these expressions, you should at least be familiar with them. It is critical that you know when someone is upset and is ready to fight you. You must understand what confronts you so that you can defend yourself appropriately.

12.16. Teasing

Key Expressions

KE1   ばかじゃない？
Baka janai?
You foolish thing!

KE2   ばーか。
Baaka.
You fool!

KE3   憎いねえ、人気者！
Nikui nee, ninkimono!
I could hate you (for it), Mr. Popular!

Explanation

GOOD-NATURED TEASING AND CONTEXT

Good-natured teasing signals intimacy. Even fighting words are used for the purpose of teasing. Because teasing and the response to teasing involve seemingly derogatory terms, it becomes critical to understand the context.

As important are the accompanying cues. Facial expressions and tone of voice are key. They communicate an ironic meaning, signaling that you are simply enjoying a good-natured teasing.

ばか AS TEASING

When someone says ばか！ 'Silly thing!' in a flirtatious way, obviously it is an expression of love. Even a phrase such as 憎 (にく) らしいひと！ [lit. 'hateful person'] can be used as a tease, only to show strong affection. We must remind ourselves that the literal interpretation is hardly enough when appreciating the meaning of "real" *Nihongo*.

12.17. Leave-Taking and Parting

Key Expressions

KE1   じゃあ、また。
Jaa, mata.
Well then.

KE2   さよなら。
         Sayonara.
         Good-bye.

KE3   バイバイ。
         Bai bai.
         Bye, bye.

KE4   失礼します。
         Shitsureishimasu.
         I'm leaving now.

Explanation

RESTRICTIONS FOR USING さよなら

Although さよなら (or the more formal さようなら) is best known as a greeting for farewell, it is important to know that among *uchi* members, one says さよなら only when the separation is for an extended period. Saying さよなら often implies that you may never see the person again.

It would be quite upsetting for Japanese parents to hear their son or daughter leave the house saying さよなら in the morning. The parents would think their child was running away from home or even ready to commit suicide! If you stay with a Japanese family, for example, the only time you should use さようなら to the family members is when leaving them for good. Schoolchildren do use さようなら to teachers at the end of the day, however, even when they will meet the teacher the next day.

LEAVE-TAKING EXPRESSIONS

1.   When leaving the house

     (a) 行ってきます。
          Itte-kimasu.
          Good-bye. [lit. 'I will go and return.']

2.   When saying good-bye to someone you meet every day or frequently

     (b) じゃあ、あした。
          Jaa, ashita.
          See you tomorrow.

(c) それではまた。
Soredewa mata.
Well then, see you again.

3. When leaving the workplace before others

(d) お先に失礼します。
Osaki ni shitsureishimasu.
Good-bye. [lit. 'Excuse me for leaving early.']

4. When leaving for a long time

(e) さようなら。
Sayoonara.
Good-bye.

(f) お元気で。
Ogenki de.
Take care of yourself.

NEGOTIATING LEAVE-TAKING

When taking leave, usually a few speaking turns are exchanged, as shown below.

(g) <conversation>
A: そろそろ帰らなきゃ。
Sorosoro kaeranakya.
I must be going.
B: えっ、そんなあ、もうちょっといてよ。
Ett, sonnaa, moo chotto ite yo.
What! Stay a bit longer, won't you?

(h) <conversation>
A: あ、もうこんな時間。帰らなきゃ。
A, moo konna jikan. Kaeranakya.
Oh, it's already late. I must go.
B: まだいいだろ。[masculine speech]
Mada ii daro.
You can stay, can't you?
A: もう遅いから。
Moo osoi kara.
It's late.

B: そう ？
Soo?
Maybe so.

A: 失礼します。
Shitsureishimasu.
I'm leaving now.

B: うん、じゃ、また。
Un, ja, mata.
Okay, well then.

A: じゃ。
Ja.
See you.

RESPONDING TO LEAVE-TAKING GREETINGS

When a family member leaves home saying 行ってきます, the remaining members respond with 行っていらっしゃい [lit. 'Go and return.'] When a co-worker leaves the office by saying お先に失礼します, the remaining co-workers will respond with お疲 (つか) れさまでした [lit. 'Thank you for your effort.']. However, if your *meue* person leaves by saying お先に, you should respond with ああどうも and not with お疲れさまでした unless that person is considered a member of your immediate work group.

Graffiti

A non-verbal sign for parting is waving left to right with your palm facing the partner. The hand gesture of flapping your fingers with your palm facing the partner, a gesture accompanying farewells in America, is, on the contrary, a sign asking someone to come toward you in Japan. (See Chapter 14 for additional discussion on gestures and hand signals.)

CHAPTER 13

Conversation Management

13.1. Conversational *Nihongo*

Explanation

Participating in casual conversation in *Nihongo* is essential in advancing your study of Japanese. First, hearing and understanding what the Japanese speaker is saying is a challenge. And when responding in Japanese, how should you behave verbally and otherwise? This chapter offers guidance for these must-do conversation activities.

CHARACTERISTICS OF CONVERSATIONAL *NIHONGO*

Conversational *Nihongo* contains the following features.

1. Short utterances, with easy-to-understand vocabulary
2. Frequent deletions, and as a result, grammatically incomplete sentences
3. A relatively free word order, with some inversions
4. Expressions sensitive to the situation, including shifting styles to meet interpersonal and personal needs with appropriate politeness levels and honorifics
5. Speaker's feelings expressed through devices such as のだ, exclamations, and interactional particles
6. Language variations used for social and expressive purposes

VOCABULARY

In speech, use 和語 (わご) more frequently, avoiding 漢語 (かんご) vocabulary. In casual conversation, for example, 苦 (くる) しむ is more likely to be used, instead of 苦悩 (くのう) する.

苦 (くる) しむ	苦悩 (くのう) する	to suffer
答 (こた) える	返答 (へんとう) する	to answer
組 (く) み立 (た) てる	構成 (こうせい) する	to structure

13.2. Taking Speaking Turns and Designing Utterances

Key Expressions

KE1   <conversation>
A: で、そのあとどうしたの？
Ｄe, sono ato doo shita no?
So what did you do after that?
B: だから、それから友だちのところへ行ったんだよ。
Dakara, sorekara tomodachi no tokoro e itta n da
yo.
So after that I went to my friend's place.

KE2   あのう、すみません。時間があったらこれを読んでおいてい
ただけません か。
Anoo, sumimasen. Jikan ga attara kore o yonde-oite-
itadakemasen ka.
Uhh, excuse me, but if you have time, could you read
this [for future purposes]?

Explanation

TAKING SPEAKING TURNS

To carry on a conversation, we must take speaking turns, maintain
them, and then yield them. At the same time we must be good listeners. How do we find the correct timing to take turns?

1.   As a rule, you should not take a turn (or attempt to take a
     turn) while the other person is speaking. Trying to get a word
     in edgewise is not generally a good idea in Japanese (or any
     other language). Taking over your *meue* partner's turn is es-
     pecially rude.
2.   If two speakers simultaneously start to speak, the *meshi-
     ta* partner should yield the turn by stopping speaking
     immediately.
3.   When your partner stops speaking apparently due to some
     trouble in speech production, allow sufficient time and assist
     in some way to avoid potential embarrassment.

4. When your speaking turn is overtly assigned, as when you are asked a direct question, it is desirable to take the turn. You have various ways to avoid answering straightforwardly if you don't want to do so. Total silence is not considered polite in this circumstance, especially toward your *meue* partner.
5. When your partner stops at a grammatically complete point such as the end of a sentence structure often ending with interactional particles, and when he or she looks at you, the floor is open to you. You are expected to take your turn.

YIELDING SPEAKING TURNS

Here are some strategies you can use when yielding your turn.

1. You can overtly yield your turn by asking a question.
2. Pause after you finish an utterance with listener-appealing devices such as interactional particles.
3. Overtly solicit your partner's opinion.
4. Make conclusive remarks if your turn is long and extensive.
5. Make eye contact with your partner at the end of your turn.
6. Use a head nod to mark the end of your turn.

DESIGNING UTTERANCES

How should our utterances be designed? Conversational utterances should take a form that fits comfortably into the ongoing activities.

1. At the beginning of an utterance, use openers to inform your partner that you are taking a speaking turn. These create a buffer zone where two people meet interactionally. You can also use this moment to prepare your utterance (see section 13.3).
2. Use prefacing expressions (see section 13.4) to warn your partner about what is coming next.
3. In between utterances, use fillers to signal your intention to continue. Fillers also show hesitation, which helps create rapport.
4. End utterances softly to minimize any possible negative impact (see section 13.6).

OTHER INTERACTIONAL STRATEGIES

In addition to the design strategies mentioned above, the frequent use of apology for sympathy-seeking purposes is a plus. Also helpful are degree words, such as ちょっと 'a bit'. These expressions make a conversation more pleasant. As a listener, sending frequent listener responses communicates your enthusiastic and supportive attitude (see section 13.11).

13.3. Openers and Fillers

Key Expressions

それで so
まあ uh
あの uh, well

Explanation

Openers are brief expressions by which you claim your speaking turn and alert others that you are about to say something. Speakers also use fillers, which are equivalent to *uhh* and *like* in English conversation. Conversational fillers may simply fill in a pause or signal the speaker's hesitation or trouble spots. Openers and fillers are useful because they allow you to hold on to your speaking turn.

KINDS OF OPENERS

1.   Marking a new topic

(それ)で so

2.   Signaling that what you are going to say is off the topic

ところで by the way
ちなみに by the way
話 (はなし) 変 (か) わるけど to change the subject

3.   Adding to the current topic

たとえば for example

PHRASES USED AS OPENERS AND FILLERS

1.   Hesitation interjections

あのう Uh, well.
まあ、そうですね。 Oh, I guess so.
ええと Well, let's see....
まあ Well, say....
なんか Uhh....

2. Expressions used while you are thinking

    (a) 何と言えばいいのか。言葉が見つからない。
        Nan to ieba ii no ka. Kotoba ga mitsukaranai.
        Uh, what should I say....I can't find the words to describe it.

    (b) うーん、むずかしい質問ですね。
        Uun, muzukashii shitsumon desu ne.
        Indeed, it's a difficult question to answer.

Graffiti

When you use openers and fillers, avoid the overuse of the same expression. It is a good idea to combine several short fillers to fill in the pauses (e.g., あのう, まあ, and ええと). You will find native speakers using these fillers quite frequently.

    Adult speech, mostly in formal masculine speech, is characterized by an inhaled hissing sound. The sound functions as both an opener and a filler. Observe masculine speech when you have access to native speakers. There is no need to imitate it.

13.4. Prefacing and Alerting

Key Expressions

KE1   ていうか、やめない、今日の買い物。
        Te yuu ka, yamenai, kyoo no kaimono.
        To tell the truth, you want to cancel our shopping today?

KE2   正直言って、絶対君は悪くない。
        Shoojiki itte, zettai kimi wa warukunai.
        To be honest, you absolutely aren't wrong.

KE3   言いたくないけど、その髪型、変。
        Iitakunai kedo, sono kamigata, hen.
        I don't want to say this, but your hairstyle is weird.

KE4   こう言っちゃなんだけど、湯川先生、今日ちょっと変だよ。
        Koo itcha nan da kedo, Yukawa sensei, kyoo chotto hen da yo.
        I shouldn't be saying this, but Professor Yukawa is a bit strange today.

KE5   実は、妙なうわさを聞いたんですが。
        Jitsuwa, myoona uwasa o kiita n desu ga.
        In fact, I heard some strange rumor.

KE6   ぶっちゃけ、俺、あいつ信じてねえし。[blunt masculine
           style]
        Butchake, ore, aitsu shinjitenee shi.
        To be frank, I don't trust him.

KE7   いきなりなんだけど、明日ひま？
        Ikinari na n da kedo, ashita hima?
        It's rather sudden, but are you free tomorrow?

KE8   私、思うんだけど、きっと会いたかったんだよ。
        Watashi, omou n da kedo, kitto aitakatta n da yo.
        I'm thinking, you know, he wanted to see you for sure.

Explanation

You use prefacing before making an important announcement or significant comment. There are a number of formulaic expressions for alerting your partner to forthcoming bad news. Phrases associated with the verb 言 (い) う 'to say' are useful for this purpose.

Psychologically, alerting is motivated by a need to bridge the gulf between *tatemae* and *honne* (see section 2.3).

PREFACING ASSOCIATED WITH 言う

1.   ていうか
        One of the most frequently used prefaces to your speech is ていうか. It is a preamble to being frank, particularly to telling the truth. ていうか appears in variations such as てか, つか, and ちゅか and is used mostly in casual speech. ていうか is also used at the utterance-final position (see section 13.6).
2.   正直言 (しょうじきい) って
        正直言って 'to be honest' is often used as a preface that the speaker is going to say something honestly without altering its content. It is also useful in a context where you reveal something contrary to what your partner is expecting.
3.   言 (い) いたくないけど
        言いたくないけど [lit. 'I don't want to be saying this, but'] in KE3 is used to show your hesitancy in revealing something. This expression is ritualized, however, and consequently the hesitation may only be in disguise.

4.　こう言っちゃなんだけど

　　こう言っちゃなんだけど 'perhaps I shouldn't be saying this, but' prefaces words that you are quite sure will be upsetting, as shown in KE4.

ADDITIONAL PREFACING

1.　実 (じつ) は

　　実は [lit. 'in fact, as a matter of fact'] is used in formal situations, particularly when you sense that the timing is right for revealing something, as shown in KE5. 実は is useful as a preface for discussing business or for announcing the main point or issue. You may use 実は as a preface to a request as well.

2.　ぶっちゃけ

　　ぶっちゃけ in KE6 is a casual and somewhat blunt expression meaning 'to tell everything without hiding'. This is used among youth, especially in very informal and familiar situations. It should be avoided in formal speech.

3.　いきなりなんだけど

　　Another strategy for communicating an out-of-context surprise is to preface it with いきなりなんだけど 'it's rather sudden, but'. As shown in KE7, you use this when what follows has little to do with what precedes and perhaps what follows becomes a sensitive issue.

4.　思うんだけど

　　When you want to share your thoughts, 思うんだけど prefaces such a desire, as in KE8. It warns your partner that what follows are your personal thoughts.

Graffiti

When you are about to say something uncertain and you are a bit hesitant, ひょっとして 'possibly' and もしかして 'conceivably' are used as prefacing. These offer a softening effect.

　　(a)　ひょっとして花火大会行った？
　　　　 Hyotto shite hanabi taikai itta?
　　　　 Did you possibly go to see the fireworks?

　　(b)　もしかして、高いとこ、こわいの？
　　　　 Moshika shite, takai toko, kowai no?
　　　　 Could it be that you're afraid of heights?

13.5. Being Artfully Vague

Key Expressions

KE1   お昼とか、いっしょに食べる？
       Ohiru toka, isshoni taberu?
       Want to eat lunch together?

KE2   時間があるから、ちょっと散歩でもしますか。
       Jikan ga aru kara, chotto sanpo demo shimasu ka.
       Since we have time, should we go for a walk?

KE3   では、改めて、事務所の方におうかがいいたしま
          す。[supra-polite style]
       Dewa, aratamete, jimusho no hoo ni
          oukagai-itashimasu.
       Well then, I will visit you at your office next time.

KE4   なんか寂しい。やっぱりあの人がいないとね。
       Nanka sabishii. Yappari ano hito ga inai to ne.
       I'm somehow lonely, after all, without her.

KE5   もう少し早い方がいいと思いますが。
       Moo sukoshi hayai hoo ga ii to omoimasu ga.
       I think perhaps it should be a bit earlier....

Explanation

Being vague does not mean that you are insincere. A certain vagueness helps make people feel comfortable. Artful vagueness comes into play when the information is presented as if it were unclear, only to avoid overly frank and straightforward opinions or news. This way, you can avoid shocking or offending your partner unnecessarily.

You should keep in mind that when you want to be vague and hesitant, you must speak in a voice that matches. Hesitant mumbling is expected, rather than speaking in a clear, proud, enthusiastic voice.

OFFERING ALTERNATIVES

1.   とか

         とか is a particle added to indicate alternatives, and as a result, it softens an utterance, as shown in KE1. とか is frequently used among young speakers.

2. でも

でも, comparable to the English *or something,* is frequently used when making suggestions and offers. でも, as shown in KE2, gives the impression that you are offering options, and accordingly, the partner can choose what he or she likes among several possibilities.

UNSPECIFYING INFORMATION

1. の方 (ほう)

の方 [lit. 'the direction of'] adds vagueness. Instead of simply saying 事務所 (じむしょ) 'office', the phrase 事務所の方 [lit. 'the direction of the office'] in KE3 adds vagueness by unspecifying the referent.

2. なんか

When revealing inner feelings, one may experience a slight embarrassment. Use なんか, as in KE4, to add the meaning of *somehow* and *somewhat.* You can use なんか as a conversation filler as well.

USING QUOTATION と思 (おも) う

You can make your assertions less blatant or offensive by adding と思う 'I think' at the end. Because と思う quotes what one thinks, it adds indirectness, giving a more reserved and less assertive impression, as shown in KE5.

13.6. Utterance-Final Strategies

Key Expressions

KE1   ちょっと時期的には早いと思いますが。
Chotto jikiteki ni wa hayai to omoimasu ga.
I wonder. I think it may be a bit too early, but....

KE2   神谷先輩、ミーティング始まりますけど。
Kamiya senpai, miitingu hajimarimasu kedo.
Mr. Kamiya, the meeting is going to start.

KE3   ほんとだよね。いい迷惑っていうかぁ。
Honto da yo ne. Ii meiwaku tte yuu kaa.
Really. It is more or less a nuisance.

KE4   すみません、忙しくて。
Sumimasen, isogashikute.
I'm sorry, I've been busy.

KE5   \<conversation\>

      A: バナナ、どうして食べないの？

           Banana, dooshite tabenai no?

           Why don't you eat the banana?

      B: だって、太るし。

           Datte, futorushi.

           Because I'll get fat.

Explanation

DANGLING CONNECTIVES

When expressing your opinion, it is advisable to add, at the end of your thought, phrases that would minimize a possible negative impact. One strategy is to add connectives. Adding connectives such as が or けど, as in KE1 and KE2, gives the impression that the utterance is incomplete or unfinished. Unfinished sentences add to a sense of one's being open to other options. By avoiding finality, these dangling connectives render statements less offensive.

ていうか AND THE LIKE

Another strategy is to add phrases such as ていうか, as shown in KE3. The utterance-final ていうか carries a tone of young people's conversational style, but its use has spread among the general population. ていうか appears in varied colloquial forms, such as ちゅか and つうか. ていうか avoids a clear presentation of your thoughts, and therefore you soften the impact of your statement.

ENDING WITH て AND たりして

As shown in KE4, you may use the て form to leave the statement vague. By not completing the sentence, the meaning is indirectly suggested.

    たりして points out one action related to the verb but with an implication that there are other options. This adds to the vagueness and to the overall softening of the impact. たりして is used, particularly in young people's casual speech, when the opinion expressed could be something unexpected or uncomfortable to the partner.

ENDING WITH ENUMERATIVE し

し appears as an utterance-final expression, as shown in B's utterance in KE5. し is grammatically used when combining two or more clauses to create an enumerative list (see section 10.2). But it can be used singularly at the end of an utterance, implying that some other information follows. This in turn gives the impression that the utterance lingers on. The utterance becomes less final and more accommodating to your partner's feelings.

13.7. Commenting on One's Own Speech

Key Expressions

KE1　だから、明日持ってくるって言ってんだろ。 [blunt style]
　　　Dakara, ashita motte-kuru tte itte n daro.
　　　So I'm telling you that I'll bring it tomorrow.

KE2　もう何度も同じことを申し上げております。
　　　Moo nando mo onaji koto o mooshiagete-orimasu.
　　　I've told you the same thing many times already.

KE3　うるさいなあ、わかってるって。
　　　Urusai naa, wakatteru tte.
　　　You are getting on my nerves. I know that, I'm telling
　　　　you.

KE4　だからできないんだってば。
　　　Dakara dekinai n da tte ba.
　　　I'm telling you, I can't do it.

KE5　あんな人に頼んだって、ダメだっつうの！ [blunt style]
　　　Anna hito ni tanonda tte, dame da ttsuu no!
　　　I'm telling you. There's no use asking him.

Explanation

By calling attention to your own words, you qualify your speech. The effect may be emphasis or hesitation. Here we will focus on the emphatic effect similar to the English *I'm telling you!* and *That's what I'm saying!* Use the utterance-final ていうか introduced in section 13.6 for hesitation.

て言ってるだろ

て言ってるだろ 'I'm saying so' and the more colloquial て言ってんだろ are blunt expressions. Similar expressions are available reflecting various politeness levels, for example, って言ってるんです, と申し上げているんです, and と申し上げております。

These phrases communicate in no uncertain terms that you have already made your point. As in KE1 and KE2, they add emphasis to your words.

って, ってば, AND っつうの

As in KE3 and KE4, in casual situations, young speakers in particular use the quotation marker って, optionally ってば. The quotation phrase っつうの is also used at the end of an utterance, as in KE5.

To mark the emphatic effect, you pronounce these phrases clearly and strongly. Note that these expressions appear as て, てば, and つうの immediately following ん.

13.8. Sharing Thoughts as Feelings

Key Expressions

KE1   \<conversation\>
    A: ミカって、彼のファン？
        Mika tte, kare no fan?
        Mika, are you his fan?
    B: そう。もう結婚してって感じ。
        Soo. Moo kekkonshite tte kanji.
        That's right. I feel like, please marry me.

KE2   \<conversation\>
    A: ねえ、東京の大学ってどんな感じなの？
        Nee, Tookyoo no daigaku tte donna kanji na no?
        Say, how do you feel? I mean about universities in
           Tokyo.
    B: どんな感じって。別にフツウだよ。
        Donna kanji tte. Betsuni futuu da yo.
        Nothing in particular. They're ordinary.

KE3   \<conversation\>
    A: でも、その計画、なんか、無理のような気がする。
        Demo, sono keikaku, nanka, muri no yoona
           kigasuru.
        But that project, I feel like it is impossible.
    B: そうかなあ。
        Soo ka naa.
        I wonder about that.

A: 絶望的って感じ。
Zetsubooteki tte kanji.
It's like, there is no hope.

Explanation

By expressing your thoughts as feelings, you solicit empathy. By making them sound like your feelings, the utterance becomes soft and emotional. As in B's utterances in KE1 and in KE2, you may use the word 感 (かん) じ 'feelings' for this purpose. 感じがする is another strategy.

ような気がする

As in A's first utterance in KE3, ような気がする 'feel like, I get the feeling like' (or a casual version, みたいな気がする) can be used to express one's thoughts. Rather than using 思 (おも) う 'think', when using ような気がする, you express the thought with less commitment, appealing more to shared feelings. ような気がする is sometimes used in a literal sense. But even then, it sustains the sense of an indirect emotional appeal.

13.9. Action-Accompanying Phrases

Key Expressions

KE1   おじゃまします。
Ojamashimasu.
Excuse me.

KE2   よいしょ。
Yoisho.
Here we go.

KE3   ハイ、どうぞ。
Hai, doozo.
Here it is.

KE4   何もかも、言ってしまおうよ。ハイ。
Nani mo kamo, itte-shimaoo yo. Hai.
Tell me everything. Come now.

KE5   \<conversation\>
A: 誰から？
         Dare kara?
         Who is going to start?
B: オレ、行きます。 [masculine speech]
         Ore, ikimasu.
         I'll do it now.

Explanation

WHEN VISITING SOMEONE

The following expressions are some of the more common phrases you are likely to use when visiting a Japanese family.

1.   At the door

     Guest: ごめんください。 Hello. [lit. 'Excuse me.']
     Host: いらっしゃい。 Welcome.

2.   As you enter the room

     Host: こちらへどうぞ。 This way, please.
     Guest: おじゃまします。 Excuse me. [said with a slight bow]

3.   When you present a gift

     つまらないものですが。 Here's something for you.

4.   When drinking or eating

     Host: どうぞめしあがってください。 Please help yourself.
     Guest: (では) いただきます。 [lit. 'Thank you, I'll help myself.']

5.   When thinking about leaving

     そろそろ 失礼 (しつれい)しますので。 I guess it's about time, I
       should be leaving.

6.   When you leave the host's home

     おじゃましました。 Excuse me....

UTTERING ACTION-ACCOMPANYING PHRASES

よいしょ in KE2 is said when you do something physically demanding. You use はい as an affirmative answer. But in many cases, はい functions as a word that punctuates actions. For example, when handing something over, you might say ハイ、どうぞ 'Here it is', as in KE3.

ENCOURAGING YOUR PARTNER

はい also encourages the consequent action, as in KE4. If you are encouraging your friends to start cleaning, you might say ハイ、そうじ、はじめてください 'Come now, start cleaning'.

ANNOUNCING YOUR ACTION

The verb 行く is used, as shown in B's turn in KE5, when declaring you are about to take an action. For example, when you are about to take your turn in a game, you may say いい？行くよ 'Ready? Here I go'.

Graffiti

Two exclamatory phrases accompany your response to what is happening, that is, the special use of きた [lit. 'it came'] and でた [lit. 'it appeared'].

For example, if you just took a sip of beer and it is shockingly good, you might say このビール、きたーッて感じ 'Boy, this beer, it's great' [lit. 'This beer feels like it came']. きたーッ is an exaggerated response to an oncoming happening.

If you and your companion were talking about baseball and if he begins his favorite talk about イチロー, then you might comment 出たよ、イチローの話 'Here it comes, his story about Ichiro' [lit. 'It appeared, his talk about Ichiro']. This expression acknowledges your partner's action as an acceptable, predictable, and tolerable action.

Both きた and でた used in this way are primarily used by youth in casual speech.

13.10. Postposing

Key Expressions

KE1	行きますか、あしたの講演。	
	Ikimasu ka, ashita no kooen.	
	Are you going, to tomorrow's lecture?	
KE2	似合ってるね、そのドレス。	
	Niatteru ne, sono doresu.	
	You look good in it, that dress.	

KE3   気をつけて、その、そこの花瓶。
        Kiotsukete, sono, soko no kabin.
        Be careful, with th... that vase.

KE4   いやだなあ、そんなこと言って。
        Iya da naa, sonna koto itte.
        It's embarrassing that you would say such a thing.

KE5   <conversation>
        A: 悪かったね、突然来て。
            Warukatta ne, totsuzen kite.
            Sorry, I came without an appointment.
        B: 大歓迎！ちょっと退屈してたし。
            Daikangei! Chotto taikutsushiteta shi.
            Welcome! I was a bit bored anyway, so....

KE6   うれしいです。あなたに会えて。
        Ureshii desu. Anata ni aete.
        Am I glad. To see you.

Explanation

FUNCTIONS OF POSTPOSING

Recall the preferred order of elements in a sentence (see section 8.14). That order may be inverted, and certain elements may be postposed for the following reasons.

1. To add something afterward, perhaps realizing there is a need to provide additional information in the postposed phrase, as in KE1 and KE2.
2. When the postposed phrase is pronounced with phonological prominence, to focus on the postposed element, as in KE3.

PRIORITIZING ELEMENTS

Another way of looking at postposing is the prioritizing of some elements at the sentence-initial position. When this inversion is used, usually it conveys a sense of urgency in that the element placed in the initial position is urgent. For example, when the speaker is emotional or excited, the feelings come first, and then later what the feelings are about is added, as in KE4 and KE5. As in KE6, you may delay the mention of certain information so that your partner may focus on the postposed element with a sense of suspense.

INVERSION AS A NORM

In some cases, the inversion is the norm. One good example is なに それ 'What (the heck) is that!', an expression of surprise, criticism, and often disgust (see section 11.8). Although this expression results from the inversion of それはなに, なに is more immediate, and consequently the inverted order has become the norm.

13.11. Listener Responses

Key Expressions

はい。 Yeah. Uh-huh, I see.
うん。 Uh-huh.
なるほど。 I see.

Explanation

WHAT TO DO AS A LISTENER

As listeners, Japanese display a great deal of feedback. Japanese listeners send frequent head nods and much encouraging brief chatter called あいづち. Sending frequent あいづち is thought to be good manners. In general, Japanese listeners send more than twice as many listener responses as Americans.

WHEN TO SEND あいづち

Your partner solicits あいづち by using final particles such as ね, expressions such as でしょ？, and brief questions such as そう思 (おも) わない？ 'don't you think so?' Your partner may end his or her speaking turn with a nod. That is a good moment to send your あ いづち.

KINDS OF あいづち

1. Conveying confirmation

   そうですか。 I see.
   そうですね。 That's right.
   やっぱり。 That's what I thought.
   なるほど。 I see.

2. Showing one's attention

    うん。 Uh-huh.
    ふーん。 I see.
    そう。 Right.
    はい。 Yeah.
    ええ。 Yes.

3. Expressing reservations or doubt

    さあ。 Well....
    (まあ) たぶん。 Perhaps....
    そうですかねえ······ Well, I am not sure....
    そう？ Really?
    そうかなあ······ I wonder....

4. Showing surprise

    ええっ？ What?
    ほんと？ Really?
    うそ！ You're kidding!
    まさか！ It can't be. Nonsense!

13.12. Clarifying Trouble Spots

Key Expressions

KE1   ええ？
      Ee?
      What?

KE2   はあ？
      Haa?
      Uh?

KE3   あした八時に···？
      Ashita hachiji ni...?
      Tomorrow at eight o'clock...?

KE4   人事課って？
      Jinjika tte?
      What do you mean by *jinjika*?

Explanation

I DIDN'T QUITE HEAR YOU

You can use ええ or はあ, with rising intonation, to convey that you did not hear what was just said. These expressions give the impression that the enunciation on the part of the speaker was unclear, and therefore the speaker is to blame. Unless it is obvious that the problem is of physical sound quality, these short expressions are to be avoided, especially toward your *meue* person.

ASKING FOR HELP

You can hear your partner's speech, but you don't quite get it. There are a few ways to ask your partner to clarify. Repeat the part you understand and trail off, as in KE3. A facial expression showing confusion would help. If you are able to pinpoint the word you did not understand, use an expression such as KE4.

ASKING FOR REPETITION

As a last resort, if you are unable to understand at all, ask your partner to speak slowly or to repeat the utterance one more time.

(a) すみません、もう少しゆっくりお願いします。
Sumimasen, moo sukoshi yukkuri onegaishimasu.
Sorry, but could you speak a little more slowly?

(b) すみません、もう一度お願いします。
Sumimasen, moo ichido onegaishimasu.
Sorry, but could you repeat it one more time?

REPAIRING YOUR SPEECH

Sometimes you realize you just made a mistake in your speech. Here are some ways to repair the errors.

(c) 三本、あ、じゃなくて四本です。
Sanbon, a, janakute yonhon desu.
Three, I mean four, please.

(d) あ、ごめん。そういうんじゃなくて。
A, gomen. Soo yuu n janakute.
Sorry. That's not what I mean.

(e) ごめんなさい。私が言いたかったのは、中止するんじゃなく
      て、延期したらってことなんです。

      Gomennasai. Watashi ga iitakatta no wa, chuushisuru n
      janakute, enkishitara tte koto na n desu.

      I'm sorry. What I wanted to say was not to cancel it but to
      postpone it.

Graffiti

Sometimes you may not understand the content of your partner's
speech, although you fully understand Japanese. Use (f) to convey that you don't really understand what your partner is talking
about.

(f) 話、ぜんぜん見えないんですけど。
      Hanashi, zenzen mienai n desu kedo.
      I don't have a clue what you are talking about.

The utterance はい？(or はあ？) can be used to express your
disbelief (except toward your *meue* person). In this case you understand what your partner said, but you are caught unprepared.

(g) \<conversation\>
      A: じゃあ、あしたもよろしくね。
          Jaa, ashita mo yoroshiku ne.
          Then I will see you again tomorrow.
      B: **はい？**あしたって聞いてませんけど。
          Hai? Ashita tte kiitemasen kedo.
          What? I haven't heard anything about tomorrow.

13.13. Echo Questions and Responses

Key Expressions

KE1   (子供が走ってる。) 子供が走ってる？
          (Kodomo ga hashitteru.) Kodomo ga hashitteru?
          (A child is running.) Did you say, "A child is running"?

KE2   (なんで？) なんでって？
          (Nande?) Nande tte?
          (Why?) You say why, but.... (what do you mean?)

KE3	(あきらめろよ。) あきらめろって‥‥‥
	(Akiramero yo.) Akiramero tte....
	(Give it up.) You tell me to give up....
KE4	(えっ？) えっじゃないよ。
	(Ett?) Ett janai yo.
	(What?) Don't say "What." Stop that nonsense!

Explanation

ECHOING YOUR PARTNER'S UTTERANCE

Commenting on your partner's speech becomes necessary for a variety of reasons. Simply repeat the partner's utterance with a rising tone, as in KE1. You use this "echo question" when requesting clarification or confirmation.

ECHO QUESTIONS WITH と

Echo questions may also accompany a quotation marker と, って, or て. Quotation offers an important function here. For example, as in KE2, by saying なんでって？ 'You say なんで, but', you raise the issue of your partner asking なんで 'Why'.

As in KE3, an echo question may function merely as an echo response. You take on a phrase mentioned in your partner's utterance as you digest the information. Or you may repeat the phrase as a potential topic for which you may add further comment. In this case, use a falling tone.

RESPONDING WITH じゃない

As in KE4, when you disapprove of what your partner says or does, you can use じゃない to deny it. In response to えっ？ 'What?', for example, you may yell out えっじゃないよ 'Don't say "What"'. It is a strong disapproval. You would use this in angry response to someone else's nonsensical utterance or behavior. Here is another situation.

(a) <conversation>
    A: だって。
       Datte.
       But.
    B: だって、**じゃねえよ**。ちゃんと説明しろよ。[blunt style]
       Datte, janee yo. Chanto setsumeishiro yo.
       Don't say "but." Explain it to me.

CHAPTER 14

Gestures and Signals

In real-life communication, verbal signs are intermingled with many non-verbal signs. Some of the non-verbal signs carry specific meanings, and it is important to know what they mean. In general, when there is a conflict of information between verbal and non-verbal signs, we take the non-verbal sign more seriously.

Think of a situation where you are saying you are sorry. But inside, you are angry and blaming someone else. Your apology will not come across as sincere, even when you repeat すみません and ごめんなさい many times, unless your posture is submissive. Bowing and casting your eye gaze downward are critical in this situation.

This chapter explains a few representative gestures and hand signals used in Japanese communication. I provide explanations only here, but you should pay attention to the visual signs observable in many sources (including Internet Web sites featuring Japanese gestures and hand signals).

14.1. Gestures and Hand Signals

1. No good

   Cross your arms to form an "X." X refers to バツ, a sign indicating that something is bad, not good, unacceptable, not permitted, etc.

2. No, that's not it

   Wave your hand right and left in front of your face.

3. Go away

   Place your hand at the two o'clock position with the back of the hand facing outward and shake your hand outward in a quick movement, as if brushing someone off.

4. Come over here

    With the back of your hand facing upward, hold your hand to the level of your eye. Then shake your hand downward toward yourself a few times.

5. Excuse me for passing in front of you

    Round your back slightly as if bowing, move in front of the person apologetically. While you do this, put one hand up in front of you (about the level of your waist), with your fingers together and the thumb up, and gently move it as if chopping something.

6. To eat

    Pretend to hold a rice bowl with your left hand. Bring your right hand to your mouth as you use the index and middle fingers to form a pair of chopsticks. Move your fingers several times, imitating the motion of bringing food to your mouth.

7. Wait, I refuse (to hear what you're saying)

    Raise your arm in front of you, slightly bending it, and show the palm of your hand to your partner. The palm should be in the upright position, as if stopping someone.

8. You

    Point to your partner with your index finger. Although this is considered rude in the United States, generally it is not in Japan. However, it is best not to point to your *meue* person with your index finger.

9. Please, this way

    Show the palm of your hand to the other person and motion with it in the direction you want to indicate.

10. Apple polishing, buttering someone up

    Rotate one fist on top of the open palm of the other hand. This motion is used as you describe someone (e.g., あいつ、これだろ 'You know, he's this, an apple polisher').

11. Lovers

    For a female lover (girlfriend, mistress), point your little finger upward (refer to [a] of Figure 3). For a male lover, put your thumb upright (refer to [b] of Figure 3). These hand gestures are not usually used by female speakers.

12. Money

    Make a circle with your thumb and index finger, similar to "okay" in America, and hold it horizontally (refer to [c] of Figure 3).

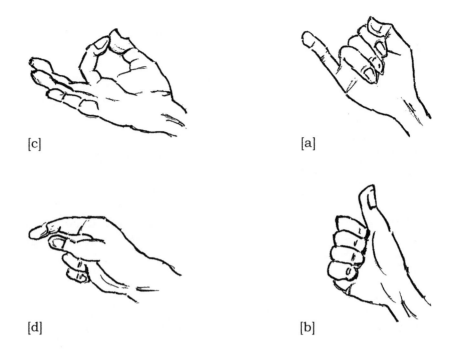

Figure 3. Examples of hand gestures.

13. How about drinking?

   Extend your thumb and index finger, forming a "C" (refer to [d] of Figure 3). Pretend you are holding a small sake cup (ちょこ), and then gesture to drink from it. This is primarily used by male speakers to invite other male friends to go out drinking.

14. I'm sorry

   Put both your hands flatly together in front of your face. Sometimes you close your eyes and pose for a moment, often saying ごめんなさい or お願 (ねが) い！You use this gesture when either apologizing or making a serious request.

15. Peace (striking a pose when taking pictures)

   The peace sign is made with the index and middle fingers shaped as a "V" and facing away from you. Use this sign not in the literal sense but when striking a pose for a photograph. Do not use this when a formal photograph is taken.

14.2. Bowing and Postures

1. Bowing

Bowing (おじぎ) is the most commonly observed body posture in Japan. From a simple quick bow to a slow and deep one, bowing is used for multiple purposes. You may bow for purposes of greeting, thanking, and apologizing. The deeper bow requires the upper body to lean forward as low as 90 degrees or even more (depending on how deeply you want to show respect), and a quick bow may be a simple nod-like acknowledgment.

When you bow to your *meue* person in formal situations, you should not raise your head too quickly, especially not before the *meue* person does.

Bowing used for parting usually takes longer, and you might keep on bowing if your *meue* person takes leave before you.

2. Sitting on the floor

正座 (せいざ)

正座 is the formal way of sitting on the floor. Sit on your knees with your legs tucked under you. This is the proper way of sitting in a たたみ room. Often you will be sitting on a 座 (ざ) ぶとん cushion instead of the たたみ itself.

Sitting in the 正座 position for hours is painful even for many Japanese. The legs fall asleep and you may not be able to stand up without help. Knowing this, often the host will say, "Please put yourself at ease." Typically the host will use 足 (あし) をくずしてください or 楽 (らく) になさってください. Thanking the host, if you are a male, assume the Indian-style position called あぐら (see below). If you are a female, sit down with legs loosely folded to one side.

あぐら

あぐら is a relaxed way of sitting on the floor. Sit down with legs crossed, assuming an Indian sitting position (or similar to the lotus position in Yoga). あぐら is not recommended for women.

3. Bowing on the floor

The most subservient posture a Japanese person would make is 土下座 (どげざ). Kneel with the upper body bent over the knees. Place both your hands on the floor in front of you.

Lower your head until it is almost touching the floor. This is a posture to show deep respect or the most serious apology. It expresses the deepest remorse. You perform 土下座 when the deepest bow is not satisfactory. Usually you are expected to put your head to the ground and keep it there until the other person tells you to raise it.

14.3. Special Hand Movements

1. じゃんけん

When randomly selecting a person for some purpose, じゃんけん is the most frequently used method. Although じゃんけん is known in many countries, its frequent use among Japanese is something to be noted. By forming rock, scissors, and paper with your hand, you show your hand at the sound of ぽん.

Usually the sequence starts with 最初 (さいしょ) はグー 'Let's start with a rock', and then everyone calls out じゃんけんぽん。Rock wins over scissors because it can crush them. Scissors cut paper, so they win over paper. But paper wins over rock because it can cover it.

グー	rock (fist)
チョキ	scissors (form a "V" with index and middle fingers)
パー	paper (open hand)

2. 指 (ゆび) きり

指きり is an action performed together by two people making promises and vows. By hooking one's little finger to the partner's little finger, the two connect to each other and promise to honor whatever they vow. The two may sing a song that goes 指きりげんまん、うそ言 (い) ったら、針千本 (はりせんぼん) 飲 (の) ます 'We are making promises; if you break them, I will make you swallow one thousand needles'.

14.4. Eye Contact

Japanese do not normally fix a direct gaze on the eyes of the person to whom they are talking. Although you are expected to look into your partner's eyes from time to time, sustained eye contact is an expression of confrontation or suspicion. Avoid looking constantly into the eyes of your Japanese listener. As a listener, you should also avoid too much eye contact. Especially if the speaker is your social superior, staring into his or her eyes consistently is considered rude. Look toward the speaker and cast your eyes in the general area of the speaker's neck and shoulders as you look into his or her eyes from time to time.

Of course, not looking into the partner's eyes at all is not a good idea. If you constantly avert your eyes from your partner's and never look into them, you give the impression that you are restless and perhaps unworthy of trust.

You might recall the Japanese words for social superiors (i.e., *meue* [lit. 'above eye level']) and social subordinates (i.e., *meshita* [lit. 'below eye level']). The direction of one's gaze reflects social status: from the lower position looking up toward *meue* and from the higher position looking down toward *meshita*. The right to gaze freely is granted to social superiors. A continuous gaze is more permissible from higher to lower eye level (i.e., from *meue* to *meshita*) but not vice versa.

14.5. Head Nods and Shakes

As you encounter Japanese speakers, you will note their frequent head bobbing. You will witness Japanese people talking on the cell phone while nodding frequently. Head nods have become so natural that Japanese aren't even aware they are nodding. In general, Japanese speakers and listeners nod almost three times more than their American counterparts.

Head nods from your listening partner function as listener responses, generally indicating that he or she is listening. They can mean "yes" if used in a context where such an answer is an option.

Nods are frequently used by speakers as well (about one-third of head nods observed in casual conversation are made by speakers). Most frequently such nods are used for emphasis or to indicate the end of one's utterance or (and this is important) the end of one's speaking turn.

Most interesting in the Japanese head nodding phenomenon is the joint and synchronic nods of the speaker and the listener. They are often repeated two to three times, as if the two are performing a head-bobbing dance together. These joint and rhythmical nods enhance the empathy and togetherness between conversation partners.

In general, head shakes are used to convey denials and negative answers.

CHAPTER 15

Rhetorical Figures of Speech

15.1. Metaphors

Key Expressions

KE1　　男は狼だ。
　　　　Otoko wa ookami da.
　　　　Man is a wolf.

KE2　　人生の花。
　　　　Jinsei no hana.
　　　　Flower of life.

KE3　　氷のように冷ややか。
　　　　Koori no yooni hiyayaka.
　　　　Cold as ice.

KE4　　シャボン玉のように消えた恋。
　　　　Shabondama no yooni kieta koi.
　　　　Love that ended like bubbles.

Explanation

UNIVERSAL METAPHORS

Some metaphors are universal across languages and cultures. For example, *cold as ice* is easily understood across many cultures.

There are two types of metaphoric expressions in Japanese. The simile uses markers, such as ような 'it is like', まるで 'it is as if', and みたい 'it resembles'. Metaphor, in a technical sense, is a straightforward linking without these markers. Here we use the term "metaphor" in a broad sense.

FLOWER METAPHORS

Perhaps one of the most culturally specific metaphors in Japanese is 花 (はな) 'flower', the cherry blossom in particular. Metaphoric idioms and expressions include the following.

(a) 高嶺の花 。
Takane no hana.
Flower on a high peek.
(unrealizable desire, an unobtainable object)

(b) 花に嵐。
Hana ni arashi.
Blossoms bring storms.
(the transient nature of glory, as symbolized by cherry blossoms blown to the ground by spring storms)

(c) 花より団子。
Hana yori dango.
Sweets are preferred to flowers.
(comically capturing human nature: although cherry blossoms are beautiful, people prefer food)

(d) 人生に花を咲かせる。
Jinsei ni hana o sakaseru.
To bring blossoms (glory, success) to one's life.

(e) 花を持たせる。
Hana o motaseru.
To let someone have flowers (i.e., glory).

In all these examples, 花 symbolizes something great, beautiful, glorious, and spectacular. Flowers, especially cherry blossoms, symbolize the transient nature of beauty, glory, and life itself.

MORE OR LESS POPULAR METAPHORS

Some metaphors appear frequently and become overused clichés. They become part of the vocabulary and are no longer considered metaphoric expressions. Because of the ubiquitous nature of the metaphor, it is important that you become familiar with some metaphors that Japanese speakers like. In creative writing, it is up to you to come up with some innovative metaphors.

15.2. Tautology

Key Expressions

KE1   勝ちは勝ち。
        Kachi wa kachi.
        Victory is victory.

KE2   仕方ないさ。子供は子供だから。
        Shikata nai sa. Kodomo wa kodomo da kara.
        What can you do? Children are children.

Explanation

Tautology is another rhetorical strategy used across languages.
When a sentence is constructed as [A is A], because it points out
something too obvious, its seeming meaninglessness demands a
special interpretation. If [A is A] is obviously the case, why is the
speaker saying so?

Tautology is a device to emphasize that, no matter what, the
fact is [A is A]. For example, 勝 (か) ちは勝ち 'Victory is victory' de-
nies the possibility that a victory may be considered anything else
and declares that no matter what people think, no matter what the
situation may be, the victory cannot be denied.

FUNCTIONS OF TAUTOLOGY

In conversation, because tautology is used to emphasize the fact
that A is nothing but A, you are often shut off from continuing on
the same topic. The strong tone of finality communicates that the
speaker refuses to repeat the points already made. With this undeniable assertive force, tautology offers this effect of finalization.

(a) <conversation>
     A: あいつ、反則しただろ。[masculine speech]
         Aitsu, hansoku shita daro.
         He broke the rules.
     B: まあな。[masculine speech]
         Maa na.
         I guess.
     A: きたねえな。[blunt style]
         Kitanee na.
         That's unfair.

B: でも、**勝ちは勝ち**。オレの負け。[masculine speech]
Demo, kachi wa kachi. Ore no make.
But victory is victory. I lost.

A: そうだけどさ。
Soo da kedo sa.
That's so, but.

B: **負けは負け**。人生ってそんなもんだよ。
Make wa make. Jinsei tte sonna mon da yo.
Defeat is defeat. Life is like that.

EXTENDED PATTERNS

In addition to [A is A], the following variations are used for tautology.

(b) 好きだから好き。
Suki da kara suki.
I love her because I love her.

(c) やるときはやる。
Yaru toki wa yaru.
When I do it, I do it with determination.

(d) いいものはいい。
Ii mono wa ii.
Good things are good, no matter what.

TAUTOLOGY AS A SILENCING STRATEGY

Because of its undeniable assertive force, tautology may be used to shun further discussion. For example, when your partner mentions that various things are involved, you may ask what those various things are, as in いろいろって？ 'What do you mean by various things?' Your partner may answer いろいろはいろいろだよ 'Various things are various things'. Although this isn't an answer, it functions as an answer, stopping further discussion.

CREATIVE USES OF TAUTOLOGY

Tautology may be creatively used. If you hear an expression such as 風 (かぜ) は風 'wind is wind', for example, at first it may not make sense. But it is not difficult to think of a situation where a statement like this does make sense. If you are trying to fly a kite and realize that you cannot control the wind, then you might say, "Well, wind is wind." It emphasizes the uncontrollable nature of wind.

15.3. Humor and Puns

Key Expressions

KE1   冬休みは、南半球へ。レッツ豪。
         Fuyuyasumi wa, minami hankyuu e. Rettsu goo.
         To the Southern Hemisphere during winter vacation.
             Let's go to Australia.

KE2   <conversation>
         A: きみ、教養あるねえ。いつから？
              Kimi, kyooyoo aru nee. Itsu kara?
              You are well-educated, aren't you? Since when?
         B: 今日よ。
              Kyoo yo.
              Since today.

Explanation

As in many other cultures, humor is important in *Nihongo* for enhancing friendliness and intimacy. Humor, however, is one of the
most difficult things to learn in a foreign language. The student
of a foreign language must not only understand the content of a
message, but also, more important, appreciate the cultural and
linguistic background before appreciating its humor. If you can
laugh simultaneously with native speakers when someone makes
a humorous statement, it is a sign that you have learned the language well.

THE WONDER OF HOMOPHONES
Typical Japanese humor comes from しゃれ 'puns'. Puns are made
with homophones, words that have the same sound. Because Japanese is rich in homophones, there are endless puns that you can
come up with.

    Of course, when you translate puns into English, they no lon-
ger function. Here are explanations of the puns given in the Key
Expressions.

1.   冬休みは、南半球へ。レッツ豪。
         This is a pun between the English expression *let's go*,
     part of which is written in カタカナ, and the sound of ゴー,

which is a part of the *kanji* compound 豪州 (ごうしゅう) 'Australia'. It is a headline that advertises Australian tourism.

2. きみ、教養あるねえ。いつから？今日よ。

This is a pun on the word 教養 (きょうよう) 'well-educated' and 今日 (きょう) よ 'it's today', which sound alike.

ANOTHER PUN

How about one more pun?

(a) <conversation>
A: このぼうし、**どいつんだ**。
Kono booshi, doitsu n da.
Whose hat is this?
B: **おらんだ**。
Ora n da.
It's mine.

Note the homophone between どいつ and おらんだ. These phrases have double meanings, どいつ (ドイツ) meaning 'whose' and 'Germany', and おらんだ (オランダ) meaning 'mine' and 'Holland'.

You can create puns like this one and see if native Japanese speakers will get them.

USING PROVERBS AND OTHER EXPRESSIONS AS SOURCES

Some puns use proverbs and common idioms as their source. For example, compare (b) and (c).

(b) 茶で食う飯も好き好き。
Cha de kuu meshi mo suki zuki.
There is no accounting for the kind of green-tea-over-rice dish people prefer.

(c) 蓼食う虫も好き好き。 (proverb)
Tade kuu mushi mo suki zuki.
There's no accounting for tastes. Some prefer nettles.

Because (b) sounds very similar to the well-known proverb (c), a typical Japanese partner would know that (b) is a pun based on (c). It incorporates the meaning of the original proverb, but (b) specifies that people like (or dislike) various kinds of おちゃづけ, a bowl of rice consisting of different condiments and green tea.

FOUR-LINE RIDDLES AND PUNS

There is a four-line riddle that plays on the pun. This pattern takes on the question-answer interaction between two people. The pun in (d) works between あき 'tiredness' and 秋 'fall season', which sound the same except for a different pitch.

> (d) <conversation>
>> A: あたらしいブーケの香、とかけて何と解く？
>>
>> Atarashii buuke no kaori, to kakete nan to toku?
>>
>> What pun can you come up with for "new fragrance of flowers"?
>>
>> B: 常夏の島、ハワイと解く。
>>
>> Tokonatsu no shima, hawai to toku.
>>
>> I'll go with "eternal-summer-island, Hawai'i."
>>
>> A: その心は？
>>
>> Sono kokoro wa?
>>
>> How so?
>>
>> B: あきが来ない。
>>
>> Aki ga konai.
>>
>> You never get tired of the fragrance (as the fall season never comes to Hawai'i).

15.4. Irony and Sarcasm

Key Expressions

KE1   お偉方
        oeragata
        the so-called great people [lit. 'great and respected people']

KE2   ご立派
        gorippa
        not so great [lit. 'extremely fine']

KE3   俺の顔に泥を塗ってくれて、ありがとうよ。[masculine speech]
        Ore no kao ni doro o nutte-kurete, arigatoo yo.
        Thanks for dishonoring me! [lit. 'Thanks for painting my face with mud.']

Explanation

The ironic (or sarcastic) use of language is universal. In each language, certain expressions and strategies are used as signals for sarcastic interpretation.

Irony and sarcasm are intended to deny literal meaning in a colorful way. Ultimately the speaker conveys another, often opposite, meaning and attitude.

IRONY AND SARCASM IN CONTEXT

In order to convey ironic (or sarcastic) intent, the speaker must send signals that would contradict the literal meaning of what he or she is saying. For example, although on the surface one may be saying ありがとう 'thanks', the tone of voice and facial expression may not indicate genuine thanks. As important is the context in which ありがとう is uttered. If a situation does not call for it and in fact the situation calls for an opposite reaction, a speech is likely to be intended as sarcasm. KE3 is such a case.

Think of a situation where you and your date end up taking care of a drunk friend. You might engage in a sarcastic conversation.

(a) <conversation>
A: よっぱらいの面倒見て、終わっちゃった。すごーく印象的
なデートだったね。
Yopparai no mendoo mite, owat-chatta. Sugooku in-shootekina deeto datta ne.
Taking care of the drunk, and our date was over. It
was a really impressive date, right?
B: 超ロマンチックだった！
Choo romanchikku datta!
It was super romantic!

MARKERS FOR IRONY AND SARCASM

Among devices that signal irony, exaggeration is the most prominent. You may use extraordinarily exaggerated vocabulary, exaggerated intonation, lengthened vowels, and repetition, which are normally unnecessary.

In English, *indeed* is often ironic as in (c).

(b) It's a lovely day for a picnic.
(c) It's a lovely day for a picnic, indeed.

In Japanese, excessively polite style functions as a signal for irony. Phrases such as お偉方 and ご立派, given as KE1 and KE2, are typically used for ironical expression.

(d)   <conversation>
    A: また、**お偉方**が何人か見学に来るらしいよ。
       Mata, oeragata ga nannin ka kengaku ni kuru rashii yo.
       Again, those "great and respected" ones are coming to observe us.
    B: いやになっちゃうね。難しい実験の最中なのにさ。
       Iya ni nat-chau ne. Muzukashii jikken no saichuu na noni sa.
       Oh, boy, that's too bad. We are in the middle of difficult experiments, you know.

Note that in the case of irony or sarcasm, positive exaggeration results in negative meaning. This contrasts with the case of teasing, where often expressions conveying negative meanings turn out to be positive in nature. For example, think of お偉方, used as sarcasm, and バカ 'a fool', used as a tease.

UNCONTESTABLE INTERACTION

Ironic comments make it difficult to come up with a counterargument. For example, your boss at work points out that a form you filled in has many mistakes. If he points it out by この書類 (しょるい)、ミスだらけだねえ 'This form has many mistakes', you may offer some excuse. But if your boss says この書類、本当 (ほんとう) にミスがないねえ 'Boy, this form has absolutely no mistakes, indeed', you would probably offer no excuse. Ironic expressions function to nullify any retort.

15.5. Idioms and Proverbs

Key Expressions

KE1   ごますり。
       Gomasuri.
       Sesame grinding.
       (apple-polishing, buttering someone up, overtly flattering, sucking up to one's superiors)

KE2　　草分け。

Kusawake.

Parting the grass.

(leading the way, going where no one has gone before, pioneering)

KE3　　井の中の蛙、大海を知らず。

I no naka no kawazu, taikai o shirazu.

A frog in the well doesn't know the sea.

(a provincial, one who has never seen the world)

KE4　　寄らば大樹の陰。

Yoraba taiju no kage.

Seek shelter in the shade of a big tree.

(securing solid protection, having friends in high places)

Explanation

Idioms and proverbs are closely associated with cultural values. Because they are ubiquitous in speech and writing, it is important that you familiarize yourself with a few examples.

(a) あいつ仕事はまったくできない。**ごますり**だけで出世した.やつなんだ。(Refer to the hand signal mentioned in section 14.1.)

Aitsu shigoto wa mattaku dekinai. Gomasuri dake de shusseshita yatsu na n da.

He can't really achieve anything at his job. He got ahead only by apple-polishing.

(b) あの先生は、日本語教育では**草分け**的な方ですよ。

Ano sensei wa, nihongo kyooiku de wa kusawaketekina kata desu yo.

That teacher, she is a pioneer in Japanese language pedagogy.

(c) 自分の意見を持たずに、**寄らば大樹の陰**で周囲に合わせてばかりいる。

Jibun no iken o motazu ni, yoraba taiju no kage de shuui ni awasete bakari iru.

He has no opinion of his own, and he goes along with people in high places, always prioritizing (his) security.

USING WELL-KNOWN PHRASES

In addition to idioms and proverbs, universally recognizable expressions appear in everyday speech. By quoting the words verbatim or by changing some just enough to make them interesting, you can achieve a special effect. For example, drawing from the expression *To be, or not to be: that is the question* from Shakespeare's *Hamlet,* you might use the following.

(d) 言うべきか、言わざるべきか、それがね。
Yuu beki ka, iwazaru beki ka, sore ga ne.
Should I say, or should I not; that's the issue.

(e) 買うべきか、買わざるべきか。迷っちゃってね。
Kau beki ka, kawazaru beki ka. Mayot-chatte ne.
Should I buy, or should I not. I just can't make up my mind.

15.6. *Yojoo,* the Lingering Effect

Key Expressions

KE1   私は降りしきる雨の中に立っていた。止みそうもない雨の中に。
Watashi wa furishikiru ame no naka ni tatteita.
   Yamisoo mo nai ame no naka ni.
I was standing in the heavy rain. In the rain that didn't seem to stop.

KE2   あの人は、帰ってくると言った。
私は、その言葉を信じている。
帰ってくる。どんなことがあっても。
きっと帰ってくる、と……

Ano hito wa, kaette-kuru to itta.
Watashi wa, sono kotoba o shinjiteiru.
Kaette-kuru. Donna koto ga atte mo.
Kitto kaette-kuru, to....

He said he would come back.
I believe in those words.
He'll come back. No matter what.
He'll surely come back....

Explanation

余情 (よじょう)

余情 is a kind of rhetorical effect often acknowledged and discussed in Japanese literature. Although the 余情 effect is usually limited to the kind of writings that would aim for a classic literary tone, its importance cannot be ignored.

余情 literally means a remaining, lingering, or sustained feeling. It is your emotional experience triggered by images created through reading certain kinds of indirect, often implicit, writings. Study the last sentences in KE1 and KE2.

INTERPRETING 余情

When interpreting 余情, the following aspects are involved.

1. Sustained visual images
2. Empathy toward the world created by the writing
3. Images associated with characters and their feelings
4. Empathy toward the writer's thoughts and philosophy

EXPRESSIONS USED FOR 余情

For the 余情 effect, you use the following strategies.

1. Postposing
2. Graphological marks such as lines with ellipses or dashes
3. Past tense
4. Metaphor and simile
5. Simple and appropriately short sentences
6. Detached, distanced writing style

CHAPTER 16

Discourse Organization

16.1. Three-Part Organization

Key Expressions

KE1   はじめ・なか・おわり
hajime, naka, owari
beginning, middle, end

KE2   序論・本論・結論
joron, honron, ketsuron
introduction, main point, conclusion

Explanation

BASIC PRINCIPLE OF ORGANIZATION

When you combine multiple sentences, you create discourse. Multiple sentences are tied together to communicate a meaningful comment or argument, and they are connected by various means. They are usually structurally organized to form a cohesive whole.

The basic and universal principle of organization is the three-part structure, that is, a beginning, middle, and end. In logical terms, they are the introduction, the main point, and the conclusion.

Obviously, not all discourse is organized this way, but it is useful to think of discourse in these three parts and to understand discourse in terms of this structure.

Note that the conclusion appears at the end. In Japanese writing, more often than not, the beginning does not suggest what the conclusion might be. This shows a sharp contrast with English writing, where in many cases the conclusion is mentioned or suggested at the very beginning. When reading, always look for the important point toward the end of the discourse.

SAMPLE DISCOURSE

What follows consists of three sentences representing each of the three elements.

はじめ beginning

(a) 仕事が忙しいとき、休憩をとらないとミスが多くなる。
Shigoto ga isogashii toki, kyuukei o toranai to misu ga ooku naru.
When you are busy, if you don't take a break, you'll make more mistakes.

なか middle

(b) そんなときこそ、ゆっくりお茶を飲むとよい。
Sonna toki koso, yukkuri ocha o nomu to yoi.
That's the time you should take it easy and drink tea slowly.

おわり end

(c) ほんの数分の気分転換が、心身をリラックスさせてくれる。
Honno suuhun no kibuntenkan ga, shinshin o rirakkususasete-kureru.
Changing your attitude for a few minutes relaxes your body and mind.

16.2. *Ki-Shoo-Ten-Ketsu,* the Four-Part Organization

Explanation

起承転結（きしょうてんけつ）is a four-part organizational principle in Japanese. It originates in four-line Chinese poetry and is frequently referred to in Japanese as a model rhetorical structure of expository (and other) writing.

ORGANIZATION

起 (き) Topic presentation: Presenting the topic at the beginning of one's argument
承 (しょう) Topic development: Following 起, developing the topic further
転 (てん) Surprise turn: After the development of the topic in 承,

introducing surprise elements indirectly relevant to, related to, or connected with 起

結 (けつ) Conclusion: Tying all of the elements together and reaching a conclusion

Example

起

忙しくて人生を楽しむ余裕がない人が増えている。

Isogashikute jinsei o tanoshimu yoyuu no nai hito ga fueteiru.

People who are too busy to enjoy life are on the rise.

承

確かに現代人は朝から晩まで走りまわっている。

Tashikani gendaijin wa asa kara ban made hashiri-mawatteiru.

It is true that people today are on the go from morning till night.

転

ところで、車で動きまわると、歩くのと違って、周りの景色を味わうことができない。

Tokorode, kuruma de ugokimawaru to, aruku no to chigatte, mawari no keshiki o ajiwau koto ga dekinai.

By the way, if you drive around, as opposed to walking, you cannot enjoy the surrounding scenery.

結

人生もそれと同じで、時間をかけないと、本当に大切なものを見逃してしまう。

Jinsei mo sore to onaji de, jikan o kakenai to, hontooni taisetsuna mono o minogashite-shimau.

Life is the same; unless you take the time, you will miss the truly important things.

In this example, 転 offers a surprise turn, something unrelated to people's busy lives. 転 introduces the topic of driving a car. But when we read 結, we realize that driving a car is an analogy leading to the conclusion. Too busy a life, similar to the case of driving a car and not walking, would result in missing the important things.

CONCLUSION AT THE END

Structuring the conclusion to appear toward the end of the discourse exhibits a striking contrast with the English deductive writing style. Deductive writing presents its thesis statement (or conclusion, opinion, or view) in the initial position.

In Japanese discourse often the conclusion is only suggested at the beginning and then presented more clearly at the very end. You must be patient when reading Japanese writing. Of course, you can always jump ahead to the very end to find the conclusion.

16.3. Paragraph Organization

Explanation

段落 (だんらく) IN JAPANESE

The 段落 'paragraph' in Japanese is similar to an English paragraph but differs in some important ways. In English, the topic sentence (placed at the initial position of the paragraph) is expected to specify the topic. It is expected to contain the writer's opinion or position, and it often provides a clue for comprehending the entire paragraph.

The concept of 段落 in Japanese remains less clear. Although the idea of a topic sentence is advocated in education, in reality, 段落 may be in form only. The topic sentence may be nonexistent or may only suggest the overall message. You may find *danraku*-like short chunks without a significant message. These are called 形式段落 (けいしきだんらく), paragraphs in form only, and appear frequently in essays.

Japanese 段落 is graphologically marked by a line change and an indention of one character space.

TYPES OF 段落

Depending on how a specific 段落 contributes to the overall meaning of a discourse, the following types are recognized.

1. Introductory 段落 (introduces the purpose or the topic of the discourse or expresses the point of view or position of the writer)
2. Background 段落 (provides background for points made elsewhere)
3. Example 段落 (offers examples and cases related to the main point)
4. Main 段落 (discusses the main point of the discourse)
5. Connecting 段落 (connects one 段落 to another 段落 smoothly by offering transitions)

6. Supplementary 段落 (adds to the preceding 段落 or adds a slightly different angle to the preceding 段落)

BASES FOR 段落 DIVISION

When should you start a new 段落? Here are some suggestions.

1. Start a new 段落 when switching topics.

    Information related to specific theme or topic
    Description of the time, place, event, characters, or actions
    Persons being quoted

2. Start a new 段落 when switching the point of view toward the topics.

    New issues (e.g., questions raised)
    New claims or points of view
    Different positions and views (e.g., opposition, criticism)
    Transition to a new stage of argument (e.g., evidence, supporting argument)

16.4. Topic Structure and Staging

Explanation

Multiple sentences with topics operate together and organize a hierarchical network of topics in discourse. In a topical network, the main discourse topic operates as a pivotal point of reference, providing the starting point for the related topics. As a reader, one strategy you can use is to trace phrases marked by topic markers such as は and も (among others).

TOPICS CREATING HIERARCHICAL ORGANIZATION

In the discourse below, you can see how topic-marked phrases construct a hierarchical organization. By tracing those topics, you can see how the overall information is organized.

(a)

　　(a1) **色は**いろいろな感情を呼び起こす。 (a2) **赤は**情熱。 (a3) **白は**清らかさ。 (a4) **ブルーは**落ち着き。 (a5) それぞれの色の特徴を生かして利用することができる。

(a6) また、**色の組み合わせも**利用できる。(a7) **黒と黄色は、**は
っきり目につく。(a8) そのため、道路標識に使われる。
(a9) このように**色は**私たちの生活に役立っている。

Iro wa iroirona kanjoo o yobi-okosu. Aka wa joonetsu.
Shiro wa kiyorakasa. Buruu wa ochitsuki. Sorezore no iro no
tokuchoo o ikashite riyoosuru koto ga dekiru.

Mata, iro no kumiawase mo riyoo dekiru. Kuro to kiiro
wa, hakkiri me ni tsuku. Sonotame, dooro hyooshiki ni
tsukawareru.

Konoyooni iro wa watashitachi no seikatsu ni
yakudatteiru.

Color evokes various feelings. Red is passion. White is
purity, and blue is calmness. We can take advantage of each
characteristic of color.

We can use combinations of colors as well. Black and yel-
low catch one's attention. Because of that, they are used for
traffic signs.

In this way color is useful to our lives.

In this piece of writing, the following phrases are marked as
topics. And they form topical hierarchy as specified below.

色 (いろ) は in (a1) (overall topic, color)
    (individual colors)
       赤 (あか) は in (a2) (sub-topic, red)
       白 (しろ) は in (a3) (sub-topic, white)
       ブルーは in (a4) (sub-topic, blue)
    (combination of colors) in (a6)
       黒 (くろ) and黄色 (きいろ) in (a7) (sub-topic, black and
       yellow)
色は in (a9) (overall topic, color)

SELECTING TOPICS AND STAGING

Generally, information already known and shared between the
communication partners is likely to become topics. However, not
all shared items become topics. The choice is based on the writer's
and speaker's "staging strategy."

I use the term "staging strategy" metaphorically to mean a
director's decision on how to present characters on a theatrical
stage. Similar to the importance assigned to different characters on

a stage, the decision to make certain items topics or non-topics offers foregrounding (and thread-sustaining) or backgrounding (non-thread-sustaining) effects. The items marked with topic markers offer information that sustains the thread, as do main characters and important issues.

In the following example, both サヤ and ヒロ constitute shared information. But only サヤ continues to be marked with the topic marker は and becomes the discourse topic. サヤ functions as a character sustaining the plot. ヒロ is an important character but does not sustain the topical thread. Metaphorically, サヤ remains on stage throughout but ヒロ is spotlighted only when introduced.

(b)

サヤとヒロはクラスメート。**サヤは**いつも明るい。ヒロが時々、いじわるをする。でも**サヤは**あまり気にしない。

サヤはひそかにヒロに恋している。今日もヒロがサヤをからかう。でも、**サヤは**それを楽しんでいるのだ。

Saya to Hiro wa kurasumeeto. Saya wa itsumo aka-rui. Hiro ga tokidoki, ijiwaru o suru. Demo Saya wa amari kinishinai.

Saya wa hisokani hiro ni koishiteiru. Kyoo mo Hiro ga Saya o karakau. Demo, Saya wa sore o tanoshindeiru no da.

Saya and Hiro are classmates. Saya is always cheer-ful. Sometimes Hiro gets nasty toward her. But Saya doesn't mind.

Saya is secretly in love with Hiro. Today again, Hiro teases Saya. But Saya is actually enjoying it.

16.5. Topic Chaining and Thread of Discourse

Explanation

CHAINING SENTENCES TO CREATE THE THREAD

Topic markers offer overt clues as to how the narrative plot or the thread of a discourse develops. Topics may consist of the agent (the person involved) or the non-agent (the issue involved). An identical initial sentence can be developed through different threads as shown below.

AGENT-TOPIC THREAD

Example (a) selects "my friend" as a topic. The topic marks the items that sustain the thread of discourse. Note 私の友達 in (a1) and 彼女 in (a4). Also to be noted is the deletion of topic in (a2) and (a3).

(a)

(a1) **私の友達**は、うそをつく。
(a2) しかも、重大なことに関してうそをつく。
(a3) 別に悪いことだとは思っていないらしい。
(a4) **彼女**は、反省も後悔もしない。

Watashi no tomodachi wa, uso o tsuku.
Shikamo, juudaina koto ni kanshite uso o tsuku.
Betsuni warui koto da to wa omotteinai rashii.
Kanojo wa, hansei mo kookai mo shinai.

My friend lies.
Besides, she lies about important things.
It seems she doesn't think it's bad.
She doesn't repent or regret it.

NON-AGENT-TOPIC THREAD

In the following discourse, "telling lies" is selected as a topic, and it maintains the thread of discourse. Pay attention to うそ in (b1), うそをつくの in (b2), and うそ in (b4).

(b)

(b1) 私の友達は、**うそ**をつく。
(b2) **うそをつくの**は、間違っている。
(b3) なるべく避けるべきだ。
(b4) しかし、時と場合によっては、**うそ**は不必要な争いを避けるのに役立つ。

Watashi no tomodachi wa, uso o tsuku.
Uso o tsuku no wa, machigatteiru.
Narubeku sakeru beki da.
Shikashi, toki to baai ni yotte wa, uso wa fuhitsuyoona arasoi o sakeru no ni yakudatsu.

My friend lies.
Telling lies is wrong.
One should avoid it as much as possible.
However, depending on the time and situation, lies are
   useful to avoid unnecessary conflict.

Sample Poem

By using topic chaining, I wrote the following poem. You can follow
how the concept of 道 (みち) 'road' is the thread for the flow of the
poem. Each line is chained to the next by the shared topic, which
forms the overall discourse topic.

(c)
   道
   地平線までまっすぐ伸びた一本道。
   道の先には何があるのか。
   道の先は、また道かもしれない。
   ただ、ここから見えるこの道は
   大きな空に届いている。
   確かにこの道の先は、無限の可能性を秘めた
   遠いどこかに続いている。

   Michi
   Chiheisen made massugu nobita ipponmichi.
   Michi no saki ni wa nani ga aru no ka.
   Michi no saki wa, mata michi kamoshirenai.
   Tada, koko kara mieru kono michi wa
   ookina sora ni todoiteiru.
   Tashikani kono michi no saki wa, mugen no kanoosei o
      himeta
   tooi dokoka ni tsuzuiteiru.

   Road
   A straight single road reaching the horizon.
   What lies ahead for this road?
   It may continue on beyond.
   Except this road I can see from here
   reaches to the expanse of the sky.
   For sure, the end of this road extends somewhere far
   to where limitless possibilities lie.

16.6. Discourse Markers

Explanation

Discourse markers are particles, connectives, adverbs, and idiomatic phrases that overtly specify discourse organization. At least five different kinds of organizational markers are available, as listed below.

1. Topic marking

    (a) 和食**といえば**、やはりすしですかね。
         Washoku toieba, yahari sushi desu ka ne.
         Speaking of Japanese cuisine, as expected, sushi is the best.

    (b) 自殺は現在の日本で**は**、深刻な問題となっている。
         Jisatsu wa genzai no nihon de wa, shinkokuna mondai to natteiru.
         Suicide has become a grave issue in today's Japan.

2. Topic development

    (c) **それでは**、次の点にしぼって考えましょう。
         Soredewa, tsugi no ten ni shibotte kangaemashoo.
         Now let's focus on the following points.

    (d) **次に**、みなさんのご意見をお聞きしたいと思います。　[suprapolite style]
         Tsugini, minasan no goiken o okikishitai to omoimasu.
         Next, I would like to hear your opinion.

3. Topic shifting

    (e) **ところで**、大阪に行った上田さんのことですが。
         Tokorode, Oosaka ni itta Ueda-san no koto desu ga.
         By the way, about Mr. Ueda, who went to Osaka.

    (f) **さて**、本題に入りたいと思います。
         Sate, hondai ni hairitai to omoimasu.
         Now I would like to get to the main point.

4. Sequencing

    (g) **まず**、問題のありかをはっきりさせよう。
         次に、いくつか解決の可能性を考えよう。
         最後に、一番いい解決策を決めよう。

Mazu, mondai no arika o hakkiri saseyoo.
Tsugini, ikutsuka kaiketsu no kanoosei o kangaeyoo.
Saigoni, ichiban ii kaiketsusaku o kimeyoo.

First, let's find out where the problem lies.
Next, let's think of a few possible solutions.
Finally, let's decide on the best solution.

5.   General conclusion

(h) 本当に勉強するつもりで大学に来る者は少ない。**つまり**、多く
     の学生たちは勉強以外の目的で、来ているのである。

Hontooni benkyoosuru tsumori de daigaku ni kuru mono
wa sukunai. Tsumari, ooku no gakusei-tachi wa ben-
kyoo igai no mokuteki de, kiteiru no dearu.

Only a few students come to the university to study. In
other words, many students come to the university
with a purpose other than studying.

PART VI

Genres

CHAPTER 17

Genre Appreciation

17.1. Genre Categories

Written discourse in the *Nihongo* world is categorized into a number of genres. First, I will divide genres based on their purpose, that is, (1) to convey information, (2) to persuade, and (3) to stir the emotions.

1. To convey information

報道文	ほうどうぶん	newspaper articles, magazine articles, reports
記録文	きろくぶん	reports based on observation (e.g., of experiments, natural phenomena, disasters)
案内文	あんないぶん	invitations, announcements, and bulletins
通信文	つうしんぶん	correspondence, letters, e-mail, text messaging
報告文	ほうこくぶん	reports of field research or observation
公用文	こうようぶん	official documents, forms, letters, and documents used for official purposes by the government
日記文	にっきぶん	diaries, records of a person's life (may fall into the category of literary works when taking the form of essays or novels)
紀行文	きこうぶん	travelogues, travel diaries, writings of travel experiences (may be considered literary works)

281

2. To persuade

論文	ろんぶん	academic theses, scholarly articles
評論文	ひょうろんぶん	criticisms
書評	しょひょう	book reviews
解説文	かいせつぶん	commentary, analysis
意見文	いけんぶん	opinion pieces
広告文	こうこくぶん	advertising
論説文	ろんせつぶん	editorials

3. To stir the emotions

詩歌	しいか	poetry, *waka* (or *tanka*), *haiku*
随筆	ずいひつ	essays
戯曲	ぎきょく	plays
童話	どうわ	nursery stories, fairy tales
民話	みんわ	folktales
小説	しょうせつ	novels
短編小説	たんぺんしょうせつ	short stories
推理小説	すいりしょうせつ	mystery novels

In the publishing industry genres are often divided into three different groups: (1) books, (2) magazines, and (3) comics. I list some representative categories.

1. 本 (ほん) Books

Fiction

純文学	じゅんぶんがく	literary novels
歴史小説	れきししょうせつ	historical novels
大衆小説	たいしゅうしょうせつ	commercial novels
ミステリー・サスペンス		mystery, suspense
ロマンス		romance novels
エッセー・随筆	ずいひつ	essays

Non-fiction

人文・思想	じんぶん・しそう	humanities, thought
社会・政治	しゃかい・せいじ	society, politics
歴史・地理	れきし・ちり	history, geography
ビジネス・経済	けいざい	business, economics
語学・辞書	ごがく・じしょ	language, dictionaries

2. 雑誌 (ざっし) *Magazines*

求人・キャリア	きゅうじん	employment, career
女性ファッション・ライフスタイル	じょせい	women's fashion and lifestyles
男性ファッション・ライフスタイル	だんせい	men's fashion and lifestyles
健康情報	けんこうじょうほう	health information
出産・子育て	しゅっさん・こそだて	childbearing and rearing
料理・グルメ	りょうり	cooking, gourmet eating
音楽・映画	おんがく・えいが	music, movies
テレビ・芸能	げいのう	television, entertainment

3. コミック *Comics*

Based on the reader

少年コミック	しょうねん	boys' comics
少女コミック	しょうじょ	girls' comics
レディースコミック		ladies' comics
成人向けマンガ	せいじんむけ	adult comics

Based on the theme

スポーツマンガ		sports comics
ファンタジーマンガ		fantasy comics
ホラーマンガ		horror comics
ＳＦ		science fiction comics
学園マンガ	がくえん	school comics
恋愛マンガ	れんあい	love comics
歴史マンガ	れきし	history comics

17.2. Mixing Genres

Although I introduced specific genres in the preceding section, different genres are often juxtaposed and integrated. In fact, if you carefully study Japanese discourse, you will find that it mostly combines multiple genres.

Mixing genres is one of the many rhetorical and expressive means available in any language. By introducing different genres into discourse, you are able to exploit them for maximum effect.

For example, observe the following discourse, in which storytelling and descriptive writing are mixed.

(a)

　むかしむかし、**あるところに**、70歳を過ぎてもみんな健康
で、野良仕事をする村があった**そうな**。

　この村とは、長野県の小さな村。そしてそこは、日本一そばが
おいしいことで知られる村である。村民は、そば粉だけからつくら
れた真っ黒のそばを一日に一度は必ず食べるのだ。

Mukashi mukashi, aru tokoro ni, nanajussai o sugite mo
minna kenkoo de, norashigoto o suru mura ga atta soona.

Kono mura to wa, Naganoken no chiisana mura. Soshite
soko wa, nihon'ichi soba ga oishii koto de shirareru mura
dearu. Sonmin wa, sobako dake kara tsukurareta makkuro
no soba o ichinichi ni ichido wa kanarazu taberu no da.

They say that once upon a time, somewhere, there was a
village where people over seventy were all healthy and worked
on the land.

This village is a small place in Nagano Prefecture. And it
is known as the place that produces the most delicious *soba*
in Japan. Once a day without fail, the villagers eat these
black noodles, made only from pure *soba* flour.

In (a), the first sentence constructs a narrative mode. The storytelling mode is particularly evident in the initial phrases むかし
むかし、あるところに 'once upon a time, somewhere'. As you know,
folktales typically begin this way. The hearsay marker そうな appearing at the end of this sentence is used exclusively when narrating a story. The second 段落 (だんらく) switches to a descriptive
style.

Introducing the discourse as if it were a folktale creates a context suitable to what follows. It provides an aura of "old" Japan,
where traditions still thrive.

You can use this storytelling mode in ordinary conversation as
well.

(b)　<conversation>

A:　新しいアパート、どんな感じ？

B:　**むかしむかし**、ある一匹の野良猫が、やっと住めるところ
　　を**見つけました**。隣近所がどんな感じか全然わからす、
　　とまどっていました。でも少しずつ、友達も**できてきま
　　した**。ってな感じかな。

A:　なに、それ。

B:　だから、少しずつだけど、住みやすく感じてるってコト。

A: Atarashii apaato, donna kanji?

B: Mukashi mukashi, aru ippiki no noraneko ga yatto sumeru tokoro o mitsukemashita. Tonari kinjo ga donna kanji ka zenzen wakarazu, tomadot-teimashita. Demo, sukoshi zutsu, tomodachi mo dekite-kimashita. Tte na kanji ka na.

A: Nani, sore.

B: Dakara, sukoshizutsu da kedo, sumi-yasuku kan-jiteru tte koto.

A: How is your new apartment?

B: Once upon a time, a stray cat at last found a place to live. She didn't know about the neighborhood and was confused. But gradually she began to make friends. That's how I feel.

A: What do you mean?

B: Don't you see? I mean that I'm getting used to it little by little.

Observe B's answer to the initial question. Instead of responding in ordinary conversational speech, B tells a story about a stray cat. Note the use of むかしむかし and formal past tense forms of the verbs. By introducing her answer as a story and by repeating the past tense in three consecutive sentences, B constructs a narrative world.

This storytelling mode creates a distancing effect. It is as if B were telling her story about someone else. But of course, it turns out to be about herself. By taking a narrative perspective complete-ly apart from the conversation-in-progress, she makes her answer that much more interesting. It allows B to reveal her inner feelings with a dramatic but somewhat distancing effect.

To appreciate the genre mixing depicted in (a) and (b), you must be able to identify the basic styles of different genres. It is beyond the scope of this book to discuss the characteristics of genres. As a student of *Nihongo,* you might try to expose yourself to as many categories of genres as possible.

In real *Nihongo* discourse, genre mixing occurs more frequent-ly than we normally think. Consider a piece of writing where the writer inserts *tanka* in an essay. You will find Japanese advertis-ing discourse that incorporates songs, conversations, and poetry. Writing that mixes the personal essay genre and an opinion piece is common as well. And of course in マンガ, you find commentary, historical accounts, folktales, and other genres mixed into the plot development of a single story.

CHAPTER 18

Selected Popular Culture Genres

This chapter contains examples drawn from authentic Japanese discourse. To appreciate these examples, you will need to use a dictionary for unfamiliar vocabulary items. Use the ローマ字 (じ) presentation and English translation provided as your guide.

I have selected the following items because incorporating "real" Japanese in your study is critical. Only through exposure to the actual everyday discourse of Japanese people can you begin to learn Japanese "for real." The examples are taken from the kind of discourse in which you, as a student of Japanese (as a foreign language), are likely to be interested. They represent today's popular culture discourse and the kind of world to which Japanese young adults are frequently exposed. I have also chosen the kind of discourse resembling ordinary natural speech, avoiding some stylized popular culture variations.

Some readings are accompanied with visual presentations as well. I hope they will help you feel that you are experiencing the world of real *Nihongo.* I should also remind you that additional (visual) information is available on the Internet. Use the titles of each sample as search keys.

18.1. Comics マンガ

やぶのてんや 『イナズマイレブン』 『コロコロコミック』 *September 2008,* 「円堂が呪われる！？」 *pp. 446–448* 小学館

『イナズマイレブン』 was originally sold as a video (RPG) game (August 2008). It was developed by レベルファイブ to be played on the Nintendo DS. The comic version was developed by やぶのてんや and started its series in the June issue of a comic magazine, 『コロコロコミック』. (The televised anime version is available; its official Web site is http://www.tv-tokyo.co.jp/anime/inazuma/.)

Figure 4. *Endoo ga Norowareru of Inazuma Irebun,* by Ten'ya Yabuno, in *Korokoro Komikku* (September 2008), published by Shogakukan.

Figure 4. *(continued)*

Figure 4. *(continued)*

『イナズマイレブン』 [lit. 'The Lightning Eleven'] is a story about a junior high school soccer team whose captain is 円堂 (えんどう). It depicts the team's formation, training, and the ultimate challenge of winning a championship. What follows is an episode titled 「円堂が呪 (のろ) われる！？」 'Endo is cursed!?'

In the next example, speech balloons are marked with < >. Other phrases appearing in the *manga* are presented in parentheses.

＊　＊　＊

（あっはっは・・・）

円堂：　　　〈いやー、昨日は　まいったよ。〉

　　　　　　〈山で特訓　してたら　ハチに襲われ　ちゃってさ~。〉

　　　　　　（はっはっはっ　はっはっ）

　　　　　　〈それにしても　豪炎寺の　おとろきよう　ったら　なかったぜ！〉

小暮：　　　〈へ□□っ　豪炎寺さんも　おどろくことが　あるんですねー。〉

豪炎寺：　　〈あのカオは　だれでも　おどろく。〉

　　　　　　（あはは　ははは）

円堂：　　　〈もしかして　幽霊とか　苦手なんじゃ　ねーの？〉

豪炎寺：　　〈オレは　そういうのは　信じない！！〉

　　　　　　〈だいたい円堂　おまえいったい　あそこで　なにをして・・・。〉

木野：　　　〈みんな　大変！！〉

　　　　　　（バンッ）

　　　　　　（マネージャー・・・。）

円堂：　　　〈どうした　また雷門夏未が　廃部とか　言い出したのか！？〉

木野：　　　〈ちがうの！！〉

　　　　　　〈うちの部に　練習試合の　申し込みが　すごいのよ！！〉

部員：　　　〈えっ！？〉

　　　　　　（どーん）

　　　　　　（こりゃすげえ！！）

豪炎寺：　　〈おそらく　帝国学園に　勝ったうわさが　ひろまったんだ。〉

　　　　　　（なるほど）

染岡：　〈帝国に勝った　おれたちに勝って　地位を　あげたいんだ
　　　　な。〉

円堂：　〈でも　これで　実践練習が　ガンガン　できるぞ！！〉

小暮：　〈今まで　相手探すのに　苦労しましたもんね…。〉

　　　　（ゴゴゴゴ…）

　　　　（な…、　なんだこれ？）

　　　　（の…、呪いの手紙！？）

　　　　（ゴゴゴゴゴゴ）

(Att hatt hatt)

Endoo:　Iyaa, kinoo wa maitta yo.

　　　　Yama de tokkunshite-itara hachi ni osoware-chatte saa.

　　　　(Hatt hatt hatt hatt hatt)

　　　　Sorenishitemo Gooenji no odorokiyoo ttara nakatta ze!

Kogure:　Heeeett. Gooenji-san mo odoroku koto ga aru n desu nee.

Gooenji:　Ano kao wa dare demo odoroku.

Endoo:　Moshikashite yuurei toka nigate na n janee no?

Gooenji:　Ore wa sooyuu no wa shinjinai!!

　　　　Daitai Endoo omae ittai asoko de nani o shite....

Kino:　Minna taihen!!

　　　　(Bantt)

Kogure:　(Maneejaa....)

Endoo:　Doo shita. Mata Raimon Natsumi ga haibu toka ii-dashita no ka!?

Kino:　Chigau no!!

　　　　Uchi no bu ni renshuu jiai no mooshikomi ga sugoi no yo!!

Buin:　Ett!?

　　　　(Doon)

　　　　(Korya sugee!!)

Gooenji:　Osoraku Teikoku Gakuen ni katta uwasa ga hiromatta n da.

　　　　(Naruhodo)

Someoka:　Teikoku ni katta oretachi ni katte chii o agetai n da na.

Endoo: Demo kore de jissen renshuu ga gangan dekiru zo!?

Kogure: Ima made aite sagasu no ni kurooshimashita mon
            ne....

            (Gogogogo....)

            (Na..., nan da kore?)

            (No..., noroi no tegami!?)

            (Gogogogogogogo)

            (Laughter)

Endoo: Well, yesterday was terrible!

            At our special training in the mountains, we got at-
            tacked by bees.

            (Laughter)

            And I couldn't believe it. Gooenji lost his cool.

Kogure: So Gooenji does get scared now and then, I see.

Gooenji: That face we saw. Everyone would be scared of it.

            (Laughter)

Endoo: Maybe you can't handle ghosts?

Gooenji: I don't believe in those things!!

            Endoo, what in the world were you doing there
            anyway?

Kino: Hey, everyone, we got trouble!!

            (Kino, the manager, makes a dramatic entry onto the
            scene.)

            (Manager....)

Endoo: What happened? Did Natsumi Raimon say something
            about abolishing our team?

Kino: No. Wrong!

            We're getting swamped. So many requests for soccer
            matches coming from other schools.

Team members: What?

            (Look. Here they are.)

            (Wow, this is something!!)

Gooenji: Perhaps the rumor has spread. We beat Teikoku
            Gakuen School.

            (Makes sense.)

Someoka: They want to gain a higher ranking by beating us, who beat Teikoku.

Endoo: But this way, we can test ourselves in practice matches!!

Kogure: We had a hard time finding teams to play against.

(Reverberating sound)

(Wha. . . . What's this?)

(A haunted letter!?)

(Reverberating sound)

* * *

FEATURES TO BE NOTED

1. Interactional particles

Comics often contain frequent interactional particles, and this section is no exception. The following list reveals their ubiquitous nature. See sections 7.10, 8.8, 11.1, and 11.5 for information on interactional particles.

まいった**よ**
襲われちゃって**さ～**
なかった**ぜ**
あるんです**ねー**
苦手なんじゃねえ**の**
すごい**のよ**
地位をあげたいんだ**な**
ガンガンできる**ぞ**
苦労しましたもん**ね**

2. Sound effects

Sound effects are used throughout, as listed below. See sections 6.9 and 11.10.

あっはっは	sound of laughter
はっはっ	sound of laughter
バンッ	sound made when a door is slammed suddenly and dramatically
どーん	sound effect when a large object makes a dramatic appearance
ゴゴゴゴ	reverberating sound of something large being moved around

3. Expressions of surprise

   Note the repetition of the initial mora in な・・・、なんだこ
れ？ and の・・・、呪いの手紙！？ This repetition expresses the
speaker's out-of-one's-control surprise (see section 11.7).

4. Use of カタカナ

   We find four words using カタカナ (see section 5.5).

   ハチ 'bee' (insect name)
   カオ 'face' and オレ 'I' (和語 (わご) in *katakana,* for colloquial
      and contemporary effect)
   バンッ！ 'door slam' (onomatopoeia)
   マネージャー 'manager' (loan word)
   ガンガン 'intensely' (mimesis)
   ゴゴゴゴ 'reverberating sound' (onomatopoeia)

   Of particular interest are カオ and オレ, which can be written in *kanji,* 顔 and 俺. In マンガ, the use of カタカナ is widespread. They add to the colloquial and with-it atmosphere.

5. For the following expressions, refer to the sections listed.

   襲われちゃって (section 9.6, Modal Verbs)
   おどろくことがある (section 10.6, *Koto* and *No* Clauses)
   もしかして (section 13.4, Prefacing and Alerting)
   苦手なんじゃねーの (section 8.13, Negative Questions)

18.2. Television Variety Show バラエティ番組

『さんタク』, *Aired on January 3, 2008,* フジテレビ

『さんタク』 is a talk show between 明石家 (あかしや) さんま and 木
村拓也 (きむらたくや). Akashiya (b. 1955, popularly known as さん
ま) is a comedian/actor/entertainer, and Kimura (b. 1972, nicknamed キムタク) is a singer/actor and member of a song-and-
dance group called SMAP.

During the New Year's holiday, for the past ten years Sanma
and Kimura have appeared in a two-hour special variety program.
The program is titled さんタク.

In this program, Sanma and Kimura talk in the studio while
various preproduced segments are inserted here and there. They
engage in different activities, such as visiting certain well-known
places, talking with celebrities, and participating in competitive
sports and games. These are incorporated into the talk-in-progress.

What follows is a short conversation that took place when

Kimura persuaded Sanma to dye his hair at a hair-coloring salon in Tokyo.

*   *   *

カラリングのお店で

スタッフ：	うちのお店、あの、シミュレーションがあって（はい）写真をとらせていただいて（はい）あのう、お顔が、ガメラ、カメラ（笑い）に出ます。
木村：	ガメラ。
さんま：	オレ、火を吹くのか。
	(スタッフと木村、さんまの冗談に、少し笑う)
木村：	いちいちいいから。やろう。
スタッフ：	ぜひ。
木村：	火を吹くのかって。
	（略）
スタッフ：	お着替えを、お願いします。
さんま：	お着替え？
スタッフ：	はい。
木村：	着替えるんですか。
スタッフ：	はい。
さんま：	着替えるの？
スタッフ：	はい、こちらのガウンに。
さんま：	なんでや。
スタッフ：	ルラックスしていただくために。
木村：	リラックス。
スタッフ：	リラックスをしていただけるために。

Kararingu no omise de

Sutaffu:	Uchi no omise, ano, shimyureeshon ga atte (hai) shashin o torasete-itadaite (hai) anoo, okao ga, *gamera,* kamera (warai) ni demasu.
Kimura:	*Gamera.*
Sanma:	Ore, hi o fuku no ka.
	(Sutaffu to Kimura, Sanma no joodan ni, sukoshi warau.)
Kimura:	Ichiichi ii kara. Yaroo.

Sutaffu: Zehi.

Kimura: Hi o fuku no ka tte.

               (ryaku)

Sutaffu: Okigae o, onegaishimasu.

Sanma: Okigae?

Sutaffu: Hai.

Kimura: Kigaeru n desu ka?

Sutaffu: Hai.

Sanma: Kigaeru no?

Sutaffu: Hai, kochira no gaun ni.

Sanma: Nande ya.

Sutaffu: Rirakkusushite-itadaku tame ni.

Kimura: Rirakkusu.

Sutaffu: Rirakkusu o shite-itadakeru tame ni.

At a hair-coloring salon

Staff member: At our store, we have this simulation procedure
               (uh huh), so we would like to take your picture if
               we could (uh-huh). Your face will appear in the
               gamera, (laughing) I mean camera.

Kimura: *Gamera.*

Sanma: Am I supposed to spew out fire from my mouth?

               (Staff member and Kimura laugh at Sanma's
               joke.)

Kimura: Don't bother with silly things. Let's do it.

Staff member: Yes, please.

Kimura: What a thing to say.... Going to spew out fire.

               (...)

Staff member: Please change into this.

Sanma: Change clothes?

Staff member: Yes.

Kimura: Is he supposed to change his clothes?

Staff member: Yes.

Sanma: Do I need to change into something else?

Staff member: Yes, into this gown.

Sanma: Why's that?

Staff member: So that you can relax.

Kimura: Relax, you say.

Staff member: So that we can make you feel relaxed.

* * *

FEATURES TO BE NOTED

1. Expressions for conversational interaction

The initial utterance by the staff member contains features typical of conversational interaction. First, note Sanma's あいづち, presented in parentheses. At the point where the staff member uses the conjunctive て and momentarily pauses, Sanma sends あいづち. This behavior helps create an engaging and friendly atmosphere (see section 13.11).

Second, note the staff member's fillers as conversation strategies. The staff member uses あの and あのう as she continues. By filling in the pause, she keeps her speaking turn.

Third, the moment when the staff member realizes she made a mistake, all three participants laugh. This joint action reflects that they are all on the same wave length, so to speak.

2. Echo questions and responses

Overall, as you find in this short segment, ordinary conversation is filled with short phrases, interaction-related brief utterances, and repetition. Repetition often occurs across speakers as echo questions and echo responses (see section 13.13). For example, Sanma's お着替え？ is an echo question, and Kimura's 火を吹くのかって is an echo response.

3. Humor and laughter

This variety program is a showcase for Sanma to display his talent for making puns and jokes (as his profession calls for). Kimura plays the part of the straight man who often tolerates (sometimes reluctantly, but mostly admiringly) Sanma's wild and crazy ways.

The joke here is based on a word the staff member has mispronounced. Instead of カメラ, the staff member says ガメラ. ガメラ sounds like a dinosaur or a monster. It could be a cartoon character that might spew fire from its mouth. Sanma's joke is based on しゃれ (see section 15.3).

4.   Speech styles and variations
     Given that Sanma is older and someone Kimura admires,
the relationship is such that Sanma is *meue* to Kimura. In
dealing with the staff at the hair-coloring salon, Kimura
makes sure to speak in a formal style (see section 12.1).
Sanma, on the other hand, speaks in the informal style and
also in the Osaka dialect. Contrast Kimura's 着替えるんですか
and Sanma's 着替えるの.
     The staff member always uses polite and supra-polite
speech. Customers are always *meue* (see section 2.3). Note
the use of お attached to 和語 (わご) in お顔がカメラに出ます
and お着替えをお願いします. Also study the honorifics appearing in the staff member's speech, as in リラックスしていただく
ために and リラックスをしていただけるために.
     Sanma plays the role of an uncontrollable joke-telling tal-
ent. He regularly mixes in his Osaka dialect with his speech
(see section 3.6). Sanma's question なんでや is a perfect
example. The Osaka dialect reminds viewers that Sanma is a
comedian from Osaka, adding texture to his character.

18.3. Television Drama テレビドラマ

『ガリレオ』, *Aired on November 5, 2007,* フジテレビ

「ガリレオ」is a television drama series aired on Fuji Television,
October–December 2007 (official Web site: http://fujitv.co.jp/
galileo/index.html). The ten-episode series is based on detective
stories by 東野圭吾 (ひがしのけいご, b. 1958), specifically his 『探偵
(たんてい) ガリレオ』and 『予知夢 (よちむ)』.
     The main characters are 湯川学 (ゆかわまなぶ), a physics pro-
fessor who insists on the logical nature of things, and 内海薫 (うつ
みかおる), a young female detective who seeks help from Dr. Yukawa. Dr. Yukawa is nicknamed Galileo; hence the title of the series.
What follows is a short exchange (taken from episode 4) between 内
海薫 and 栗林宏美 (くりばやしひろみ), an assistant in Dr. Yukawa's
physics lab.
     The = in this example indicates the takeover of the speaking
turn by the listener immediately after the partner's speech.

                               *   *   *

栗林 :   あ、しまった！
内海 :   なに、やってんですか。

栗林：	実験用のセパレーター作ってんだよ、湯川先生に頼まれて。
内海：	へえ、そういうこともやるんですね、助手って。
	（栗林、助手と言われて不愉快そうに内海を睨みつける）
	半田ごての使い方ぐらい慣れなきゃ。
栗林：	半田ごてじゃありません。これはプラスチックウェルダーって言うんです。超音波でくっつけるんです。
内海：	超音波？
栗林：	中学の工作とは違うんだよ。だいたいなんであんたここで油うってんだ？
内海：	だから、湯川先生に＝
栗林：	＝だからどこ行ったか知らないって。
内海：	他殺説の根拠をはっきりさせてもらわないことには＝
栗林：	＝今日は帰ってこないなあ、きっと。
内海：	栗林さんってどうしていつも非協力的なの！
栗林：	だって、俺、関係ないもん＝
内海：	＝もう、ただでさえイライラしてるのにもう。
栗林：	俺だって２０年ストレスためっぱなしだよ！
	（ポーズの後）
内海：	かわいそうに。
栗林：	かわいそう言うな！

Kuribayashi:	Att, shmatta!
Utsumi:	Nani, yatte n desu ka.
Kuribayashi:	Jikkenyoo no separeetaa tsukutte n da yo, Yukawa-sensei ni tanomarete.
Utsumi:	Hee, sooyuu koto mo yaru n desu ne, joshu tte.
	(Kuribayashi, joshu to iwarete fuyukaisooni Utsumi o niramitsukeru.)
	Handa gote no tsukaikata gurai narenakya.
Kuribayashi:	Handa gote jaarimasen. Kore wa purasuchikku werudaa tte yuu n desu. Chooonpa de kuttsukeru n desu.
Utsumi:	Chooonpa?
Kuribayashi:	Chuugaku no koosaku to wa chigau n da yo. Daitai nande anta koko de abura utte n da?

Utsumi: Dakara, Yukawa-sensei ni=

Kuribayashi: =Dakara doko itta ka shiranai tte.

Utsumi: Tasatsusetsu no konkyo o hakkirisasete-morawa-
                 nai koto ni wa=

Kuribayashi: =Kyoo wa kaette-konai naa, kitto.

Utsumi: Kuribayashi-san tte dooshite itsumo hikyooryo-
                 kuteki na no!

Kuribayashi: Datte, ore kankei nai mon=

Utsumi: =Moo, tada de sae irairashiteru noni moo.

Kuribayashi: Ore datte nijuunen sutoresu tameppanashi da yo!

                 (Poozu no ato)

Utsumi: Kawaisoo ni.

Kuribayashi: Kawaisoo yuu na.

Kuribayashi: Oh no, I did it again!

Utsumi: What are you doing?

Kuribayashi: I'm making a separator for the experiment. Dr. Yu-
                 kawa asked me (to make it).

Utsumi: I see. Such things you do, I mean, being an
                 assistant.

                 (Kuribayashi, upset at the phrase "assistant,"
                 stares at Utsumi)

                 You must get used to the soldering iron, you know.

Kuribayashi: Not a soldering iron. This is called a plastic welder.
                 Joining parts with a supersonic wave.

Utsumi: Supersonic wave?

Kuribayashi: It's different from junior high school craft class.
                 (Come to think of it) in the first place, what are you
                 hanging around here for?

Utsumi: So, I wanted to see Dr. Yukawa=

Kuribayashi: =I'm telling you, I don't know where he went.

Utsumi: I must have him clarify his theory that the victim
                 was murdered=

Kuribayashi: =He won't be back today, for sure.

Utsumi: Why are you, Mr. Kuribayashi, always so
                 unhelpful!

Kuribayashi: I have nothing to do with your business=

Utsumi: =I'm stressed out already and on top of that, now you (make me more upset).

Kuribayashi: I'm stressed out too, after twenty years of pent-up pressure!

(after a pause)

Utsumi: Poor thing.

Kuribayashi: Never say "Poor thing."

* * *

FEATURES TO BE NOTED

1. Conflict situation

This segment illustrates a conflict situation between two people, Utsumi and Kuribayashi, who know each other fairly well. Utsumi, being younger and a guest, maintains a formal style almost always. Kuribayashi mixes formal and informal styles.

The conflict starts when Kuribayashi's frustration peaks. He asks だいたいなんであんたここで油 (あぶら) うってんだ？using the informal style. The use of あんた and the critical tone of the utterance adds to the bluntness.

Utsumi answers by starting her utterance with だから, with a don't-you-get-it attitude. Before she finishes her turn, Kuribayashi interrupts by starting his utterance with だから. These and other turn-taking mishaps in this segment illustrate that two people are in conflict (see section 13.2). They exchange some harsh words. The ultimate is when after a pause Utsumi says かわいそうに. Kuribayashi refuses this characterization. He responds with an abrupt command かわいそう言うな！(see section 12.12). Sympathy coming from a young detective is something Kuribayashi simply will not tolerate.

Utsumi and Kuribayashi can fight like this because they know that these verbal spats are not going to cause permanent damage to their relationship. They are both releasing stress by sniping at each other.

2. Echo questions

When Kuribayashi explains that he was making a separator using a plastic welder, Utsumi repeats the question by echoing Kuribayashi's word (see section 13.13).

栗林： 超音波でくっつけるんです。
内海： **超音波**？

Echo questions often function to establish a topic. Although the atmosphere is unfriendly, at least they carry on an engaged conversation at this point.

3. Postposed elements

This segment contains the following postposed elements (see section 13.10).

(a) 栗林：実験用のセパレーター作ってんだよ、**湯川先生に頼まれて**。

(b) 内海：へえ、そういうこともやるんですね、**助手って**。

(c) 栗林：今日は帰ってこないなあ、**きっと**。

When pronounced with stress as in the examples above, postposing communicates the importance of the elements in question. In (a), Kuribayashi's insistence on the fact that he was asked by Dr. Yukawa is significant. In (b), Utsumi emphasizes that Kuribayashi is an assistant (he has been an assistant too long). In (c), Kuribayashi insists that Dr. Yukawa "for sure" won't be back.

4. *No da* sentences

This segment contains the following *no da* expressions (see section 9.12). Some of them appear in casual んだ, in question sentences, and in shortened の.

やってんですか (question on shared information)
作ってんだよ (explanation)
やるんですね (emphasis)
言うんです (emphasis)
くっつけるんです (explanation)
違うんだよ (emphasis)
油うってんだ (question on shared information)
非協力的なの (question on shared information)

The basic function of のだ and んだ is to appeal to the assumed common understanding or knowledge between you and your partner. They offer reason or cause, express emphasis, and ask questions based on shared information.

5. Deletion of grammatical particles

Given that this segment is a part of casual conversation, we find some deletion of grammatical particles.

なに (を) やってんですか
セパレーター (を) 作ってんだ
なんであんた (は) ここで油うってんだ

どこ (へ) 行ったか知らない
だって俺 (は) 関係ないもん
ストレス (を) ためっぱなし
かわいそう (と) 言うな

18.4. Print Advertising 広告

A. キユーピー株式会社「中華スープの素」『オレンジページ』 (December 2, 2007, p. 202), オレンジページ

This print advertising appears in 『オレンジページ』 [lit. 'Orange Page'], a monthly magazine targeted at housewives. The magazine features articles on cooking and other domestic matters. The following advertisement addresses readers who may be in the market for a soup mix.

* * *

1. 台所の　野菜を　ゆでる。
2. スープの　素を　加える。
3. 弱火で　3分！

にんじん、ねぎ、しいたけなど、お家にある野菜をゆで、そこに3分クッキングの中華スープの素を入れるだけ！弱火で3分加熱すれば、とてもおいしい中華スープが手軽に作れます。和風スープ、チャウダー、ミネストローネもあります。おいしいスープで野菜をたっぷり召しあがってください。

1. Daidokoro no yasai o yuderu.
2. Suupu no moto o kuwaeru.
3. Yowabi de sanpun!

Ninjin, negi, shiitake nado, ouchi ni aru yasai o yude, soko ni sanpun kukkingu no chuuka suupu no moto o ireru dake! Yowabi de sanpun kanetsusureba, totemo oishii chuuka suupu ga tegaruni tsukuremasu. Wafuu suupu, chaudaa, minesutoroone mo arimasu. Oishii suupu de yasai o tappuri meshiagatte-kudasai.

1. Boil vegetables you can find in your kitchen.
2. Add the soup mix.
3. Cook at low heat for three minutes.

Boil vegetables you have in your home, such as carrots, onions, shiitake mushrooms, and so on, and all you need to do is to add the three-minute Chinese soup mix. Cook it for three minutes at low heat, and you will have easily prepared

Figure 5. Advertising for Chuuka Suupu no Moto (by Q. P. Corporation), in *Orange Page* (December 2, 2007), published by Orenji Peeji.

a delicious Chinese soup. Also available are a Japanese soup mix, a chowder mix, and a minestrone soup mix. Enjoy eating a lot of vegetables served in delicious soups.

* * *

FEATURES TO BE NOTED

1. loan words

    This advertising contains many loan words, as listed below (see section 6.2).

スープ	soup
クッキング	cooking
チャウダー	chowder
ミネストローネ	minestrone

    In addition, the brand name is a loan word from Cupid (i.e., キューピー). The title of the magazine itself is coined from the English words "orange" and "page" (i.e., オレンジページ). These foreign-sounding phrases give a fashionable impression and are widely used (see section 6.3).

2. Informal non-past

    Note the use of the non-past tense for procedural descriptions (see section 8.3). The numbered directions appearing as headlines are given as if they were a part of a cooking recipe.

3. Addressing the consumer

    The main body of the copy takes on a friendly but formal style to address the consumer. The last sentence uses the honorifics (respectful forms) 召しあがってください, adding to the overall level of politeness (see sections 12.2 and 12.7).

4. Exclamatory phrases

    Advertising copy often uses short sentences and phrases. Exclamatory phrases appear frequently. They are concise, emphasize only critical information, and carry with them dramatic and emotional effects (see section 11.3).

    弱火で3分! and にんじん、ねぎ、しいたけなど、お家にある野菜をゆで、そこに3分クッキングの中華スープの素を入れるだけ! are such examples. We can assume that でできます and です, respectively, are deleted from the full statements. These sentences without predicates add to the immediacy and dramatic effect of the copy.

5. For the following expressions, refer to the sections listed.

お家 (section 12.2, Politeness and Honorifics)
野菜をゆで (section 10.2, Connecting Clauses)
加熱すれば (section 10.3, Conditionals)
作れます (section 9.5, Potential and Ability)
召しあがる (section 12.2, Politeness and Honorifics)
召しあがってください (section 12.7, Making Requests)

B. 政府広報　「飲酒運転は、止めなかったあなたも同罪です。」『*MEN'S NON-NO*』*(February 2008, p. 111)*, 集英社

This is a campaign against drunk driving sponsored by the Japanese government. The advertisement strongly communicates the message through its headline and copy.

* * *

飲酒運転は、止めなかったあなたも同罪です。
酒を飲み、運転しなければ起こらない犯罪。
それが、飲酒運転による事故です。
止めなかった人も罪は同じ。懲役や罰金が科せられます。
取り返しのつかない悲劇を、もう起こさないでください。
絶対にしない。絶対にさせない。飲酒運転は犯罪です。

Inshu unten wa, tomenakatta anata mo doozai desu.
Sake o nomi, untenshinakereba okoranai hanzai.
Sore ga, inshu unten ni yoru jiko desu.
Tomenakatta hito mo tsumi wa onaji. Chooeki ya bakkin ga
　　　kaseraremasu.
Torikaeshi no tsukanai higeki o, moo okosanaide-kudasai.
Zattai ni shinai. Zettai ni sasenai. Inshu unten wa hanzai desu.

As for drunk driving, if you haven't stopped the driver, you are
　　　guilty of committing the same crime.
A crime that does not happen unless you drink and drive.
That is the accident caused by driving while intoxicated.
The person who doesn't stop it is committing the same crime. And
　　　will be imprisoned and fined.
Do not repeat a tragedy you can never mend.
Never do it. Never let others do it. Drunk driving is a crime.

* * *

FEATURES TO BE NOTED

1. Clausal modification and clausal explanation

   This advertisement notably takes on a complex sentence structure of clausal modification (see section 10.4) and clausal explanation (see section 10.5).

   Examples of clausal modification are [止めなかった] あなた and [止めなかった] 人. Examples of clausal explanation are [酒を飲み、運転しなければ起こらない] 犯罪, [飲酒運転による] 事故, and [取り返しのつかない] 悲劇. The portion that is bracketed modifies or explains the noun immediately following it. Clausal modification and clausal explanation make it possible to pack rich information into a relatively small number of phrases, a useful strategy for advertising headlines and copy.

2. Passives and causatives

   Although Japanese passives and causatives are used in a limited way, the examples appearing in this text are quite effective. See sections 9.9 and 9.10 for passives and causatives.

   懲役や罰金が科せられます communicates the negative impact of being punished, and 起こさないでください communicates the power the driver has, that is, not to cause an accident.

   An interesting contrast is observed in the pair of sentences 絶対にしない and 絶対にさせない. Here, drunk driving is something that one *would not do* and *would not let others do*. The difference between しない and させない is significant, and that is realized by simple verb conjugation.

3. Topic chaining

   The headline and the copy of this advertisement illustrate how a topic can be maintained by chaining relevant words (see section 16.5). More specifically, the writer uses repetition, paraphrasing, and a 漢字 (かんじ) connection for topic chaining.

   First, note the repetition. The phrase 飲酒運転 appears three times. Given that we are exposed to 飲酒運転は at the very beginning, we sense that the text is about 飲酒運転. And the overall topic is sustained partly with the repetition of the identical phrase.

   Paraphrasing is a useful way to maintain cohesion without excessive repetition. The expression 酒を飲み運転 paraphrases 飲酒運転. Observe the interesting repeated use of 漢

字 (i.e., 罪). The words 同罪, 犯罪, and 罪 are used as they are chained to the idea of crime (罪).

18.5. Magazine Essay 雑誌エッセー

中丸雄一 「理想はお互いに尊敬し合えるオシャレな関係」『明星』 *(January 2008, p. 33)*, 集英社

This is a short essay appearing in an entertainment magazine. The essay is credited to 中丸雄一 (なかまるゆういち) (b. 1983), a member of a song-and-dance idol group, KAT-TUN. The magazine contains many photographs of teen idols, talents, and entertainers. The photographs are accompanied by essay-like pieces that "confess" how those celebrities feel. Obviously, these pieces are produced for the fans' consumption, and they contain funny, pleasant, uncontroversial, friendly, and not-so-serious comments.

* * *

　ま~寒くなってきたから、なんとなく人肌恋しい季節ではありますね、うん。で、なんでしたっけ？　あぁ恋？　恋ね。いちばん語るの苦手な分野だ・・・。あんまり恋に積極的なほうでもないんでね。無理!!って思うことのほうが多いんでね。本当に好きな人の前に出ると、すごーく不自然になってしまったり・・・。気になってる人がいても、俺じゃ申し訳ない気がして、逃げ腰になっちゃったり。そうなると、会話なんてもってのほか、目も見られずに、一方的な恋で終わってしまうわけですよ。たとえ、がんばって話して、少し仲よくなっても、それ以上はビビッてしまうとかね。自分でもどうしてこうなのかよくわかんないけどホントに不器用だなって思う。

Maa, samuku natte-kita kara, nantonaku hitohada koishii kisetsu de wa arimasu ne, un. De, nan deshita kke? Aa koi? Koi ne. Ichiban kataru no nigatena bun'ya da....Anmari koi ni sekkyokutekina hoo demo nai n de ne. Muri!! tte omou koto no hoo ga ooi n de ne. Hontooni sukina hito no mae ni deru to, sugooku fushizen ni natte-shimattari....Kininatteru hito ga ite mo, ore ja mooshiwakenai kigashite, nigegoshi ni nat-chattari. Soo naru to, kaiwa nante motte no hoka, me mo mirarezu ni, ippootekina koi de owatte-shimau wake desu yo. Tatoe, ganbatte hanashite, sukoshi nakayoku natte mo, sore ijoo wa bibitte-shimau toka ne. Jibun demo dooshite koo na no ka yoku wakannai kedo hontoni bukiyoo da na tte omou.

Well, it's getting colder, and it is a season when you miss someone close to you. Right. And what was it? Ah, love? Love, isn't it?

The kind of thing I am at my worst talking about....I'm not too aggressive about love. Impossible! Too many times, I have felt that way. When I face someone whom I truly like, I become very awkward....Even when I have someone I'm a bit attracted to, I feel I'm not good enough, and I tend to withdraw from her, like. In that situation, not to mention talking with her, but even looking at her eye to eye become impossible, and the love ends as one-sided love, as you see. Even when I dare to talk and we become a bit close, I'm too afraid to go further, really. I don't understand why I'm this way, and I realize how awkward I am.

* * *

FEATURES TO BE NOTED

1. Speech-like writing

   The style used in this essay is 新言文一致体 (しんげんぶんいっちたい), where formal and informal forms are mixed. The entire text carries with it a friendly, speech-like quality (see section 3.9).

   The overall friendliness expressed in the writing is supported by the sound changes listed below.

ないんでね	instead of ないのでね
多いんでね	instead of 多いのでね
すごーく	instead of すごく
俺じゃ	instead of 俺では
なっちゃったり	instead of なってしまったり
わかんない	instead of わからない
って思う	instead of と思う

   In addition, note the use of final particles

   人肌恋しい季節ではあります**ね**
   恋**ね**
   積極的なほうでもないんで**ね**
   思うことのほうが多いんで**ね**
   終わってしまうわけです**よ**
   それ以上はビビッてしまうとか**ね**

2. Mixing styles

   The writer mixes formal and informal styles (see section 12.1). The formal styles (ありますね, なんでしたっけ？ and わけですよ) address the reader directly. On the other hand, sentences that whisper his inner response appear in the informal

style (分野だand 思う). By mixing styles, the writer presents
information with different degrees of significance. This strategy communicates the overall structure of the discourse as
well.

3. Conversation in writing
      Another feature supporting 新言文一致体 is to incorporate
conversation within the written text. Note the initial portion.

  ま~寒くなってきたから、なんとなく人肌恋しい季節ではあります
    ね、うん。で、なんでしたっけ？　あぁ恋？　恋ね。

      Here, the sentence starts with ま~, an opener, and ends
with うん, a marker for the end of a speaking turn. Then the
writer carries on a pseudo conversation, で、なんでしたっけ？
あぁ恋？恋ね. This one-sided conversation assumes that the
reader has come up with the answer 恋. In response to the
imagined answer, 恋 becomes the topic.

4. Unfinished sentences
      The following sentences take the kind of final expressions
that leave them unfinished (see section 13.6). Note the use
of ellipses, the use of で and たり. They all contribute to the
overall impression of conversational writing.

  いちばん語るの苦手な分野だ・・・。
  積極的なほうでもないんでね
  思うことのほうが多いんでね
  すごーく不自然になってしまっ**たり**・・・。
  逃げ腰になっちゃっ**た**り

5. てしまう expressions
      Notice the frequent use of てしまう expressions. These ex-
pressions convey that the action was completed with a sense
of regret, appealing to the feeling that things have occurred
beyond the writer's control (see section 9.8).

  すごーく不自然に**なってしまったり**
  逃げ腰に**なっちゃったり**
  終わってしまう
  ビビッてしまう

6. カタカナ and youth language
      The text also uses カタカナ, as in ビビる and ホントに. The
writer chooses カタカナ to add to the text a youth-oriented,
with-it attitude.

18.6. Cell-Phone Novel ケータイ小説

美嘉『恋空』(上 2006, p. 274), スターツ出版

ケータイ小説 (しょうせつ) 'cell-phone novels' began to appear in 2001, when ケータイ 'cell phones' became widespread in Japan, particularly among the youth. Because text messaging is restricted in character space, ケータイ小説 use short and simple sentences, without traditional 段落 (だんらく) divisions. Unlike traditional novels, ケータイ小説 are presented horizontally. Even when they are published as books, they follow the horizontal format.

ケータイ小説 differ from online novels in their convenience. Because ケータイ小説 can be read anywhere (e.g., while waiting for a bus or sitting on a park bench), they are even more accessible than online novels. Many ケータイ小説 are accessible on the Internet as well.

The popularity of the ケータイ小説 is supported by their theme. They are usually assumed to be based on the writer's personal experience. They are narrated from a first-person perspective. Writers (mostly female) are thought to be in their teens or early twenties. They have gone through some of the typical life experiences of youth, such as love relationships, breakups, pregnancies, domestic violence, juvenile delinquency, school bullying, and suicide. More recently, ケータイ小説 have become more diverse and now include science fiction and fantasy.

After some ケータイ小説 became very popular, publishers began to take notice. The earliest novel that became well known beyond its cell-phone readers was "Deep Love" by Yoshi.

『恋空』, by 美嘉, was available at a cell-phone site [魔法 (まほう) のiらんど] in 2003–2004. It became so popular that in 2006 it was published in two volumes as a hardcover book. Following the text messaging format, the books took on the horizontal writing style, a style unusual for Japanese novels. 『恋空』was also produced as a television drama series and a movie in 2007.

The story traces the seven years of a love-breakup-love relationship between Mika (the writer) and Hiro, who meet in their first year of high school.

* * *

新しい涙の味
もうすぐ高校二年生も終わる。
テストもギリギリでクリアし、補習もまぬがれて今回は難無く三学期を終える事ができた。

「明日から春休みだけど怠けないで勉強しろよ」

先生の言葉に生徒達は歓声をあげ、一斉に教室を出る。

美嘉は友達に別れを告げるといそいそと靴を履き替え、小走りで学校を出た。

・・・高校生活もあと一年か。

天気いいなあ~!! ラララぁ♪」

こんな気分のいい時は自然に歌を口ずさんでしまう。

バス停の前に到着し、時間を確認しようとポケットに手を入れたが、携帯電話がない。

・・・あ!! そう言えば机の中に入れておいたままだ。

歩いてきた道を戻り、再び学校へ歩き始めると、前方から仲のよさげなカップルが歩いてきた。

そのカップルとちょうどすれ違った瞬間・・・

「美嘉ちゃんだよね？」

美嘉はカップルの女の方に声をかけられて振り返った。

・・・この顔、忘れられるはずもない。

咲。ヒロの元カノの咲だ。

Atarashii namida no aji

Moo sugu kookoo ninensei mo owaru.

Tesuto mo girigiri de kuriashi, hoshuu mo manugarete konkai wa nannaku sangakki o oeru koto ga dekita.

"Ashita kara haruyasumi da kedo namakenaide benkyooshiro yo."

Sensei no kotoba ni seito-tachi wa kansei o age, isseini kyooshitsu o deru.

Mika wa tomodachi ni wakare o tsugeru to isoisoto kutsu o hakikae, kobashiri de gakkoo o deta.

....Kookooseikatsu mo ato ichinen ka.

"Tenki ii naa!! Ra, ra, raa □"

Konna kibun no ii toki wa shizenni uta o kuchizusande-shimau.

Basutei no mae ni toochakushi, jikan o kakuninshiyoo to poketto ni te o ireta ga, keitai denwa ga nai.

....A!! Soo ieba tsukue no naka ni irete-oita mama da.

Aruite-kita michi o modori, futatabi gakkoo e aruki-hajimeru to, zenpoo kara naka no yosagena kappuru ga aruite-kita.

Sono kappuru to choodo surechigatta shunkan....

"Mika-chan da yo ne?"

Mika wa kappuru no onna no hoo ni koe o kakerarete furikaetta.

....Kono kao wasureru hazu mo nai.

Saki. Hiro no moto kano no Saki da.

The taste of new tears.

Soon, my junior year of high school will end.

Barely, but I passed exams, and I wasn't forced into extra review classes; this time I could end the third semester safely.

"From tomorrow, the spring break starts. Don't forget to study hard."

Students screamed with joy as the teacher said that, and everyone left the classroom at the same time.

I said my good-byes to friends, changed shoes, and left school almost running.

....One more year as a high school student.

"What nice weather. La, la, la."

On such a pleasant day, I end up singing a song.

I arrived at the bus stop, and I put my hand in my pocket to check the time, but I couldn't find my cell phone.

....No!! That's right, I left it inside my desk drawer.

I traced back along the road I had come, and as I began walking again toward the school, I noticed an intimate couple approaching.

The moment when I passed by that couple,...

"You're Mika, aren't you?"

said the woman of the couple, and so I turned my head toward her.

....This face, it is impossible to forget.

It was Saki. Saki, Hiro's ex-girlfriend.

* * *

FEATURES TO BE NOTED

1. Narrative tense

As you have probably noticed, this segment contains both past and non-past tenses (see sections 8.3 and 8.4). Below the main predicate verbs are categorized into the two tenses.

Non-past: 終わる, 出る, 口ずさんでしまう, ない, ままだ, ない, 咲だ

Past: できた, 出た, 歩いてきた, 振り返った

Non-past tense sentences describe what is happening "now." They may refer to an event happening "now" or the feelings and thoughts of the writer (following the first-person perspective). Inner-thought sentences include the following.

・・・高校生活もあと一年か。

・・・あ!! そう言えば机の中に入れておいたままだ。

・・・この顔、忘れられるはずもない。

Past tense sentences describe what happened from the writer's perspective. Unlike English, where narrative normally takes the past tense, in *Nihongo,* the tense shift is relatively free.

2. Exclamatory phrases

To dramatize the story, noun phrases without predicates appear, as in そのカップルとちょうどすれ違った瞬間...and 咲 (see section 11.3).

3. カタカナ and youth language

カタカナ appear for words that are typically associated with youth language. The effects are multiple, including loan words, sound effects, first names, and special words (see sections 5.5 and 6.2).

クリアする	to clear (i.e., to pass), クリアas a loan word
ラララぁ	sound-based phrase, rhythm-taking, expressing happiness
ヒロ	nickname; the hero is 弘樹 (ひろき) but is called Hiro, which is transcribed as ヒロ
元カノ	ex-girlfriend, a combination of 元 (もと) and 彼 of 彼女 (かのじょ) 'girlfriend', written with カタカナ

The expression テストもギリギリでクリアする is youth language, and so is the phrase 仲のよさげなカップル. Note also the use of 元カノ, a phrase frequently used among youth.

4. Note the use of □ (see section 3.10).
5. For the following expressions, refer to the entry sections listed.

事ができた (section 9.5, Potential and Ability)
勉強しろ (section 12.12, Giving Orders and Commands)
別れを告げると (section 10.2, Connecting Clauses)
歩き始めると (section 10.2, Connecting Clauses)
声をかけられて (section 9.9, Passives)
忘れられる (section 9.5, Potential and Ability)
はずもない (section 9.6, Modal Verbs)

PART VII

Learning *Nihongo*

CHAPTER 19

Methods

19.1. Taking Classes

If it is at all possible to take structured courses in the Japanese language, you should do so. Learning in a classroom offers the kind of experience difficult to duplicate otherwise. You will meet a teacher who is a native or near-native Japanese speaker. You will get acquainted with people who share your interest in learning *Nihongo*.

Taking classes can offer the following.

1. A systematic introduction to and the learning of sounds, scripts, and grammar
2. Enacted interaction practices focusing on communication strategies
3. Cultural information related to topics covered in the lessons
4. Up-to-date audio and video materials developed for language-learning purposes
5. Group activities such as discussions, skits, and interviews
6. Drills, exercises, creative assignments, and classroom participation to enhance your performance
7. Quizzes and examinations to assess your ability
8. Direct access to instructors who can offer assistance and advice

High schools, colleges, and private language schools offer various classes, covering the beginning to the most advanced levels. They sometimes offer courses for specific purposes, such as writing, conversation, and business Japanese. It is advisable to take the basic language courses first and follow the programs through to make sure your knowledge and experience are constructively accumulative.

You may have access to Japanese courses offered as distance-learning classes or on the Internet. Although limited, these courses will prove useful, nonetheless.

19.2. Learning on Your Own

If you have no available Japanese courses near you and you are on your own, there is no need to despair. You can purchase textbooks as well as audio and visual materials. You can enroll in online courses and make use of information available on the Internet. Googling "learning Japanese" will lead you to an array of useful sources. Once you have familiarized yourself with the core knowledge of Japanese language learning, you can sort out useful and not-so-useful information.

You are never completely alone when learning Japanese. Although it takes determination, it is possible to learn basic Japanese on your own. Such an experience will test you, but it is possible to become proficient in Japanese even when you study it on your own.

Whether you are taking a course or not, what is important is to reach out for various resources. By accessing pedagogical resources, you will learn various methods. Learning is a creative process. By experimenting with different methods, you will find the right combination most agreeable and suited to you.

Keep in mind that as in everything else in life, unless you truly want to learn Japanese, you will not succeed. And unless you enjoy the process, you will not last. If you know what you truly want to do and if your desire is to learn Japanese, you have already taken the first critical step.

19.3. Language Skills

Language students are expected to master reading, writing, speaking, and listening. These four basic skills are not completely isolated. In fact, reading and writing are based on similar knowledge, and speaking and listening are synergistic. In addition, given the prominence of visual images in communication, learning how to read them is also essential. Although certain programs tend to emphasize specific skills, it has been my experience that unless you develop each of these skills, you will not come out proficient in *Nihongo*.

19.4. Reading

What to Read

As a general rule, choose materials that cover the topics personally interesting to you. What you already know about a topic will serve as background knowledge when reading a Japanese text. Your prior knowledge will be a big help when you get stuck.

Obviously, what you can read depends on your proficiency level. With material too difficult for your level, you may simply be overwhelmed. Be kind to yourself. Different reading materials specifically prepared for students of Japanese as a foreign language are available.

If you want to read authentic material, choose simple texts first (such as those targeted at junior high school and high school students). I do not recommend children's books for adult students of Japanese. Although they seem deceptively easy, baby words and children's vocabulary differ from adult language and are often useless to adult learners. If possible, it would be a good idea to seek advice from your language teacher as to what specific books are most appropriate.

I usually recommend short stories by 星新一 (ほししんいち) for his short, simple, and straightforward writing style. If you are a mystery novel fan, perhaps works by 赤川次郎 (あかがわじろう) are more accessible than others. Some of the current works of 東野圭吾 (ひがしのけいご) may also interest you.

If you have access to libraries with a Japanese language collection, check out what they have. Most libraries hold collections of modern literature published by major Japanese publishers. You will recognize the names of some authors. Among the works, choose short fiction with relatively short sentences and simple sentence structures.

Libraries may also subscribe to major Japanese journals and magazines. Look through them and read simple articles, essays, advertising, and so on.

The magazine industry in Japan produces an array of weekly and monthly magazines for specific readers. Magazines for youth carry articles in colloquial language with current vocabulary. Read these magazines to keep up with the most current language. Magazines often carry concise articles with concrete examples. The writing style is direct and clear. You may find this kind of writing useful for your study.

If you have access to brick-and-mortar Japanese bookstores (including second-hand bookstores), browse through them. You will be amazed at the vast variety of publications available. You may ask the sales staff to recommend something for you.

Of course, bookstores on the Internet (e.g., http://www.amazon. co.jp/ and http://www.kinokuniya.co.jp/) provide a wealth of information. You have access to practically every possible publication in Japan. Information is available in English, but to take full advantage of what's out there, you must already be proficient in Japanese. Still, such sites offer an opportunity to browse through the endless lists of publications in Japanese.

Japanese newspaper companies offer Japanese language Web sites. Look for the Web sites of major newspapers as listed below.

朝日新聞 (あさひしんぶん) http://www.asahi.com/
毎日新聞 (まいにちしんぶん) http://www.mainichi.jp/
読売新聞 (よみうりしんぶん) http://www.yomiuri.co.jp/

Once you reach these sites, you will have access to different types of writings, news, editorials, essays, sports articles, popular culture items, interviews, special features, and so on.

Major publishing houses regularly publish new titles in established series called 新書 (しんしょ), with endless titles of non-fiction paperbacks. For example, Iwanami Shoten publishes 岩波新書 (いわなみしんしょ), and Shinchoosha publishes (新潮新書しんちょうしんしょ). The 新書 series cover everything from philosophy and religion to music and art. Each book (reasonably priced) is written by an expert in the field and usually provides relevant information in plain, non-technical Japanese. By selecting up-to-date publications in these series, you will access what is topical in the contemporary Japanese publishing world.

In the literary market, after a couple of years as hardcover publications, novels are published as reasonably priced paperbacks called 文庫 (ぶんこ). Here again, major publishing houses publish series; for example, Kadokawa Shoten publishes 角川文庫 (かどかわぶんこ), and Bungei Shunjuusha publishes 文春文庫 (ぶんしゅんぶんこ).

Also available are electronic versions of some literary works, accessible through the Web site 青空文庫 (あおぞらぶんこ) at http://www.aozora.gr.jp/.

How to Read

Depending on the purpose, your reading strategies may differ. Here I assume you are reading as a part of your language education and perhaps for information as well as for enjoyment.

When reading something new, gauge the entire task before attacking the first sentence. Consider the genre. Book information is available on booksellers' Web sites. Having a general idea of what you are reading is a great help.

When reading, you must use all kinds of knowledge about the Japanese language. By this I mean that you must know the words, grammar, rhetoric, and discourse organization used in a text. Fortunately, you have already gained knowledge in all these areas. Although this book contains only the most basic (and simplified) information, you will find information related to reading in Chapters 6 through 13, as well as Chapters 15 and 16.

Perhaps I should mention two important clues for reading. First, find the topic of a discourse by observing phrases marked by topic markers and repetition. These are key words around which a particular paragraph or discourse develops. Second, always pay attention to what is stated at the end. Whether it is the end of the paragraph or the end of an entire piece, the conclusion is likely to be presented or repeated there.

Regarding the physical activity of reading, sometimes read out loud. Think of the meaning as you read. This will help you read better and appreciate the meaning at the same time. After reading Japanese works, always write something down about them. This process will force you to fully understand what you have just read and help you to make it your own. This way, you will be reading the text "for real." It will offer an opportunity to review the vocabulary as well.

19.5. Writing

Scripts

Practicing Japanese scripts is actually quite enjoyable. For those of you who have been exposed to nothing but the Latin alphabet, the Japanese writing system will offer a new way of understanding what writing is.

When learning scripts, don't just look at them. Always write them by hand, and repeat writing them. Follow the correct stroke order and the method of fixing and releasing your strokes. You must learn Japanese scripts through your body, not just through your mind. Through repeated practice, Japanese scripts will become second nature. The more time you spend practicing, the better you will become. I recommend that you learn handwriting first and then start writing electronically.

Writing Practice

Your writing practice should start with sentences, paragraphs consisting of a few sentences, and simple memos. Keeping a simple journal in Japanese will help you write something on a regular basis.

Later, when you begin writing compositions or essays, construct each sentence according to the word and grammar rules you learned in Chapters 7 through 11. Then use devices to connect sentences appropriately, as discussed in Chapter 10. You should also follow one of the overall discourse organizations presented in Chapter 16.

Once you have finished writing, you should edit what you wrote, preferably several times. If you have someone who can correct your writing, make use of such an opportunity. You will benefit from one-to-one instruction when learning how to say what you want to say.

Writing is generally more challenging than reading. Unlike reading, writing requires you to create something from nothing. If it is too difficult at first, you might imitate some written texts. By changing certain parts, you can gradually proceed to your own writing. Through this exercise, you will build confidence, and you will be able to write something new on your own.

19.6. Speaking and Listening

Speaking correctly involves not only a knowledge of Japanese grammar but also its use. Take advantage of the strategies you learned in Chapters 12 through 14.

If you are to participate in conversation, preparing something to say beforehand is a good strategy. At the early stage of learning, it is extremely difficult to create something in Japanese on the spot. An ongoing conversation changes from one moment to the next, and it is difficult to catch up with what others are saying. At first, making your own comments will seem almost impossible. By the time you have come up with something to say, the topic will have moved on, and what you have just prepared will no longer be relevant. Preparation may not work all the time, but without it, you will be less successful.

To participate in conversation, you must be able to comprehend what your partner is saying. Do not be afraid to ask questions if you don't understand (see section 13.12). At first you may not be able to pinpoint what you don't understand. But it is always better to clarify uncertain points as soon as possible. I have experienced awkward moments in English conversation when I didn't quite get something but was forced to pretend as if I did.

Even when your Japanese is not perfect, it is best to say something—anything you can come up with. Make your partner wait for what you can produce. Being shy and keeping quiet will not make you a competent Japanese speaker.

There are interactive audio and visual language materials, some available on the Internet. Make use of these resources so that you become familiar with the speed and tone of conversational Japanese.

Form a conversation group where you gather with other students learning Japanese. If you know people who speak Japanese, invite them. Arrange some sort of exchange so that the Japanese speakers may benefit from what you offer in return.

To practice listening, if you have opportunities to attend (or view) lectures given in Japanese, go and take notes and write summaries.

Overall, it is always a good idea to combine different practices so that you engage in multiple skills in *Nihongo*.

19.7. Memorization

One of the methods of learning anything is mimicking and memorization. Although these two aspects are sometimes taken to be too rudimentary and boring, a certain amount of memorization is necessary in language learning. To achieve this, the best way is to appeal to both the short-term and the long-term memory. The more you repeat what you learn, the clearer the stored information will be and the longer it will stay stored. When you are learning a foreign language, you should spend some time every day reviewing old things while learning new things.

If you are a native speaker of a Western language, *Nihongo* vocabulary will not be cognate to your native language. This means that you will not be able to guess at a meaning too easily. For example, if you are familiar with Spanish, learning Italian vocabulary is easier because there are so many cognates. When learning Japanese words, you will have to memorize word by word (except perhaps for a few loan words).

Making vocabulary cards is a good idea. Memorizing basic sentences is another workable strategy. You can use these basic sentences as guides for creating new ones. The conjugation of verbs and adjectives must be memorized. Although Japanese conjugations are not as complex as those of the Romance languages, learning them to the level that you can immediately come up with correct forms is a formidable task.

Memorization is always helped when you actually access memory. The more you retrieve what is stored in your memory, the more accurate and long-lasting your memory will become.

When you try to memorize, do not just look at words to memorize. Say those words, write them, and then use them in sentences. Repeat those sentences out loud. This way, you will stimulate your many senses.

19.8. Creative Practice

Creative practice is the most fun part of language learning. Why not write a short story in Japanese? *Haiku* and *tanka?* How about making a short speech in Japanese? How about writing a Japanese song (to a melody you are familiar with)? If you are attending a class, creating a skit or a play will offer some enjoyable and memorable experiences.

One of the things I did as a student of English (while I was studying English in Japan) was to describe everything I saw in English. This turned out to be quite difficult, but I was trying to live life as an English speaker. People around you may wonder about your mental health when you go about mumbling things in Japanese. But that is not your concern. You are carrying on an important mission.

You may also think of participating in Internet sites where some of what you practice may be shared with others. For example, a Web site where students (both Japanese and foreign) post their compositions may provide you with an opportunity to share your writing and to compete with other students (e.g., Web site さくぶん at http://www.sakubun.org/).

19.9. Exposure to Japanese Language and Culture

Exposure to the *Nihongo* world and culture will stimulate you in many ways. It is rewarding to know that the Japanese scripts you learned actually appear in a Japanese advertisement, for example.

If you live near a major college library, you have access to books and magazines written in Japanese. If you live in or near major cities, there are Japanese bookstores (e.g., Kinokuniya, Sanseido, and Book-off).

There are American publishers focusing on Japanese and Asian books (e.g., the University of Hawaiʻi Press) and distributors located in America (e.g., Kodansha America, Inc.).

And of course, you can use the Japanese search engine (http://www.goo.ne.jp/) to look for an endless amount of information presented in Japanese, including visual materials.

Visiting museums and art exhibits related to Japanese culture is always an exciting experience. Japanese movies will reveal interesting social and cultural aspects of Japan.

Some cable television networks offer Japanese language programs worldwide. These programs will give you opportunities to listen to various styles and strategies used in many different Japanese genres.

19.10. Interaction with Native Speakers

Interacting with native or near-native speakers of the Japanese language is a must in language learning. Ultimately, you must feel comfortable communicating with these people.

If you are in a university, look for organizations associated with Japanese students. You can arrange learning exchanges. You can learn Japanese from the Japanese student, and in turn, you can teach English (or other subjects).

When you become proficient in Japanese, Internet chat rooms will be a good place to go to test your Japanese in real-life, if not virtual, communication. Corresponding through e-mail with a Japanese e-friend can provide a real-life communication opportunity without your having left your room. Access to native speakers from abroad is possible through reasonably priced international phone calls (some via the Internet) or through video phone services. Interaction with native speakers in a real sense adds excitement to your learning process.

Always remember, however, that native speakers are not necessarily good language teachers. Know that although they have full command of the language, they are not trained to look at Japanese from a foreign speaker's perspective. I have witnessed many situations where native Japanese speakers make up wrong grammatical rules and insist on unrealistic social customs. Take your native speakers' advice with a grain of salt. Even then, you have a lot to learn from them.

Always remember that although the varieties of language native speakers use may not be the standard Tokyo speech, they are not "wrong." Whatever they say, as long as they communicate, they are correct, in the sense that their language is functional. When I first learned English, I witnessed an American boy pointing to a bicycle and calling it a bike. My English teacher in Japan would not allow me to use the word "bike." But I learned quickly that whatever the little boy said was "real." Non-native speakers have a lot to learn from native speakers, indeed.

19.11. Thinking and Feeling in *Nihongo*

Your ultimate goal in acquiring Japanese is not only to master the language per se, but also to think and feel in Japanese. That means your cognitive and emotional processes must evolve in Japanese. This is difficult to achieve unless you are in an environment where Japanese is spoken on a daily basis.

This may be possible if you are enrolled in an immersion program, an environment where you are forced to speak Japanese 24–7. And if you go and live in Japan and you surround yourself not with foreigners but with Japanese speakers, you can enjoy such an environment.

When you live in a Japanese-speaking environment, you will begin to "breathe" in Japanese. You will literally live like a Japanese person, going through every aspect of life in Japanese. And that experience will change you. It will change you not in the sense that you are a totally different person, but in the sense that you are no longer a monolingual person. Mastering a foreign language reaches to the core of your being. For better or worse, it is a life-changing experience.

To learn Japanese for real, beyond the methods suggested so far, you must remain creative. Your desire to learn something new every day is the most important motivation. Try to gain knowledge that you didn't have twenty-four hours earlier. As long as you are committed, you will eventually master Japanese to such a level that you will be amazed at yourself!

CHAPTER 20

Tools and Resources

Given the fluid nature of information on Japanese-language learning, I will touch on only a few tools and resources. Search for up-to-date detailed information on the Internet. If possible, it is always a good idea to ask your instructor about the reliability of information on the Internet. In most cases, reliable sites are those sponsored by textbook publishers, Japanese-language programs at colleges and universities, and Japanese-language and cultural associations and organizations.

20.1. Textbooks

Although there are a number of Japanese-language textbooks available, below I list a few elementary ones. Many of the textbooks come with workbooks and CDs, as well as their own Web sites for additional information, tools, and exercises.

Secondary school

Japanese for Young People I, II, III. Association for Japanese-Language Teaching. Kodansha International, 1998, 1999, 2001.
Yookoso. Yasu-Hiko Tohsaku. McGraw-Hill, 1994, 2004, 2006.

College

Genki I, II. Eri Banno, Yutaka Ohno, Yoko Sakane, Chicako Shinagawa, and Kyoko Tokashiki. Japan Times, 1999.
Nakama I, II. Seiichi Makino, Yukiko Abe Hatasa, and Kazumi Hatasa. Houghton Mifflin, 1998, 2000.

General/Adult

Japanese for Busy People I, II, III. Association for Japanese-Language Teaching. Revised 3rd edition. Kodansha International, 2007, 2008.

20.2. Dictionaries

Dictionaries come in three different forms: print, electronic, and online. Here are some representative ones.

Dictionaries in Print

Kodansha's Communicative English-Japanese Dictionary. Kodansha International, 2006.
Kodansha's Furigana Japanese-English Dictionary. Kodansha International, 2001.
Kodansha's Furigana English-Japanese Dictionary. Kodansha International, 2001.
Oxford Starter Japanese Dictionary. Oxford University Press, 2006.

Electronic Dictionaries

Electronic dictionaries are easy to carry and offer features that are quite helpful. Brand-name companies such as Canon, Casio, Seiko, and Sharp produce electronic language devices. These products come with several different kinds of dictionaries already installed. One feature that you might look for is handwriting recognition. This is quite handy because otherwise you must look for the 漢字 (かんじ) reading first (by using radicals and stroke numbers), which can be extremely time-consuming. With the handwriting recognition feature, you simply copy the 漢字 you don't know by hand, and the dictionary will recognize it.

Casio EX-word DATAPLUS 4 XD-SP6600
Canon WordTank G70
Sharp PW-N8100
Seiko SR-G9000
Nintendo DS (Japanese dictionaries available)

Online Dictionaries

There are a number of free online dictionaries available, including the following. Some allow ひらがな, カタカナ and 漢字 input; others allow only ローマ字 (じ) input.

http://jisho.org.
http://www.englishjapaneseonlinedictionary.com
http://www.saiga-jp.com
http://www.polarcloud.com/rikaichan/

20.3. Reference Books

Although there are many reference books written in Japanese, they are not immediately accessible to the beginning student. As I stated in the preface, this book contains simplified information. Detailed information about Japanese language and linguistics is widely available, including in my own books. The following reference books in English are representative.

Backhouse, A. E. 1993. *The Japanese Language: An Introduction.* Oxford: Oxford University Press.
Chevray, Keiko Uesawa, and Tomiko Kuwahara. 2000. *Schaum's Outline of Japanese Grammar.* New York: McGraw-Hill.
Cipris, Zeljko, and Shoko Hamano. 2002. *Making Sense of Japanese Grammar: A Clear Guide through Common Problems.* Honolulu: University of Hawaiʻi Press.
Iwasaki, Shoichi. 2002. *Japanese.* Amsterdam: John Benjamins.
Johnson, Yuki. 2008. *Fundamentals of Japanese Grammar.* Honolulu: University of Hawaiʻi Press.
Makino, Seiichi, and Michio Tsutsui. 1986. *A Dictionary of Basic Japanese Grammar.* Tokyo: Japan Times.
———. 1995. *A Dictionary of Intermediate Japanese Grammar.* Tokyo: Japan Times.
———. 2008. *A Dictionary of Advanced Japanese Grammar.* Tokyo: Japan Times.
Maynard, Senko K. 1990. *An Introduction to Japanese Grammar and Communication Strategies.* Tokyo: Japan Times.
———. 1997. *Japanese Communication: Language and Thought in Context.* Honolulu: University of Hawaiʻi Press.

———. 1998. *Principles of Japanese Discourse: A Handbook.* Cambridge: Cambridge University Press.

———. 2005. *Expressive Japanese: A Reference Guide to Sharing Emotion and Empathy.* Honolulu: University of Hawai'i Press.

———. 2009. *An Introduction to Japanese Grammar and Communication Strategies.* Revised. Tokyo: Japan Times.

Maynard, Senko K., and Michael L. Maynard. 1993. *101 Japanese Idioms: Understanding Japanese Language and Culture through Popular Phrases.* Hightstown, NJ: McGraw-Hill.

———. 2009. *101 Japanese Idioms.* With an MP3 disk. New York: McGraw-Hill.

McClure, W. T. 2000. *Using Japanese: A Guide to Contemporary Usage.* Cambridge: Cambridge University Press.

Shibatani, Masayoshi. 1990. *The Languages of Japan.* Cambridge: Cambridge University Press.

20.4. Writing Tools

If you are taking a structured Japanese course, depending on the program, you will be learning ひらがな, カタカナ, and 漢字 at different stages. However, you are most likely to learn ひらがな first, followed by カタカナ. 漢字 are usually taught half way into an elementary course. It is key that you actually write the characters (many times). Just looking at them is not only boring but also ineffective. The following are helpful writing tools.

Lampkin, Rita. 1990. *Easy Kana Workbook: Basic Practice in Hiragana and Katakana for Japanese Language Students.* McGraw-Hill.

Hadamitzky, Wolfgang, and Mark Spahn. 2003, 2004. *Writing Japanese Kanji and Kana: A Self-Study Workbook for Learning Japanese Characters,* vols. I and II. Charles E. Tuttle.

In addition, information on ひらがな, カタカナ, and 漢字 is widely available on the Internet (e.g., http://www.kanjisite.com). Some Web sites show stroke orders, and they are particularly useful when learning on your own.

20.5. Audio and Visual Materials

Free access to audio and video materials in Japanese is available at Fujisankei Communications International, Inc. (official Web site http://www.fujisankei.com). Fujisankei airs Japanese-language news and other programs from its New York headquarters to an American audience. Other audiovisual materials in Japanese are widely available on sites such as http://www:youtube.com.

Through Internet radio you can access NHK radio news, updated daily at http://www.nhk.or.jp/r-news/, and 文化放送（ぶんかほうそう）radio programs at http://www.joqr/bbqr/indet.php/.

Audio books are available on the Internet as well, for example, at http://www.e-kotoba.com.

The audiovisual presentation of Japanese songs (on television and some on the Internet) is often accompanied with words at the bottom of the screen. However, depending on the songs and singers, the sounds may be overly stylized. You will find some good samples among folk songs (not stylized traditional songs) and pop music (i.e., J-pop).

Japanese television variety shows, some available on http://www.youtube.com, come in various forms, and many are captioned in Japanese scripts. These captions are especially useful when you don't quite understand or catch the words spoken in real time.

Japanese movies, anime, and TV programs can be purchased (on DVDs) from Japanese video stores, some located within the United States. They are also available through the Internet. Some movies are suitable for Japanese learners. They contain contemporary speech styles representing different demographics in near-natural social situations. Recent useful movies include the following: *HERO* (2007), *Closed Note* クローズド・ノート (2008), 恋空 *(Koizora)* (2008), and *KIDS* (2008). Recent television dramas include the following: たったひとつの恋 *(Tatta Hitotsu no Koi)* (2006), 有閑倶楽部 *(Yuukan Kurabu)* (2007), ガリレオ (2007), *CHANGE* (2008), and 流星の絆 *(Ryuusei no Kizuna)* (2008).

Once you have access to these audiovisual materials, view them repeatedly, pausing and replaying wherever necessary. Use information available on the Internet about a specific movie or television series. Many of these are produced from novels and comic books. If you refer to these original works, you will better understand the content.

If you are interested in listening practice, Japanese sounds are created on the Internet at sites such as http://www.neospeech.com.

20.6. Japanese Language Organizations

There are local, regional, national, and international organizations related to Japanese-language education. The following are well known.

Association of Teachers of Japanese (ATJ)

http://www.colorado.edu/ealld/atj/

An academic association of teachers of Japanese. Members are mostly from the United States, but membership is open to students and scholars worldwide. The organization publishes the academic journal *Japanese Language and Literature* (I serve on the Editorial Advisory Board) and holds its annual conference in conjunction with the Association of Asian Studies annual conference. It is currently housed at the University of Colorado (279 UCB Humanities 240, Boulder, CO 80309–0279). Visit its Web site for a variety of up-to-date very useful information related to Japanese-language learning. This Web site mostly offers information for teachers, but some information is useful for students.

National Council of Japanese Language Teachers (NCJLT)

http://www.ncjlt.org

A professional association of Japanese teachers. Active promotion of the teaching and learning of the Japanese language in K–16 in the United States. Partner organization of ATJ.

NCJLT
P.O. Box 3719
Boulder, CO 80307–3719

Japan Foundation

http://www.jpf.go.jp

The Japan Foundation (国際交流基金 こくさいこうりゅうききん) is a Japanese government entity (an independent institution under the jurisdiction of the Foreign Ministry of Japan) that undertakes the international dissemination of Japanese culture. It promotes cultural exchanges, overseas Japanese-language education, and intellectual exchanges. The Japan Foundation maintains overseas branches in nearly twenty countries, and it has its own local Web sites. For students of Japanese, the foundation's *Nihongo Kyoiku Tsushin* newsletter may be of interest (http://www.jpg.go.jp/j/japanese/survey/tsushin/index/html). On the Japan Foundation site, you will also find useful content such as *Erin's Challenge! I Can Speak Japanese.*

20.7 Contests and Scholarships

Speech Contests

Japanese-language speech contests are held in many cities worldwide. They are sponsored through the Japan Foundation, local businesses, and cultural organizations. Search on the Internet for the contests near you, and find out how you can participate. Some contests offer substantial prizes, such as a round-trip ticket between the United States and Japan.

Bridging Scholarships

http://www.colorado.edu/eale/at/Bridging/scholarships.html

The U.S.-Japan Bridging Foundation provides scholarships through the Association of Teachers of Japanese to assist students to study in Japan. The foundation awards approximately twenty scholarships a year to meet the travel and living expenses of students while they are in Japan. There are two application deadlines per year (fall and spring).

20.8. Placement and Proficiency Tests

Once you learn some Japanese, you will need to be placed at the right level to continue studying. For this purpose, formal or informal placement tests and interviews are conducted at various institutions.

Japanese Language Proficiency Test

The Japanese Language Proficiency Test (JLPT) is a worldwide test supported by the Japan Foundation, with its official Web site at http://www.jflalc.org.

The JLPT is a standardized test to evaluate and certify the language proficiency of non-native Japanese speakers. The test is held once a year (in December) and has five levels, beginning at level 5 and progressing to level 1. The JLPT is administered by Japan Educational Exchanges and Services in Japan. Overseas it is co-sponsored by the Japan Foundation and local cultural exchange and educational institutions. In the United States contact the JLPT Administration Committee at the Japan Foundation, Los Angeles.

AP Japanese

Some high school students who have studied Japanese may take the Advanced Placement Japanese Language and Culture Exam conducted by the Educational Testing Service. The AP Japanese exam assesses students' interpersonal communication skills, their abilities to present and interpret language in spoken and written forms, and their functional familiarity with Japanese culture. Students are tested through Internet access on listening, reading, writing, and speaking skills. Information on content and possible credit transfers is available at the College Board Web site (http://www.collegeboard.com/student/testing/ap/sub_japaneselang.html).

Depending on the policies of specific universities, some credits can be transferred. In many cases a score of 4 is approximately equivalent to the completion of elementary Japanese, and a score of 5 possibly equates with the completion of a part of intermediate Japanese. Regardless of the AP test results, most college programs require a placement test. It is unwise to take courses lower than the level at which you are placed. Not only is it demoralizing, but you will also not receive credit.

20.9. Study and Work in Japan

High School Study Abroad Programs

For high school students, there are programs under the Rotary Club, American Field Service, and Youth for Understanding. Additional financial assistance to study in Japan may be available through local communities and Japanese companies. Search on the Internet for up-to-date information.

College Exchange Programs

UNIVERSITY AND COLLEGE PROGRAMS

There are a number of exchange programs between U.S. colleges and Japanese universities. The college you attend is likely to have some study abroad program offered in Japan.

CONSORTIUM OF COLLEGES

If your college does not have a study abroad program, look for a consortium of colleges that accepts students from non-member colleges. Choose a semester, a year, or summer to suit your need.

The Inter-University Center for Japanese Language Studies (http://www.stanford.edu/dept/IUC) is a consortium of American universities that sponsors study abroad in Yokohama. It is possible for students from non-member institutions to apply for the program.

JAPANESE UNIVERSITIES

Japanese universities offer Japanese-language programs for students from abroad. They include the following: Kansai Gaidai, International Christian University, Nanzan University, Ritsumeikan University, Senshu University, Sophia University, and Waseda University. Access their Web sites for up-to-date information.

Japan Exchange and Teaching Program (JET Program)

http://www.us.emb-japan.go.jp/JETProgram

Although you may find opportunities to work in Japan through other means, the JET Program is probably one of the most rewarding. It is a Japanese government initiative that brings college graduates (mostly native speakers of English) to work in Japanese elementary, junior high, and high schools. There are three kinds of participants: Assistant Language Teacher (ALT), Coordinator for International Relations (CIR), and Sports Exchange Adviser (SEA). Participants come from forty-some countries, most prominently from the United States, where three thousand participants a year are recruited. The majority of JET participants teach English at junior high or high schools in various rural areas of Japan. The one-year contract is renewable.

Career Opportunities

Once a year, a career forum, a job fair for bilingual candidates (usually Japanese and English), is held in Los Angeles and Boston. Information is available at http://www.careerforum.net.

To the Reader,

Congratulations! You have taken a significant first step in learning Nihongo *by reading this book. Obviously, you have not read this book in one sitting or even in one month. But by now, you have gained a significant amount of knowledge. Learning something new is a precious gift given to us all. But, among all things, learning a foreign language will reward you in special ways. Whatever you do with your life, this experience will guide you on both personal and professional levels. So let me send you off with these ubiquitous words:* がんばってください！

Appendixes

Appendix 1

VERB CONJUGATION

	U-Verbs	*RU-Verbs*
Informal		
Non-past (basic)	書く	食べる
Past	書いた	食べた
Non-past negative	書かない	食べない
Past negative	書かなかった	食べなかった
Formal		
Non-past	書きます	食べます
Past	書きました	食べました
Non-past negative	書きません	食べません
Past negative	書きませんでした	食べませんでした
て form	書いて	食べて
Conditional	書けば	食べれば
Volitional	書こう	食べよう
Passive	書かれる	食べられる
Causative	書かせる	食べさせる
Abrupt command	書け	食べろ

Irregular verbs

Informal		
Non-past (basic)	来 (く) る	する
Past	来 (き) た	した
Non-past negative	来 (こ) ない	しない
Past negative	来 (こ) なかった	しなかった
Formal		
Non-past (basic)	来 (き) ます	します
Past	来 (き) ました	しました
Non-past negative	来 (き) ません	しません
Past negative	来 (き) ませんでした	しませんでした

	U-Verbs	*RU-Verbs*
て form	来 (き) て	して
Conditional	来 (く) れば	すれば
Volitional	来 (こ) よう	しよう
Passive	来 (こ) られる	される
Causative	来 (こ) させる	させる
Abrupt command	来 (こ) い	しろ

Be-*verb*

Informal

Non-past	だ	
Past	だった	
Non-past negative	ではない	じゃない
Past negative	ではなかった	じゃなかった

Formal

Non-past	です	
Past	でした	
Non-past negative	ではありません	じゃありません
Past negative	ではありませんでした	じゃありませんでした
て form	で	
Conditional	なら (ば)	
Volitional	でいよう	
Abrupt command	でいろ	

Existential verbs

Informal

Non-past (basic)	ある	いる
Past	あった	いた
Non-past negative	ない	いない
Past negative	あった	いなかった

Formal

Non-past	あります	います
Past	ありました	いました
Non-past negative	ありません	いません
Past negative	ありませんでした	いませんでした
て form	あって	いて
Conditional	あれば	いれば
Volitional		いよう
Abrupt command		いろ

Appendix 2

ADJECTIVE CONJUGATION

	い *adjective*	な *adjective*
Informal		
Non-past (basic)	新しい	便利な
Past	新しかった	便利だった
Non-past negative	新しくない	便利ではない
		便利じゃない
Past negative	新しくなかった	便利ではなかった
		便利じゃなかった
Formal		
Non-past	新しいです	便利です
Past	新しかったです	便利でした
Non-past negative	新しくないです	便利ではないです
		便利じゃないです
	新しくありません	便利ではありません
		便利じゃありません
Past negative	新しくなかったです	便利ではなかったです
		便利じゃなかったです
	新しくありませんでした	便利ではありませんでした
		便利じゃありませんでした
て form	新しくて	便利で
Conditional	新しければ	便利なら (ば)

Appendix 3

PREDICATES FOR "REACTIVE" DESCRIPTION

Natural Phenomena

降る	雨が降る。	Rain falls.
吹く	風が吹く。	Wind blows.

Sense/Perception/Physical Condition

する	においがする。	It smells.
かわく	のどがかわく。	I'm thirsty.

Existence/Possession

ある	大きい建物がある。	There is a large building.
	お金がたくさんある。	He has a lot of money.
いる	子供がいる。	There is a child.

Emotional Response

好きな	あの人のことが好きだ。	I like that person.
欲しい	お金が欲しい。	I want money.

Spontaneous Occurrence

見える	海が見える。	The ocean can be seen.
聞こえる	音楽が聞こえる。	The music is heard.

Potential

できる	テニスができる。	I can play tennis.
わかる	日本語がわかる。	I can understand Japanese.
かかる	時間がかかる。	It takes time.

List of Author's Works

Senko K. Maynard

泉子・K・メイナード

Books Written in English

1989. *Japanese Conversation: Self-Contextualization through Structure and Interactional Management.* Norwood, NJ: Ablex.

1990. *An Introduction to Japanese Grammar and Communication Strategies.* Tokyo: Japan Times.
(1998. Thai translation of *An Introduction to Japanese Grammar and Communication Strategies* [Tokyo: Japan Times]. Parts I and II. Translated by Preeya Ingkaphirom Horie and Kanok Singkarin. Bangkok, Thailand: Samakkhiisaan.)

1993. *Discourse Modality: Subjectivity, Emotion and Voice in the Japanese Language.* Amsterdam: John Benjamins.

1993. *101 Japanese Idioms: Understanding Japanese Language and Culture through Popular Phrases.* With Michael L. Maynard. Lincolnwood, IL: Passport Books.

1997. *Japanese Communication: Language and Thought in Context.* Honolulu: University of Hawai'i Press.

1998. *Principles of Japanese Discourse: A Handbook.* Cambridge: Cambridge University Press.

2002. *Linguistic Emotivity: Centrality of Place, the Topic-Comment Dynamic, and an Ideology of Pathos in Japanese Discourse.* Amsterdam: John Benjamins.

2005. *Expressive Japanese: A Reference Guide to Sharing Emotion and Empathy.* Honolulu: University of Hawai'i Press.

2007. *Linguistic Creativity in Japanese Discourse: Exploring the Multiplicity of Self, Perspective, and Voice.* Amsterdam: John Benjamins.

2009. *101 Japanese Idioms* (with MP3 disk). With Michael L. Maynard. Republished. New York: McGraw Hill.

2009. *An Introduction to Japanese Grammar and Communication Strategies.* Revised. Tokyo: Japan Times.

Books Written in Japanese

1993. 『会話分析』くろしお出版
1997. 『談話分析の可能性：理論・方法・日本語の表現性』くろしお出版
2000. 『情意の言語学：「場交渉論」と日本語表現のパトス』くろしお出版
2001. 『恋するふたりの「感情ことば」：ドラマ表現の分析と日本語論』くろしお出版
2004. 『談話言語学：日本語のディスコースを創造する構成・レトリック・ストラテジーの研究』くろしお出版
2005. 『日本語教育の現場で使える　談話表現ハンドブック』くろしお出版
2008. 『マルチジャンル談話論：間ジャンル性と意味の創造』くろしお出版
2009. 『ていうか、やっぱり日本語だよね：会話に潜む日本人の気持ち』大修館書店

Dissertation

1980. "Discourse Functions of the Japanese Theme Marker *Wa*." Northwestern University.

Articles, etc., Written in English

1981. "The Given/New Distinction and the Analysis of the Japanese Particles *Wa* and *Ga*." *Papers in Linguistics* 14, 1, 109–130.
1981. "Teaching *Wa* from a Discourse Perspective." *Proceedings of the Sixth Hawaii Conference on Japanese Linguistics and Language Teaching*, 89–98.
1982. "Hiroshima Folktales: Text-Typology from the Perspective of Structure and Discourse Modality." *TEXT: An Interdisciplinary Journal for the Study of Discourse* 2, 375–393.
1982. "Theme in Japanese and Topic in English: A Functional Comparison." *Forum Linguisticum* 5, 235–261.
1982. "Analysis of Cohesion: A Study of the Japanese Narrative." *Journal of Literary Semantics* 11, 19–34.
1983. "Flow of Discourse and Linguistic Manipulation: Functions and Constraints of the Japanese and English Relative Clause in Discourse." *Proceedings of the Thirteenth International Congress of Linguists*. Ed. Shiro Hattori and Kazuko Inoue, 1028–1031. Tokyo: Tokyo Press.

1984. "Functions of *To* and *Koto-o* in Speech and Thought Representation in Japanese." *Lingua* 64, 1–24.

1985. "Choice of Predicate and Narrative Manipulation: Functions of *Dearu* and *Da* in Modern Japanese Fiction." *Poetics* 14, 369–385.

1985. "Contrast between Japanese and English Participant Identification: Its Implications for Language Teaching." *International Review of Applied Linguistics* 23, 217–229.

1985. Review of *Ellipsis in Japanese,* by John Hinds. *Journal of Pragmatics* 9, 847–851.

1986. "The Particle *-O* and Content-Oriented Indirect Speech in Japanese Written Discourse." In *Direct and Indirect Speech, Trends in Linguistics, Studies and Monographs.* Vol. 31. Ed. Florian Coulmas, 179–200. Berlin: Mouton de Gruyter.

1986. "Interactional Aspects of Thematic Progression in English Casual Conversation." *TEXT: An Interdisciplinary Journal for the Study of Discourse* 6, 73–105.

1986. "On Back-Channel Behavior in Japanese and English Casual Conversation." *Linguistics* 24, 1079–1108.

1986. Review of *Japanese Women's Language,* by Janet Shibamoto. *Journal of Asian Studies* 45, 860–862.

1987. "Thematization as a Staging Device in Japanese Narrative." In *Perspectives on Topicalization: The Case of Japanese Wa.* Ed. John Hinds, Senko K. Maynard, and Shoichi Iwasaki, 57–82. Amsterdam: John Benjamins.

1987. "Interactional Functions of a Nonverbal Sign: Head Movement in Japanese Dyadic Casual Conversation." *Journal of Pragmatics* 11, 589–606.

1987. "Review of *Japanese,*" by John Hinds. *Linguistics* 25, 1192–1196.

1987. "Variability in Conversation Management: Fragmentation of Discourse and Back-Channel Expressions in Japanese and English." Microfiche, ED 283 407. Educational Resources Information Center (ERIC), U.S. Department of Education, Office of Educational Research and Improvement.

1987. "Pragmatics of Interactional Signs: A Case of *Uh-huh*'s and the Like in Japanese Conversation." *Fourteenth LACUS (Linguistic Association of Canada and the United States) Forum,* 67–76.

1989. "Functions of the Discourse Marker *Dakara* in Japanese Conversation." *TEXT: An Interdisciplinary Journal for the Study of Discourse* 9, 389–414.

1990. "Understanding Interactive Competence in L1/L2 Contrastive Context: A Case of Back-Channel Behavior in Japanese and English." In *Language Proficiency, Defining, Teaching, and Testing.* Ed. Louis A. Arena, 41–52. New York and London: Plenum Press.

1990. "Conversation Management in Contrast: Listener Response in Japanese and American English." *Journal of Pragmatics* 14, 397–412.

1990. "TEXT: An Open Forum for International Scholarship." *TEXT Special 10th Anniversary Issue, Looking Ahead: Discourse Analysis in the 1990s* 10, 61–62.

1990. "Expression of Appeal in the Utterance Design of Japanese Conversational Language." *Journal of Japanese Linguistics* 12, 87–114.

1991. "Pragmatics of Discourse Modality: A Case of the Japanese Emotional Adverb *Doose.*" *Pragmatics* 1, 371–392.

1991. "Pragmatics of Discourse Modality: A Case of *Da* and *Desu/ Masu* Forms in Japanese." *Journal of Pragmatics* 15, 551–582.

1991. "Discourse and Interactional Functions of the Japanese Modal Adverb *Yahari/Yappari.*" *Language Sciences* 13, 39–57.

1992. "Speech Act Declaration in Conversation: Functions of the Japanese Connective *Datte.*" *Studies in Language* 16, 63–89.

1992. "Cognitive and Pragmatic Messages of a Syntactic Choice: A Case of the Japanese Commentary Predicate *N(o) Da.*" *TEXT: An Interdisciplinary Journal for the Study of Discourse* 12, 563–613.

1992. Review of *Aspects of Japanese Women's Language,* edited by Sachiko Ide and Naomi Hanaoka McGloin. *Discourse & Society* 3, 519–522.

1992. "Where Textual Voices Proliferate: A Case of *To Yuu* Clause-Noun Combination in Japanese." *Poetics* 21, 169–189.

1992. "Toward the Pedagogy of Style: Choosing between Abrupt and Formal Verb Forms in Japanese." In *Japanese-Language Education Around the Globe.* Vol. 2. Ed. Japan Foundation Japanese Language Institute, 27–43. Urawa, Japan: Japan Foundation Japanese Language Institute.

1993. "Interactional Functions of Formulaicity: A Case of Utterance-Final Forms in Japanese." *Proceedings of the Fifteenth International Congress of Linguists.* Vol. 3, 225–228. Quebec City: Laval University Press.

1993. "Declaring Speech Act in Conversation: A Study of Japanese Connective *Datte.*" *Proceedings of the Fifteenth International*

Congress of Linguists. Vol. 1, 355–357. Quebec City: Laval University Press.

1993. "The Meaning of Teaching Japanese in the United States." *The Breeze* (Japan Foundation Language Center Newsletter), September, 3–4.

1994. (Abstract) "Images of Involvement and Integrity: Rhetorical Style of a Japanese Politician." *The Association for Asian Studies, Abstracts of the 1994 Annual Meeting.* Ann Arbor: Association for Asian Studies, 127.

1994. "Images of Involvement and Integrity: Rhetorical Style of a Japanese Politician." *Discourse & Society* 5, 233–261.

1994. "Thematic Suspension and Speech Act Qualification: Rhetorical Effects of Stray Interrogative Clauses in Japanese Text." *Poetics* 22, 473–496.

1994. "The Centrality of Thematic Relations in Japanese Text." *Functions of Language* 1, 229–260.

1995. "'Assumed Quotation' in Japanese." *Gengo Hen'yoo ni okeru Taikeiteki Kenkyuu, oyobi sono Nihongo Kyooiku e no Ooyoo.* Ed. Misato Tokunaga, 163–175. Tokyo: Kanda Gaikokugo Daigaku.

1995. "Commentary Questions in Japanese: Cognitive Sources and Pragmatic Resources." *Studies in Language* 19, 447–487.

1995. "Interrogatives That Seek No Answers: Exploring the Expressiveness of Rhetorical Interrogatives in Japanese." *Linguistics* 33, 501–530.

1995. Review of *Situated Meaning: Inside and Outside in Japanese Self, Society, and Language,* edited by Jane M. Bachnik and Charles J. Quinn, Jr. *Language in Society* 24, 611–614.

1995. "Japanese Discourse, a New Journal." *Japanese Discourse: An International Journal for the Study of Japanese Text and Talk* 1, 1–5.

1995. "Conversation Analysis and the Essence of Language." *Japanese Discourse: An International Journal for the Study of Japanese Text and Talk* 1, 47–52.

1996. "Contrastive Rhetoric: A Case of Nominalization in Japanese and English Discourse." In *Contrastive Semantics and Pragmatics.* Ed. Katarzyna Jaszczolt and Ken Turner, 933–946. Oxford: Elsevier Science.

1996. "Multivoicedness in Speech and Thought Representation: The Case of Self-Quotation in Japanese." *Journal of Pragmatics* 25, 207–226.

1996. "Presentation of One's View in Japanese Newspaper Columns: Commentary Strategies and Sequencing." *TEXT: An Interdisciplinary Journal for the Study of Discourse* 16, 391–421.

1997. "Manipulating Speech Styles in Japanese: Context, Genre, and Ideology." *Proceedings of the Fifth Princeton Japanese Pedagogy Workshop,* 1–24. Ed. Seiichi Makino.

1997. "Analyzing Interactional Management in Native/Non-native English Conversation: A Case of Listener Response." *International Review of Applied Linguistics and Language Teaching* 35, 37–60.

1997. "Synergistic Structures in Grammar: A Case of Nominalization and Commentary Predicate in Japanese." *Word: Journal of the International Linguistic Association* 48, 15–40.

1997. "Meta-Quotation: Thematic and Interactional Significance of *Tte* in Japanese Girls' Comics." *Functions of Language* 4, 23–46.

1997. "Textual Ventriloquism: Quotation and the Assumed Community Voice in Japanese Newspaper Columns." *Poetics* 24, 379–392.

1997. "Shifting Contexts: The Sociolinguistic Significance of Nominalization in Japanese Television News." *Language in Society* 26, 381–399.

1997. "Rhetorical Sequencing and the Force of the Topic-Comment Relationship in Japanese Discourse: A Case of *Mini-Jihyoo* Newspaper Articles." *Japanese Discourse: An International Journal for the Study of Japanese Text and Talk* 2, 43–64.

1998. "Understanding and Teaching Japanese Discourse Principles: A Case of Newspaper Columns." In *Japanese-Language Education Around the Globe.* Vol. 8. Ed. Japan Foundation Japanese Language Institute, 67–86. Urawa, Japan: Japan Foundation Japanese Language Institute.

1998. "Ventriloquism in Text and Talk: Functions of Self- and Other-Quotation in Japanese Discourse." (Keynote Speech.) *Japanese/Korean Linguistics.* Vol. 7, 17–37. Ed. Noriko Akatsuka et al. Stanford, CA: Center for the Study of Language and Information.

1998. Review of *Love, Hate and Everything in Between,* by Mamiko Murakami. *Journal of the Association of Teachers of Japanese* 32, 2, 69–71.

1999. "Discourse Analysis and Pragmatics." In *The Handbook of Jap-*

anese Linguistics. Ed. Natsuko Tsujimura, 425–443. London: Blackwell.

1999. "On Rhetorical Ricochet: Expressivity of Nominalization and *Da* in Japanese Discourse." *Discourse Studies* 1, 57–81.

1999. "A Poetics of Grammar: Playing with Narrative Perspectives and Voices in Japanese and Translation Texts." *Poetics* 26, 115–141.

1999. "Grammar, With Attitude: On the Expressivity of Certain *Da*-Sentences in Japanese." *Linguistics* 37, 215–250.

2000. "Speaking for the Unspeakable: Expressive Functions of *Nan(i)* in Japanese Discourse." *Journal of Pragmatics* 32, 1209–1239.

2000. "Expressivity in Discourse: Cases of Vocatives and Themes in Japanese." *Language Sciences* 23, 679–705.

2001. "Sources of Emotion in Japanese Comics: *Da, Nan(i),* and the Rhetoric of *Futaku.*" In *Exploring Japaneseness: On Japanese Enactments of Culture and Consciousness.* Ed. Ray T. Donahue, 225–240. Westport, CT: Ablex.

2001. "Mitigation in Disguise: *Te-yuu-ka* as Preface to Self-Revelation in Japanese Dramatic Discourse." *Poetics* 29, 317–329.

2001. "Falling in Love with Style: Expressive Functions of Stylistic Shifts in a Japanese Television Drama Series." *Functions of Language* 8, 1–39.

2001. "In the Name of a Vessel: Emotive Perspectives in the Reporting of the *Ehime Maru-Greeneville* Collision in a Japanese Newspaper." *Journal of Linguistics* 40, 1047–1086.

2004. "Poetics of Style Mixture: Emotivity, Identity, and Creativity in Japanese Writings." *Poetics* 32, 387–409.

2005. "Thematization as a Staging Device in the Japanese Narrative." Reprinted in *Japanese Linguistics: Pragmatics, Sociolinguistics and Language.* Ed. Natsuko Tsujimura, 143–164. London: Routledge.

2005. "Another Conversation: Expressivity of *Mitaina* and Inserted Speech in Japanese Discourse." *Journal of Pragmatics* 37, 837–869.

2008. "Playing with Multiple Voices: Emotivity and Creativity in Japanese Style Mixture." In *Style Shifting in Japanese.* Ed. Kimberly Jones and Tsuyoshi Ono, 91–129. Amsterdam: John Benjamins.

Articles, etc. Written in Japanese

1987.「日米会話におけるあいづちの表現」『言語』11月号 88–92.

1991.「文体の意味：ダ体とデス・マス体の混用について」『言語』2月号 75–80.

1993.「アメリカ英語」『日本語学』特集『世界の女性語、日本の女性語』13–19.

1994.「『という』表現の機能：話者の発想・発話態度の標識として」『言語』11月号 80–85.

1997.「アメリカ英語」『女性語の世界』井出祥子編集　明治書院 130–140.

1998.「パトスとしての言語」『言語』6月号 34–41.

2001.「心の変化と話し言葉のスタイルシフト」『言語』6月号 38–45.

2001.「日本語文法と感情の接点：テレビドラマに会話分析を応用して」『日本語文法』1, 90–110.

2003.「談話分析の対照研究」『朝倉日本語講座』Vol. 70『文章、談話』佐久間まゆみ編集　朝倉書店 227–249.

2005.「会話導入文：話す『声』が聞こえる類似引用の表現性」『言語教育の新展開：牧野成一教授古希記念論文集　鎌田修他編集　ひつじ書房 61–76.

2005.『新日本語教育事典』担当事項　会話のしくみ (337–338)、レトリック (361–362)、命題 (584–585)、モダリティの研究 (585–586)、トピック・コメント (581–582) 水谷修他編集、日本語教育学会編　大修館書店.

2006.「指示表現の情意：語り手の視点ストラテジーとして」『日本語科学』19, 55–74.

2006. (ブログ)　　　「言語についての誤解と正解」言語学出版社フォラム http://www.gengosf.com/dir_x/modules-wordpress/index.php?p=16.

2007.「言語学と日本語教育学：知の受容から知の創造へ」『日本語教育』132 23–32.

Subject Index (English)

Subject Index and Key Phrases (Japanese)

(Listed according to the あいうえお *order)*

About the Author

Senko K. Maynard was born and educated in Japan, graduating with a B.A. from Tokyo Gaikokugo Daigaku (Tokyo University of Foreign Studies). She spent her high school senior year in the United States as an American Field Service Scholarship recipient, and later continued her education in the United States as a graduate student. After receiving a doctorate in linguistics from Northwestern University, she taught Japanese language and linguistics at the University of Hawai'i, Connecticut College, Harvard University, and Princeton University. She is currently Professor II of Japanese language and linguistics at Rutgers University. Professor Maynard has published more than eighty articles and reviews in American, Japanese, and international journals, and is the author of seventeen books in English and Japanese. Recent books include *Expressive Japanese: A Reference Guide to Sharing Emotion and Empathy* (University of Hawai'i Press, 2005); *Linguistic Creativity in Japanese Discourse: Exploring the Multiplicity of Self, Perspective, and Voice* (John Benjamins, 2007); *Maruch Janru Danwaron: Kanjanrusei to Imi no Soozoo* (Kuroshio Shuppan, 2008); and *Te Yuu ka, Yappari Nihongo Da yo ne: Kaiwa ni Hisomu Nihonjin no Kimochi* (Taishukan Shoten, 2009).

Production Notes for Maynard / *Learning Japanese for Real*
Cover design by Julie Matsuo-Chun
Interior design and composition by Wanda China with display type
in Meiryo and text in Bookman Old Style
Printing and binding by Sheridan Books, Inc.
Printed on 50# House Opaque, 606 ppi